T0243374

The Golden Rule

Reader reviews

'Dr Pollock writes in such a pleasant, conversational style that the book is easy reading even when its content is hard-hitting'
P.J.G *****

'A superb book in which the author clearly cares about the reader every bit as much as she does her patient'
Pete *****

'This is a book written for all ages. Informative, intriguing and beautifully written by a doctor with true insights into growing old'
Michael *****

'The most brilliant book imaginable on the subject of getting old. An absolute must for anyone with elderly parents, relatives or friends (or indeed if you're heading into your own twilight years!)'
Clare *****

'Really well written, insightful and informative. I wish we all had a Dr Lucy on hand'
Carrie *****

'With two parents getting older and frailer, this book has given me ideas of how to tackle those difficult conversations that do need to be had. As Lucy says, it is BECAUSE I love you that we need to talk about this'
Joanne *****

'Profound – really necessary for the mental well-being of all elderly people'
Derek *****

'Informative, funny, touching and so perceptive'
Sarah *****

'You're writing about me and my friends – thank you'
Sue *****

'Kind and insightful. A must-read for all "apprentice old people"!'
Von *****

The Golden Rule

Lessons in living from a doctor of ageing

DR LUCY POLLOCK

MICHAEL  JOSEPH

PENGUIN MICHAEL JOSEPH

UK | USA | Canada | Ireland | Australia
India | New Zealand | South Africa

Michael Joseph is part of the Penguin Random House group of companies
whose addresses can be found at global.penguinrandomhouse.com

First published by Penguin Michael Joseph, 2024

002

Copyright © Lucy Pollock, 2024

The moral right of the author has been asserted

Set in 13.5/16pt Garamond MT
Typeset by Falcon Oast Graphic Art Ltd
Printed and bound in Great Britain by Clays Ltd, Elcograf S.p.A.

The authorized representative in the EEA is Penguin Random House Ireland,
Morrison Chambers, 32 Nassau Street, Dublin D02 YH68

A CIP catalogue record for this book is available from the British Library

HARDBACK ISBN: 978–0–241–59351–6

www.greenpenguin.co.uk

For Flora, Ben and Letty

Contents

Author's Note

Many people in this book – my patients, their families, friends and carers – seem very real to me. I can see their expressions, and can hear their voices. And yet none of them are real – they are woven together from multiple tiny threads of reality drawn individually from the cloth of others' lives. Names, occupations, medical details, settings and family structures have been adjusted to preserve confidentiality, and although each person is imagined, I hope they will seem real, for each has a story to tell. My colleagues, however, are entirely real, as are the situations in which we find ourselves, including the events described in Chapter 11.

1. The Oscillating Narrative

'Darling!' Mum greets me from her kitchen as I step through the front door. 'There's a letter for the post.'

It's April 2021. I hang my coat on the newel post and peel off my jumper. Mum's hall radiator thrums. Two woolly hats, one inside the other (they are worn simultaneously), are tucked between the radiator and the wall. A third hat, also well warmed, contains her house key.

The letter is in the grip of a big old bulldog clip, which is attached by string and a lump of Blu-Tack to a cage on the back of the door, installed years ago by an observant occupational therapist who had noticed my stepdad falter as he bent to pick post from the floor. Today's letter, the one Mum wants me to take to the postbox, must have an overseas destination, for she has added a wobbly parade of lower-denomination stamps to her customary second-class offering, by way of encouragement to the Royal Mail. She has chosen one of her better envelopes. The writing is off centre – the envelope will have shifted under her hand and she won't have had the strength to straighten it – but the delivery instructions are clear.

The President. The White House. The USA.

Mum has always had a strong sense of agency. She asserts control over her life. She makes swift, firm and irrevocable decisions, which have often involved a disregard for her own well-being or that of others that could result in anything from mild inconvenience to serious physical harm. As she has become older, her ability to influence events has diminished. She cannot travel, visit a shop with ease or make her signature fizzy soup ('It's fine. I've boiled it up'). She can no longer organise a fund-raising event or even confidently use the telephone. But she can write letters and does so: to friends and acquaintances (she is meticulous about letters of condolence), but also to the BBC, the Archbishop of Canterbury, the Prime Minister, the Queen. The recipients are, in general, polite. The BBC sends the transcript of the radio play she requested. Someone at Number Ten thanks her for the information she supplied (what this was, I have no idea) and assures her that the Prime Minister's dog, Dilyn, is quite well. The letters from the ladies-in-waiting at Buckingham Palace are naturally an exercise in courtesy: *Her Majesty the Queen would like to thank you for writing to her again.* I wonder how the White House will shape up.

'I've kept a copy. See what you think,' says Mum, and points to it.

To write this letter, I know that she will have first risen from her kitchen chair. She will have turned sideways on its cushion and leaned forward to place a tea towel over the corner of the table, to pad it a little, and she will have gripped this corner with her right hand, while pushing herself up with her left hand beside her hip. She will have moved on puffy feet – stripey socks and Velcroed sandals – holding first her chair, then the table, then kitchen sideboard, door frame and bookcase, into a small dining area which now acts as a study. She will have called Tracey, who is cleaning the bathroom, to adjust another chair for her. The view from Mum's bungalow is beautiful, across her small garden and the river to the grassy meadows and willows beyond, but she is unable to straighten up enough to see it. Her view these days is of the floor, the bottom two shelves of the bookcase, sometimes the face of a carer when they crouch beside her. She'll have summoned a specific sheet of paper and will have folded four pieces of kitchen roll to place under her wrist. She will have covered each of her dusky fingers (this takes some time) in little caps that she has made out of papery surgical tape and will then have wrapped her hand in another tea towel, soft worn linen, before picking up her pen to write.

Mum does not reliably recall the names of her nine grandchildren. She tells embarrassing, inaccurate stories of my own past, and that of my brother and sister, peppered with grandiose claims of heroism. Her house is filled with scraps of paper on which she has written aphorisms, Bible quotes, jokes that make no sense. I wonder what she needs to tell the leader of the free world. I read the letter.

Dear President Biden, I beseech you to reconsider your policy of withdrawal from Afghanistan.

Now it's September and I listen to the radio on my way to work. Mum's letter to the President, coherent and passionate, outlined her concern that the withdrawal of American troops would leave thousands – millions – of women and children at the mercy of the Taliban. Subsequent events have already borne out her fears. I turn the radio up. The Chief Rabbi is talking about the refugee families arriving in Britain from Kabul, and how their children will adapt to life in the UK. He observes how vital it is that they learn English quickly, as kids do, and assimilate British values – he speaks optimistically of tolerance, freedom of expression, kindness. But he talks also of the importance of their Afghan heritage, of maintaining pride in their origins and traditions. He mentions the work of an American psychologist, Marshall Duke. Dr Duke, the Rabbi explains, carried out a study of children, asking them what they knew of their parents and grandparents. Where did they come from? How did they meet? Had they suffered misfortunes – illness, financial hardship, the loss of a home or of a homeland? Subsequent assessment of these children revealed that those who knew more about the older members of their family were happier, less anxious and better able to cope with upsets and challenges. On further analysis, those children whose families had weathered storms long before they were born – children who knew that life holds bad times as well as good – were the most balanced, contented and resilient of all. Duke's team have a phrase for those family tales of loss and recovery: the oscillating narrative.

The radio programme moves on to the weather, the traffic lights change, and I start looking for my car parking permit, tucked between a bottle of hand sanitiser, dodgy biros and a handful of spare face masks by the gearstick.

Later that day, I'm hovering in the office that my colleague Peter shares with four of our fellow geriatricians. Right now the others are out on the wards or in clinic, seeing the older people for whom we care, and Peter's trying to do something on his computer – answer an email, write a report – but he can see that I'm going to interrupt him.

'What's up then?'

'Sorry, Peter, you're busy, but tell me something. We all know young people are good for old people. Four-year-olds visiting care homes, lovely stuff. But why are old people good for young people?'

Peter stretches, clasping his long fingers together and turning his hands palm upwards above his head. 'I think it's like a roller coaster. When you're young, you're on the roller coaster, but you don't really know it. When things go wrong, when you're at the bottom of the ride – you know, fail an exam, split up with a girlfriend – you feel like life's at an end, and you can't believe it'll ever get better.'

He picks up a circular piece of metal from his desk. It's part of a bicycle that the chain hooks round, and he turns it in his hands as he thinks aloud. 'But older people, they're at the end of the ride. In fact, they might have stepped right off the roller coaster. They can see the whole picture, the ups and downs. It's about perspective.'

At home that evening I look up Marshall Duke's original paper. It's called 'Knowledge of Family History as a Clinically Useful Index of Psychological Wellbeing and Prognosis'. One of its co-authors is Professor Robyn Fivush, from Emory University, whose work focuses on the ways in which families reminisce about past experiences. She has a particular interest in auto-biographical narratives, the stories that inform our perception of ourselves. She studies how these stories and our response to them might enhance or inhibit our emotional and social understanding and define how we cope with stressful and traumatic events. In their paper, the authors were careful not to draw simplistic conclusions from their findings. Children who knew the most about their family history did indeed turn out in other measures to have lower anxiety and higher self-esteem.

They also had fewer behavioural problems. However, as the authors explained, it would not be enough simply to teach children some key facts about their individual family sagas and hope this would fix their worries. Rather, of course, it is the way in which family stories are told that builds confidence and strength. The children who could answer family history questions confidently also had more cohesive families.

The authors looked into how information gets handed across generations and found it was usually by mothers and grandmothers, and often at family gatherings – meals, holidays, celebrations. They acknowledged that the link may well be no more than a correlation – families that can muster kitchen tables, festive meals and holidays probably have a head start when it comes to providing stability and confidence – but their data suggested that the effect was about more than just financial security, and material poverty does not prevent a family from being cohesive and celebrating anniversaries, although it may make it harder. In later research Professor Fivush explored the idea that children do best when they have been allowed to develop a strong sense of what she called 'the intergenerational self'. She describes how that intergenerational self is grown, the essential elements passed down the line from grandparent to parent to child, and she highlights the role of stories that provide strength and guidance.

*

There is a steady stream of people coming in and out of Don's room, which is right in the middle of the Acute Medical Unit (AMU). Time-lapse photography would show a complex, dense web outside its door. Nurses and young doctors pass Don's room on their way to and from other bays; Health Care Assistants carry pans to the sluice; paramedics deliver new patients to the unit. The radiographer trundles by with a portable machine for the man in the next room, who is too sick to go downstairs for his chest X-ray. The floor outside Don's room, a node between the ward reception desk, two bays and a corridor, is cleaned and polished by Nali in the morning and Steffan in the afternoon. Jeffrey comes past with the food trolley, but Don is beyond food. A trio of medical students consult their notes outside his room, allocating patients to one another, people with whom they'll spend an hour or so laboriously asking a tick list of questions – weight loss, alcohol consumption, cough (dry, productive, with blood?) – and carrying out a detailed examination for signs important or arcane (the students do not yet differentiate). Don is not on the list of suitable recipients of their attention and the students disperse. The phlebotomist passes by with her trolley of butterfly needles and blood test tubes, and she too does not disturb Don. The people flowing in and out of Don's room are his family, and during my day on duty I see them slip quietly past one another. There are no protracted corridor conversations, no overt displays

8

of grief, but there is contact – palms that meet, sliding over one another as brother passes brother. A quick hug, the squeeze of an arm. A teenage grandchild arrives and another leaves. There are brief smiles. Eyes glisten.

I met Don this morning. He is seventy-nine and has pancreatic cancer and is dying. He is known to the palliative care team, and in recent weeks they have discussed with him where he would like to die, offering the option of care at home. Don has been clear. He has confided in the team that his wife Maureen is a worrier. Things – places, objects – take on special meanings for her. She will never be able to sleep in the house in which Don has died. He therefore does not wish to die at home. The palliative care team hoped to provide a bed in the hospice for his last days, but events have moved too quickly; there is no space there, so here he lies, in a room surrounded by the purposeful chaos of one of the busiest places in the hospital.

Late in the evening, before leaving, I knock at Don's door and let myself in. I'm hit by a wave of serenity. Two daughters, shoulder to shoulder on plastic chairs, and a man who is Don's son maybe, whose hand rests on the back of a younger lad, a grandson – spotty and handsome in a dark hoody and clean white trainers, leaning forward, elbow on knee, chin on palm. And Don in the centre, yellow-grey, eyes closed, perhaps asleep or perhaps away, far away, deep in his past or his future.

Don's eldest daughter Lisa steps out of the room

with me. She is pale and composed, in a silvery knitted top. Her toes are tanned and wear pretty rings. I check in – is he comfortable?

'I think he's fine,' she says, and catches herself, blinks and smiles. 'I mean, dying, but you know . . .'

I reply that I know what she means and I'm glad he's OK, and I ask how Maureen is doing, and Lisa explains that the family are taking it in turns to sit with her, at home, because Mum doesn't do hospitals. Then I say, 'Lisa, I hope you don't mind me saying but there is a lot of love in that room.'

She looks at me and raises her eyebrows for a moment. 'Dad –' she starts then stops and looks at the ceiling, but she doesn't look really because she is squeezing her eyes closed. She breathes in through her nose and sighs slowly out, then opens her eyes and speaks again. 'Dad grew up in care. He didn't get any love. And he always said he would give his family all the love he didn't get.'

Out of nowhere – out of a childhood that did not include family meals, kindly grandparents, a shared past – Don has created for his own family a beautiful story, a narrative that's already been handed to his grandchildren. The story does not have to be all happy to be a good one and a true one, a story that provides strength and guidance.

In November that year, I walk along a cliff path and think about stories. I've come away from home to rest for a moment beside the sea, and my thoughts are jumbled because Mum isn't well and I feel bad for taking myself further from her, and work is pressing because the hospital is full, more full than ever, with two beds in each single room, and we are trying to set up a new service, to offer better treatment in their own homes for older people, the frailest, those who are most likely to become confused by a change of scene and who do not thrive in hospital. There are issues of workforce, training, communication. The IT is awful. We must make plans: how to safely and swiftly supply medicines, oxygen, equipment and staff beyond the familiar setting of the hospital. There are meetings, endless meetings.

The blackberries are over, and down on the slippery stones at the bottom of the cliff the seal pups are fat. I try to think of the earliest stories I can remember – fables, myths, parables – that might have shaped my own understanding. I think of primary school, of a coat hook with a lion sticker and my own plasticine tin, and I think of Aesop's Androcles, who escaped from slavery and pulled a thorn from the paw of a lion, meeting the lion again in the gruesome Roman circus, where the lion was supposed to eat him but declined to do so, remembering Androcles' kindness, and how the Emperor was impressed by their tale and set them both free. I am six and I want to be Androcles. I can feel the rough weave of my garment and noble courage courses through me as I hold the huge putrid paw and find the thorn with my brave fingers. But also I can smell my father's tweed jacket as he sits on my bed, reading aloud Saki's story of Bertha, a little girl who is so horribly good that she wins medals for punctuality, conduct and obedience. Bertha is pursued by a wolf (the wolf espies her in the distance on account of her spotlessly clean pinafore) and she hides in a bush, but the clanking of her enormous medals gives her away and she is devoured.

I look out to sea, where a tanker is moored as it waits for its turn at the nearby refinery. I think of Frankie, for whom we cared in the storm of the pandemic. She had COVID and then pneumonia, and she got very ill indeed, and then she had a heart attack, and then she got better, and over that time snippets of Frankie's life emerged. Among those looking after Frankie was Salimah, a doctor who the Medical Staffing department had rustled up from somewhere, not one of our allocated trainees but an extra pair of hands to work on an extra ward, a courageous young doctor who had trained in a language not her own and was now in a country far from home.

Salimah spent lots of time with Frankie, her head with its neatly tied scarf bent over Frankie's arms, searching for a tiny undamaged vein in which to insert a drip to deliver more antibiotics, and they told one another things. Salimah was delighted. 'Frankie worked in fashion,' she said. 'For Dior! Finding fabric all over the world!'

I saw Frankie on my ward round, as she sat on the edge of her bed, gathering her strength and will for a moment of standing to hold a frame and move her feet round, one step, one step, one step, to turn and to sit with relief in a high-backed chair and wriggle a little to loosen her dressing gown, which I noticed was a baby blue fine-knit cashmere with a collar of detailed brocade. I commented on her amazing life, and Frankie shook her head reprovingly. 'Not all roses, Dr Pollock.' She glanced at her neighbour, asleep in the next bed, and leaned forward. 'My first two husbands were complete shits.' She grinned then looked away and caught her top lip in her teeth, frowning as she recalled a precise moment of shittiness before she winked. 'And then I found a keeper . . .'

We are surrounded now by images of perfection. Our children are bombarded with messages both overt and subtle, and the barrage does not let up as we move into adulthood. Messages fly at us from advertisers, TV programmes, Instagram; from teachers, parents, government; from our peers and eventually, disastrously, from deep within ourselves. We must have the perfect body, the perfect teeth, the perfect clothes, the perfect exam results, the perfect degree and the subsequent perfect job, the perfect relationship, unsullied by fatigue or jealousies. We must have the perfect home and the perfect holiday: the cocktail bar, the infinity pool. Yet most older people have lived lives like Frankie's, full of events both joyous and tragic, and older people have a perspective that the rest of us might struggle to see.

Back on the cliff path, I watch the wind blowing across the dried grasses and evergreen gorse of the headland, and see the small birds buffeted, hopping between twigs and making short flights to their hidden places of sanctuary. I think about what we can learn from the stories of others and how we can gain the information and confidence we need to influence our own futures and to find new ways to make the most of long lives.

It is spring. I get home from work one day and our son is in the kitchen, come to use the gym equipment my husband set up in the barn during lockdown. He takes off the orange top he's been wearing all day, a heavy garment with metal wires knitted into its fabric, smeared with green and brown stains. He's working on the railways, chainsawing trees and strimming scrub, and I'm so proud of him for finding his balance again after a year of anxiety and disorientation, a crisis of confidence, a good degree abandoned. He asks about my day and I sigh — we've had a bit of a time of it today on my ward, because George died last night and Horace went this morning, and June died too just before I left for home, and none of them were unexpected but three at once . . . And my son spreads his arms, beckoning me into a hug. His chin is on my head, and he says, 'That's the thing about your job, Mum. It's not so much life and death, as death and death.'

Oh, my darling boy, you make me laugh. My job is all about life. It's about people and warmth and kindness, and about pain and loneliness, and complicated medicine, and overstretched services, and best-loved dogs and Elton John or Clara Schumann. And making a donation to save the whales, and setting a timer on Alexa for pills or pavlova, and going to the pub or to the library or to Valencia. It's about a nervous doctor from Oman scanning his notes for an error, and a physio from Romania who is married to a stove fitter from down the road, and a nurse from Zimbabwe with waist-long braids tied back in a scrap of orange light. It's about benches in memoriam and woods where bluebells grow, and worries that make us breathless in the night, and playground slides and boat trips and macramé and motorbikes. It's about disproportionately disabling corns on toes and a strange pain in a rib and plans for a wedding. It's about frustrated neighbours, ratty sisters, trust between strangers. It's about watering the tomatoes on a balcony seven floors up and the warmth of the sun on a sleeve and finding new shoes for an old husband.

This book is about many things I have learned from my patients and their families and carers. It is a book of stories – stories about courage, fear, trust, malevolence, laughter, grief and good and bad behaviour. Stories about better ways of providing care, about communities and services that make a difference. How do we find a balance between our search for perfection and the necessity of accepting that life in very old age might present intractable problems? How do we make things better while learning still to cherish imperfect lives? What can we piece together from our own experience, and from that of our family, and from friends and strangers about getting older?

What are stories for? To entertain. To explain, to illuminate. To comfort. Above all, stories help us to make sense of our lives. Stories show us that we are not alone. Here is a book of stories about things we can learn from those who have gone before us. Stories that offer optimism, honesty and strength – good advice for our future selves.

2. Advice for My Future Self

When I had our first baby, we lived in London. She slept in her basket in a cupboard and my husband and I bathed her in a washing-up bowl. A couple of months later, in the winter, we moved, as you do with a tiny baby (why not throw every aspect of your life into disarray at once?), into our new, very old house in the country, a house which was missing several windows and still had a digger in the front room – a small one, my husband assured me, but it was unquestionably yellow and with hydraulics, which is a digger all the same. I realised one evening that our baby needed a bath and somewhere in the move the washing-up bowl had got lost and my husband was still working in London and would not be back until late. I surveyed the bathroom. Its mouldy carpet had been torn up, leaving mangy patches of underlay on grey floorboards with dust and nails, and the radiator was tepid and the cast-iron bath was big and deep and cold.

I put her towel on the radiator and lined up the baby shampoo and the soft sponge, and I ran the bath and tested the water temperature with my elbow, as I had been taught to do, and unwrapped my baby (the most beautiful baby in the world, because one baby must be and why should she not be mine?) and I knelt by the bath and lowered her into the water, my right hand behind her little head, left hand under her bottom very carefully. I suddenly thought, *Perhaps I shall have a funny turn, a seizure or a stroke, and my baby will drown,* and as I thought this, her tiny perfect mouth drooped down at the corners. *What is the matter?* I thought. Her beautiful forehead crinkled and I thought, *The water is too hot. Or too cold? Maybe she is unaccountably allergic to the water of Somerset?* Then tears sprang at the edge of her eyes, which searched my face as I gazed down at her, and I realised I must lift her out, quickly, right now, and as I reached for the towel so that I could wrap her up and make her safe, I caught my reflection in the window. It was a dark night and there was no curtain, and my face was taut with fear and worry. My poor baby. I looked down at her and smiled and trickled warm water from my fingers until her expression changed, first to uncertainty and then to a smile. She gave a wriggle, a kick of her little legs. Together we grew what we needed. Security. Confidence.

It strikes me now, that we are doing to older people what I did to my baby many years ago. We are looking at our ageing population and at individual older people – even or perhaps especially those whom we love – with concern, anxiety or even panic. In turn, older people look back at the rest of us, thinking, *What is it you are seeing? Why are you all looking worried? What is so wrong with us?* And that is not right. We do not need to gaze on older people in a way that causes them to be fearful. It is not fair and it is not helpful.

It is also very unwise to develop at any stage of our lives a prejudice against our future selves.

There's a programme at present in the NHS in England to identify unwarranted variation in performance and results between hospitals – waiting times, say, or the effectiveness of a particular operation – and to put in place the work needed to address those variations. The project is called GIRFT – Getting It Right First Time – but when I was first told of this programme I was distracted and misheard it as Getting It Right Third Time, which too often feels like a more accurate description. And perhaps it reflects a realistic assessment of our learning about our new longevity. We know a great deal now about the medical interventions that add years to our lives, but we have so much yet to learn about complexity, about quality of life and what matters and making the most of it – about being older for longer and adding life to those years.

The extension of life expectancy way beyond that of previous generations has caught us on the hop, and we need to harness energy, ingenuity and resourcefulness to make the most of a long life. What have we learned so far?

The huge increase in average lifespan over the last century was driven by medical advances that allowed *young* people to live longer, advances which tackled the big causes of premature death. Catastrophic infectious diseases that carried us off in infancy have largely been eradicated through vaccination and the provision of clean water, and deaths in midlife due to heart disease or cancer have become less frequent as both preventive and curative treatments have evolved. But now our scientific progress is allowing *old* people to live longer. The challenge has changed; we need to live well, as well as to live long.

In the kitchen one evening, I listen to a lecture online. Eamon O'Shea is the just retired professor of health economics at the University of Galway, Ireland, his life's work the study of dementia, inequality and ageing. Professor O'Shea has his sleeves rolled up for retirement. He asks us to think of our childhood and adolescence, our life as a young adult, at university or in a first job – the first two and a bit decades of our lives. He reminds us that at sixty-five we have on average a similar amount of time left during which we can be active, fulfilled and contented. Time enough for us to use what we've learned and learn some more. Luck will play its part, but we also have choices.

'When I'm eighty,' Eamon says cheerfully, 'it's no good just being on life's pitch – I want to be playing in the game.'

There's a strong and growing body of evidence about five simple behaviours that increase our lifespan – physical activity, ditching cigarettes, eating a healthy diet, restrained consumption of alcohol and embracing some sort of cognitive challenge. We can all guess that the pandemic did no favours to the nation's waistline. We all know too, that it's easy to become despondent about exercise, to feel that we are too old, too tired, that we are beyond donning trainers and gym shorts – but it may be helpful to know that trainers and gym shorts aren't what we need, for even a modest increase in physical activity, achievable without shedding our usual clothes, improves our chances of living well and preserving our independence. Importantly we also know that as well as living longer, people who maintain four or five of these good behaviours also spend fewer years living with dementia. We know what's good for us. But Professor O'Shea's not just talking about exercise and clean living. He alludes to friendship, creativity, curiosity – the things that make us human.

Two further influences are becoming apparent that shape how we age. The first is social connection. It's taken a pandemic to highlight the centrality of human relationships, yet the evidence was there already: that we need one another, that loneliness kills. We instinctively know that we can become bewilderingly connected *to* everything – the internet, the news, the latest mini-series – at the same time as finding ourselves dangerously connected *with* no one. And the evidence is building. We know that increasing separation from families, friends, neighbours and communities is bad for our health, that social isolation, which is growing in many countries, is bad for well-being and bad for happiness at any age – loneliness hurts younger people too. We know that we can change this – that we can build communities that foster connection, warmth and kinship.

Finally and fascinatingly it is increasingly clear that our attitude to getting older affects how we age. Professor Rose Anne Kenny has run The Irish Longitudinal Study on Ageing (TILDA) since 2009, and alongside their insights regarding diet and muscle building, sleep and cold-water swimming, friendship and laughter, Professor Kenny and her team have studied the effect our attitude towards ageing can have on how well we get on later in life.

Some of Professor Kenny's research is described in her book, *Age Proof*, which is peppered with gripping studies. In one exercise adults aged fifty and over were asked to say how much they agreed with statements such as 'As I get older I can take part in fewer activities' and 'I feel left out of things', alongside positive statements like 'As I get older I get wiser' or 'As I get older there is much I can do to maintain my independence'. Professor Kenny's team adjusted for the fact that some participants had medical conditions or life circumstances that would affect both their answers and their chance of successful ageing, and they did good statistical work to take account of these factors. They watched their participants for eight years and found that those with poor attitudes were more likely to experience accelerated physical and cognitive ageing. Conversely people who were already frail but who had positive attitudes towards getting older maintained mental abilities that were as good as their non-frail peers. These people weren't unrealistic, just positive. And it's not just one study. It's repeatedly been shown that our attitudes to ageing affect how we physically age, even while we are young. Further research scrutinising the human genome is beginning to shed light on the biological mechanisms that make this happen – molecular changes in the genes that control ageing, molecular changes brought about by *thinking*. What we think about getting older actively changes our chance of living longer healthier lives. It sounds nuts but it's true.

Professor Kenny's research is backed up by evidence from the United States which demonstrates dramatically that how we feel about getting older affects not just our future abilities but also influences how well older people live right now. Dr Becca Levy, a professor of psychology and epidemiology at Yale has, like Professor Kenny, studied the effect that our beliefs about ageing have on our behaviour. Her research repeatedly challenges negative cultural stereotypes about older people. Dr Levy is even-handed – she acknowledges the devastating effects of conditions related to biological ageing, but her studies and experiments consistently demonstrate that ageing is also a deeply social and psychological process.

I described one of her experiments badly to a charming mathematician I once met on a train. In Dr Levy's book, *Breaking the Age Code*, she explains how older people were given 'priming' sessions before sitting a memory test. During the priming session, participants were exposed to a series of words associated with either positive stereotypes of old age, such as 'wise', 'alert' and 'learned', or negative words, such as 'senile', 'confused' and 'Alzheimer's'.

The mathematician listened as I explained that the older people who had seen the positive words – for no more than ten minutes – performed better on the subsequent memory test than those who had witnessed the negative words.

'I'm not surprised,' he told me. 'The same happens with children, of course. If you tell them they can solve a maths problem, they tend to do a lot better than if you say, this one's too difficult for you.'

But I had got something important wrong. Later, I reread Dr Levy's work. In the 'priming' sessions, the study participants had been asked to focus on a bullseye in the centre of the screen, while the positive or negative words were flashed above or below it, so fast they were unaware of the words, which looked like just a blur. The participants had no idea what words they had been shown, but they had perceived and absorbed the messages, and their ability to do the memory tests was damaged or enhanced by what they had *unconsciously* seen. Dr Levy's experiment, since repeated across five continents, is one of many that demonstrate that our memory – and, beyond that, our health and behaviour and happiness – is influenced by our view of ageing, which in turn is affected, subtly but profoundly, by the attitudes held by those around us.

I am driving through our village on my way back from the river, where the dog and I have been walking, and I am flagged down by Mike. I squint up at him as the car window descends, for Mike is tall and the sun is setting behind him.

'Lucy! I just read your book. It's brilliant,' says Mike, and I am chuffed, because I had written a book to help older people and their families – stories that explain how to tackle worries like whether one might be taking too many medicines, dilemmas about driving, conversations concerning resuscitation – and I like Mike and value his praise. He is retired now. He was one of our local GPs and he once told me how his role was made clear to him early on when he had just joined the practice fresh from training. He had been signing letters when he overheard a conversation between the surgery's most experienced receptionist and a new patient, who was filling in the registration documents.

'Which doctor do you want to see?' the receptionist asked.

The patient replied, 'I don't know. What have you got?'

And the receptionist put her hands firmly together and leaned towards the new patient through the hatch to tell him, 'Well, you can have the old one, or the young one, or the clever one.'

Now Mike leans on my car, his big hand on the door frame, and I remember how tenderly those hands held my son when he was a baby and unwell, and how tactfully Mike had suggested that it might be a good idea for me to take him to hospital that very day, and Mike had refrained from pointing out that another mother, one more observant or attentive, might have sought help sooner. I remember how calm and unhurried his conversation was with the paediatrician on duty as he made arrangements for my son's urgent assessment.

Mike is beaming at me, backlit by the sun. 'Great book. It's all true. And it's useful, and it's funny.' He pats the car and straightens up. 'Anyway, well done.'

He puts his hand on the small of his back, and pushes his shoulders back, and winces. 'Only problem is, now I feel as if I've read the script and I'm not sure I want a part in the play.'

Oh, Mike! I do not wish to see him disconcerted. And he is not alone.

*

We come to a paradox. So much of the tremendous work about ageing comes down to Plan A. Positive attitudes, healthy lives – in the end, Plan A is 'Don't get old'. And that is a very good plan, but we need a backup. We rightly admire and celebrate the nonagenarian wing walkers, the poets and artists and CEOs who show the rest of us how to age well, but we must not pretend that this is the only story. Ageing is inevitable; we might slow the rate but we cannot evade the process. We're all aware that for many older people and their families, ageing holds fears and real difficulties. We must not pretend that older people don't ever have to contend with multiple medical problems or that soon these problems won't exist. We can't tell ourselves that many older people, including our future selves, won't end up in hospital, or in and out of hospital, or in a care home. We can't pretend that no one ever becomes frail or needs help, even those who were hitherto fit and active. And we know we haven't got this right so far. Let's be honest, we too often see older people – parents, grandparents, spouses, friends – being treated in ways we would not wish to be treated ourselves. It's tricky to maintain a positive attitude to ageing if deep down we are afraid. So we need a Plan B.

Every day in my work I see older people being offered care and treatment that is thoughtful, effective and kind. But it isn't consistent, and there is much we can change. And all of us have a role in this – not just people who work in healthcare. We can all play our part – older people, those who love and care for them, and any one of us who suspects that at some point in the future we may become old. We can do so much better.

It's a popular thing at present to be asked to go back in time to advise one's teenage self. Knowing what you know now, what advice would you give to yourself at eighteen? I put the question to Molly, who has dropped in for tea on her way to visit her grandson's new baby.

'God, what an awful idea,' she says. 'If I knew then what I know now, I wouldn't have been able to enjoy my twenties.'

I listen to a Mancunian woman on the radio. She's wheezing and laughing at the same time. 'If I knew then what I know now,' she says lugubriously, 'I'd have kept me legs in a jug.'

But later I wonder, instead of advising my eighteen-year-old self, what advice would I give my *eighty*-year-old self? If I could write a birthday card now, to open on my eightieth birthday, what would I say?

I pull out a piece of paper and stare at it.

Don't worry too much about what people think, I write.

I come back to the piece of paper through the day, adding directions. *Be kind. Be interested in other people. Enjoy small pleasures. Do your bloody pelvic floor exercises.*

This morning I looked in my diary: *29 June. Let Martin know*, I have written. I have no recollection who Martin is, nor what I should let him know.

I add a note to my eightieth birthday advice: *Don't sabotage yourself by writing stupid stuff in your diary. Make things clear.*

I try my new question out on everyone. I am merciless in my interrogation of friends and colleagues.

'Make sure you have beauty in your life,' says Cory. 'Flowers. A painting. Try to be in a lovely place.'

Charlotte pauses as we walk together across the moor. 'Oh, that's a good one. Try to spend time with your friends.'

Katherine and I have chatted about her daughter's A level choices and whether their cat is pregnant, and she's chastised herself for her lockdown weight gain before I say, 'Here's a question – what would be your advice to your eighty-year-old self?'

'Ooh,' says Katherine immediately. 'Keep fit.'

I suddenly realise that my question is a trap. We may be able to recall the hopes and fears of our eighteen-year-old self and we may have some wise but too late advice for that long-ago teenager, yet when it comes to projecting ourselves into the future, our own future, something different happens.

I ask my question again, testing my new theory. We're walking out of a dance class one evening in early spring. I love it; I stay in the back row and go left when everyone else has gone right and I tread on my own toes. I ask Selina for her advice and she laughs.

'Make the most of it. Get something out of every

day – like tonight, the birds singing in the dusk and the moon all lit up.'

But I ask Frances the same question and she sets down the pan she has pulled from the oven. Her kitchen is full of lists and bills, and there is a mother-in-law who is demanding, impervious to the effect she has on others. Frances wipes the sweat from her forehead with the inside of her arm and says, 'Try not to worry.'

'Be curious,' says Karen, and later she lends me a book about the history of fabric and I learn of the strips of linen that bound the mummy of Tutankhamun, and the woollen sails of the Vikings.

Tess has come to stay the night before a wedding and has unpacked her trouser suit and borrowed the iron. I pose my question: what advice would you give your eighty-year-old self?

Tess moves the tip of the iron to press a pleat precisely into place.

'Make an effort,' she says firmly.

The men I ask look wary – perhaps they are less confident of their longevity than women.

Nicholas is reserved. He considers the question before answering. He has weathered storms and sadness, and says, 'Will I actually be around?' Then he sets his shoulders and continues. 'Yes, OK. No regrets. That's my advice. Keep looking forward.'

My theory seems to be holding up under scrutiny. Even Ed's response is consistent. He puts up his hand to push my question away. 'Why ever would I want any-one's advice when I'm eighty?' Ed has been iconoclastic since the day he was born and has never been one for following advice, not even his own.

I think about each answer and realise that, of course, almost all of us are giving our future selves the advice we would give ourselves right now. The advice I offer my eighty-year-old self is the advice I might do well to follow today.

Iona is only twenty-three, settling into a new job in a city far from friends and family. Her advice is sage.

'Try not to forget the things you used to enjoy,' she suggests. 'Like, I loved singing at school, and I com-pletely forgot about it at uni, but now I've joined a choir.'

I think of Frances, my worrier friend, and I guess that by the time Frances is eighty her troublesome mother-in-law is unlikely to remain troublesome but other concerns may well have moved in to fill the gap that mother-in-law has left. I think of Rose Anne Kenny's work and the evi-dence that our individual attitude to health and well-being has such a profound effect on what happens to us as we get older, and I wonder whether Frances will ever be able to follow her own advice and learn not to worry. I wonder whether she might be able to start right now.

My Aunt Virginia thinks hard when I ask her to advise her older self.

'I'm a bit closer to eighty than you are,' she says. Virginia is in her early seventies.

'This question really matters to me.'

She turns a piece of paper over in her hands as she formulates her answer, and as she speaks I recognise that this is advice she has already given herself, and has followed.

'I'd say take a look at the traits you've got, the ones you've inherited and the ones you've grown for yourself. Then work out which ones you want to keep and do something about the rest.'

I love Virginia's answer. It's courageous and optimistic, and I know she is right. Our personality traits are strong. Some are built in but others we have allowed to take root; we can review our behaviours and make choices. As we've moved into midlife I've watched my own generation – family and friends – and I've seen patterns emerge that I recognise, because they are patterns that I see in my patients, people who are in their late seventies and beyond. I've watched people grow beautiful behaviours – generosity and patience, curiosity and grace – and I have seen bad behaviours allowed to set seed – selfishness, spite, a sourness that curdles the kindness right out of that person and blights the lives of those around them. And I have realised that some of these are lifelong traits, knitted into our DNA, and others have developed in response to events and experiences. But in either case a different way of being can be achieved by a willed change in direction, an active decision to step on to a different path.

The same is true of our collective behaviour, how our society does things. In the same way as my aunt reviewed her habits, choosing which to build up and which to discard, we can decide what we value. We can look at the way in which we treat older people today and we can think about the way we would like to be treated ourselves in the future. We can decide what changes we need to make and work together to make them now. We can strengthen communities, our sense of belonging. We can decide to look out for one another, invest in housing and transport, in access to outdoor spaces, creative projects, the performing arts. We can create opportunities for generations to meet and to learn and enjoy being with one another. And we can bring a strong lens to focus on healthcare. We can commit to Plan A, taking care of ourselves as we gain years, and at the same time we can develop our Plan B. We can acknowledge that sad and difficult things happen in old age – loss and debility cannot be eradicated, but situations we fear can be made less fearful if we talk about them, if we recognise that there are different ways of doing things, and if we work together to make changes that will help older people right now and will make life better for ourselves in the future.

We can celebrate good things that are happening already and we can embrace new approaches with confidence. We can acknowledge and call out thoughtless care, inflexible systems and bad behaviours. We must demand a shift in power. We must challenge and push aside healthcare that does not listen, that doesn't take the time to understand our goals and wishes. Older people today, and you and I in the future, deserve to be heard.

We can get this right. We can acknowledge that life in old age may be messy and complicated, but that there is also room for laughter, confidence, fulfilment.

I try my question out on Jane. She is a psychotherapist whose insights have provided me stability and comfort and helped me to change my behaviour. What is her advice for her eighty-year-old self?

She tips her head on one side and regards me carefully.

I want to wriggle. Jane's perception is both ferocious and compassionate. I try to guess what she will be thinking – she will not be planning to make a demand. Jane does not readily give advice. Instead I know she will be thinking about that eighty-year-old woman, weighing her up. Jane will be thinking about what will be good, what will be helpful and true, for her own future same-but-different self to read on that birthday.

The moment passes. Jane blinks and straightens up. She claps her hands together.

'Wow. What a ride.'

3. Silver Platter

The river close to our house runs slowly and the fields are flat and end at the water's edge in an abrupt drop fringed with strappy reeds. The cattle, Charolais cross salted caramel, cannot drink here where the bank is steep. But at intervals a small muddy bay curves into the field, a patch of shallow water, and we watch, my husband and the dog and I, while a drama plays out as slowly as the river runs. The bullocks are coming to drink but a swan is standing in the shallow water by the little muddy beach, preening himself with deliberate care, choosing one feather at a time to ruffle and adjust, and the lead bullock comes nearer, dewlap swaying. The bullock pauses and the swan pauses also, then bends his head back to his plumage, tucking his beak again into his chest feathers to tease out a wrinkle that none of us can see. The bullocks are huge – born in the winter on Exmoor, they have been brought down to fatten here by the river and now in late summer they have great slabby shoulders and kneecaps as big and thick as breadboards, and the bullock at the front lowers his head and watches the swan, then takes another step. The swan straightens up. The bullocks behind shift uneasily – one comes

forward to stand by the muscled rump of his leader, and
for a moment everything is still. Then the lead bullock
takes another step, and in an instant the swan extends
his head and plucks a long reed leaf from the bank and
lays it swiftly on the mud, his neck snaking. The reed lies
there, a green line beyond which none shall pass. The
bullocks blink as they absorb this message. They take a
step back and swing away. The swan watches them go.
He stretches his wings. He resumes his business with
the feathers.

'Young lady, you can bring that tablet to me on a silver
platter and I will not be taking it.'

Mrs Goldman and I look down at the red and white
pack of pills on the desk between us, and I look again
at my notes, where I have written Mrs Goldman's blood
pressure, which I have just checked, and checked again,
hoping for a better result, but the second reading was
rather worse than the first, so I have had to write *197/98*
and drawn a circle round the result. Mrs Goldman and
I have reached an impasse.

I pull a face and Mrs Goldman says, 'Don't you pull
faces at me. That tablet makes me feel bleurgh.'

It's 1994. Mrs Goldman and I first met a few weeks
ago on the ward where I'm the new registrar. I've been
qualified for four years. My consultant does a ward round
twice a week – the rest of the time I'm in charge. Mrs
Goldman had been admitted following a severe bout

of gastroenteritis, for which she held her fishmonger responsible. She had been dehydrated when she first came in with a very low blood pressure, but two days of intravenous fluid and rest had allowed her insides to recover, and the nurses had recorded her blood pressure as it climbed steadily back to normal levels and then went on climbing, past the upper limits of normal and inexorably higher. *188 systolic, 195, 204.* I had discussed Mrs Goldman's hypertension with my boss and sent her urine off to the lab to be tested for protein – none, a good thing – and I had turned the ward lights down so that I could squint with an ophthalmoscope into her eyes, looking for signs of pressure in the blood vessels of her retinas, but her arteries were smooth and her retinal tissue unblemished. I had retrieved an ECG machine from the cardiology ward in the new block, wheeling it down in the swish lift, then along the basement corridor, its ceiling lined with mysterious ducts and redundant cables, past bed frames and stained chairs with paper labels Sellotaped to them reading 'condemned' in a variety of misspellings, and back up again in the clanky lift to the geriatric ward in the old block, and I'd lined up the little rubber suction pads along Mrs Goldman's bony ribs and recorded a bad ECG because one suction pad had fallen off and there wasn't any gel left in the bottle and I wasn't going back to cardiology for more, so I'd apologised to Mrs Goldman and used some of my spit to get the last pad to stick and her ECG was perfect, with no signs of the heart strain that a woman of ninety-two should have with a blood pressure that high.

By rights, a consistently elevated blood pressure should be causing damage. We know that middle-aged people with even mildly raised blood pressure are more likely to run into cardiovascular trouble than those whose blood pressure remains low. Too much salt, crummy diets lacking fruit and vegetables, obesity, lack of physical activity, excessive alcohol or caffeine – all contribute to a hypertensive tendency, and yet there are those who live a saintly life, running marathons on unsalted lettuce, despite which their blood pressure rises, as there's a substantial genetic component to this condition, with an additional mean genetic kick for those of black African or black Caribbean descent. There's also an association with deprivation that isn't explained by other factors – as with many other diseases, treatment of hypertension demands treatment of inequity. And hypertension causes harm. Over time, the excess pressure in blood vessels causes changes to the delicate tissue that lines each artery. Arteries which in youth are stretchy and elastic, flexing with each heartbeat, instead become stiff. As the lining of each artery thickens, the canal through which blood can flow narrows and can become blocked entirely. The heart, trying to push blood through those thickened arteries, is put under strain and its muscle grows bigger – a bad thing, as the heart muscle outstrips its own blood supply and becomes enlarged but ineffective. The most delicate arteries often show the damage first – those that provide the filtering mechanisms of the kidney suffer early, causing protein to leak into the urine. The layers of the retina at the back of the eye develop telltale signs of stressed blood vessels – tiny bleeding points, fluffy pale 'cotton wool spots' made of dead and dying nerve fibres whose blood supply has dried up. And high blood pressure increases the risk of heart attacks and of stroke in both its devastating forms, the commoner version due to blockage of an artery and the less common haemorrhagic stroke that results from a burst blood vessel. So we are right to worry about hypertension, and considerable efforts are made to detect and treat it, because in the right people treatment can reduce the risk of the premature disability and death caused by heart attacks and strokes.

Mrs Goldman's blood pressure was too high and I was determined to bring it down. She may not have signs of organ damage yet, but she surely would soon. And I was young, embarking on my training in geriatric medicine and I was avowedly non-ageist, and I would pit my skills against Mrs Goldman's blood pressure as staunchly as I would for that of a fifty-year-old.

'It's time I went home,' Mrs Goldman had informed me on the ward, as she packed her nightdress and washbag into a neat suitcase. Her red coat with gold buttons was ready on the bed. Not so fast, Mrs G! I had looked through her notes – I wasn't the first person to worry about her blood pressure. She'd been given a beta blocker, atenolol, a few years previously, but her heart had slowed dramatically, causing her to feel light-headed and the atenolol had been stopped. Her GP had then tried a water tablet, a thiazide diuretic, great for calming high blood pressure, but Mrs Goldman's sodium level had taken a dive, so bendroflumethiazide was added to the list of medications she couldn't take. But I had a new one up my sleeve, amlodipine, a calcium channel blocker, only quite recently available in the UK, and I had told Mrs Goldman to take one tablet a day until I saw her in outpatients to ensure they were working.

And now here she is, sitting in clinic in her red coat in the chair opposite my desk, and neither of us is happy.

'When you say "bleurgh", Mrs Goldman, can you describe a bit more what you mean?'

Mrs Goldman puffs her pale cheeks and lets out a thoughtful breath. She has lively brown eyes and she taps the packet of pills – gold rings, a charm bracelet sliding down her fine-boned wrist.

'Good for nothing. Washed out, washed up.'

'Light-headed?'

'No, not that. Just bleurgh.'

'Swollen ankles?' I ask, and I lean down to peer at Mrs Goldman's ankles under the desk – tiny shapely ankles in fifteen-denier tan stockings above shiny patent court shoes.

'No,' says Mrs Goldman.

I open the desk drawer and get out a copy of the British National Formulary, the BNF, to look up the potential side effects of amlodipine, and feeling bleurgh is not listed. I check with Mrs Goldman about breathlessness, cramps, flushing, headaches or tummy upsets, but she denies all these, and there's only one side effect left, which is asthenia, which doesn't count as I have not heard of it.

I come clean with Mrs Goldman. 'I'm not sure what else we can do. I'll talk with the boss after clinic. I'm sorry these ones didn't work for you.'

Mrs Goldman pushes the tablets gently across the desk. 'You keep these, Dr Pollock. And I think the best thing you can do for me is leave me alone. I've got to ninety-two with that blood pressure and I think maybe it suits me.'

After clinic, I go to the library and get a dictionary and look up asthenia. It means weakness.

Over the years I've kept an eye out for that word 'asthenia'. It's a strange situation, because medics use fancy words all the time and we all know, for instance, that 'paraesthesia' means pins and needles, and 'fasciculation' means twitching of muscle visible under the skin, which happens when muscles have lost their nerve supply and don't know what to do so they just fidget, and 'diplopia' means double vision, and we use words like 'paraesthesia', 'fasciculation' and 'diplopia' when we're talking to one another, rather than using layman's terms. We seem to have a blind spot for 'asthenia', though, because when we mean weakness, we say weakness, and it's really only in the BNF that asthenia is used, and a great many doctors don't know what it means, and I think they gloss over it, as I did. Weakness is a side effect that matters, especially perhaps to older people who may have problematic weakness already, and some years ago I wrote to the BNF to ask whether they would consider dropping the word 'asthenia' and use 'weakness' instead, but they explained that they base the list of side effects in the BNF on the information provided by the drug manufacturer in what is called the Summary of Product Characteristics that every manufacturer must supply for each drug, and I am not even going to speculate as to why any drug manufacturer might choose to use the word 'asthenia', which no one understands, rather than 'weakness', which everyone does. Asthenia now appears as a potential side effect for over 400 drugs in the BNF.

This is not to say that everyone on any of those drugs will become weak. Most people on most drugs do not get any side effects at all. Drugs are largely safe and effective. Amlodipine in particular, as one of the most commonly prescribed antihypertensives in the world, has saved countless lives, and is an important and useful drug. But no drug is right for everyone.

I have never forgotten Mrs Goldman, her light step as she left the clinic, and her polite and firm refusal to take the tablets I thought would be good for her. I've never forgotten the dignity with which she adjusted the power balance in that clinic room. I didn't meet her again, so I don't even know whether 'bleurgh' for Mrs Goldman did mean weakness. It might have meant something quite different that wasn't on the list of side effects in the BNF, and in those days I might have told myself that Mrs Goldman's dissatisfaction with my pill was in her head. But now I know that if a patient feels an effect of a drug, whether positive or negative, they feel the effect of the drug. A feeling that is 'in our head' is still a feeling, and no one else can tell us that we don't have it. So when my patient perceives that they have a side effect nowadays I explore that, and I might work out that the feeling is due to some other issue that needs different attention and that the pill is, in fact, not responsible, or I might be able to reassure my patient that the feeling is not sinister and that the medication might be worth taking all the same if it is helping, at which point the side effect may often resolve. Or we may try a drug holiday to see if that makes a difference. Or I may accept that the side effect is indeed a side effect for that person, and we shall find another way round the problem, which in some circumstances might mean leaving my patient, like Mrs Goldman, well alone. Mrs Goldman also taught me my first lesson in sharing decisions with my patients.

*

Almost three decades later, I'm in trouble on Twitter. A cardiologist has described my behaviour as dangerous. Another has declared that I cannot be treating people with heart failure properly. I receive a private message suggesting – extremely politely – that my recent post might be considered an example of bullying. The sender of this message explains that a doctor reading my original post might recognise him or herself, despite the emphatic absence of any personal detail and he asks whether I would give permission for my tweet to be used as an example of inappropriate social media behaviour in a talk he is giving. I am chastened and accede willingly to his request. I have indeed publicly criticised the treatment plan of another doctor – a doctor I do not know, in a hospital in which I do not work, and I had not considered the possibility that this doctor might identify themselves as the subject of my denunciation and be distressed.

The trouble started, as trouble often does, with a drug chart. It is estimated that around one in five hospital admissions of those aged over sixty-five is medication-related, and that around 80% of these medication-related admissions are preventable.

I have a day's work in one of the community hospitals. There are not enough doctors – indeed, for this fortnight there are no regular doctors to provide medical care for the forty patients here, and someone may be coming tomorrow from the other side of the county, but right now there are new patients who have not been seen for days and Pearl is one of them. I am looking at the list of her drugs and at another list of her medical problems, and the lists are both long and sit uneasily together. I pull her notes from the cabinet and read a sad story, and I walk round to the bay to say hello to Pearl.

Pearl is in her chair looking out of the window – there are trees moving in an autumn wind that has blown up this morning. There is a *Take a Break* magazine on her bedside table, and Jelly Babies, and a cardboard sick bowl that is being used to hold Pearl's glasses and comb, and a white plastic pot for her dentures labelled with a Sharpie: her name and a smiley face.

I sit on Pearl's bed and ask how she is feeling.

'Oh, I am not so bad.'

I ask whether she is breathless at all or in any pain.

Pearl shakes her head.

'I know this sounds like a silly question, Pearl, but do you know where we are at the minute?'

Pearl nods, then looks around uncertainly and back at me, her eyebrows raised a little for me to supply the answer.

'It's hard to keep track, isn't it, when you've not been well,' I say, and I tell her the name of the community hospital to which she was transferred a few days ago from another hospital. It should be closer to home but it isn't because the system is overstretched and our patients get little choice now about where they go for

rehabilitation. Pearl's family will be facing a long journey to visit, but they have visited, because someone has
brought those Jelly Babies. There's a carton too of a protein drink with a straw. I pick it up – it's still full – and I
ask Pearl whether she might be able to drink some and
she scrunches her face like a child faced with spinach.
I ask if there is anything she does fancy and she gives
a little apologetic shrug. Then I ask if there is anything
that is worrying her, and she leans towards me and looks
sideways to check that no one is listening.

'This is . . . These people . . .' Her words tail off and
she looks at the magazine and cannot figure it out.

Here is the sad story from Pearl's notes. She was
admitted after a fall, a hip fracture. She'd only just
returned home after breaking the other hip a few weeks
ago – home to Ronald, with equipment (a commode, a
walking frame, a raised toilet seat), and they had been
offered care but Ron had said he would manage: Pearl
was not so good with strangers coming in. Ron had
indeed managed but Pearl had fallen again, walking with
her frame between her bed and chair. And last time
Pearl's kidneys had played up after her hip repair and
she'd needed some extra intravenous fluid, and this time
her oxygen level had dropped suddenly after her operation and a young doctor had been called to see her in the
night and requested blood tests alongside a chest X-ray
and a CT scan to check that Pearl did not have a pulmonary embolism, a blood clot on the lung, which she

didn't, and she was given some antibiotics in case there was an infection and her oxygen level had improved the next day, maybe because of the antibiotics or because it would have anyway, as Pearl had been sleepy when her oxygen level was low, what with the anaesthetic and the painkillers. But among her blood tests the doctor had asked for a BNP level, looking for a substance released into the bloodstream by a heart that is struggling. A raised level might indicate heart failure, which could explain that low oxygen reading, even though Pearl didn't have any other signs of heart failure. Pearl's BNP level was sky-high.

There's national guidance now, acknowledging that a very high BNP level is associated with a poor prognosis in people with heart failure, and the guidance requires that someone with a high BNP must have an echocardiogram, a heart scan, promptly, and Pearl had had that scan and it showed that her heart muscle was indeed not working properly. When the big chamber of the heart – the left ventricle – squeezes, it should send at least half the blood it contains around the body to limbs and organs and brain. But when the heart muscle is weak, it delivers a dwindling amount of blood and Pearl's heart was sending less than 20% of its contents around her body with each beat. This condition is called heart failure with reduced ejection fraction (HFrEF, pronounced *hef-ref*) and its treatment has been transformed in the last thirty years by a series of drugs.

Here in the community hospital Pearl's chart now includes all four medications that have been shown to improve outcomes in people with HFrEF, including the newest, which is actually two drugs in one pill. Thus five new medicines, alongside the ones she was taking already, to treat a condition she undoubtedly has. So why have I become so enraged that I have written and sent an angry tweet?

I realise now that I am not angry with the doctor, a cardiologist who wrote up these medicines for Pearl before she was transferred to the community hospital. No, let me be honest, I am angry with him, but I also recognise that his motivation was good, that he wanted to protect Pearl from harm. He knows that in trials these medicines have been shown to reduce the chance of a patient dying during the trial period and they improve a patient's chance of avoiding a further hospital admission with worsening heart failure. I too know those facts. I've read the trials and the subsequent guidelines. But that cardiologist should also know that Pearl or someone like her would not meet the inclusion criteria for these trials. He should know that to be included in these trials she must have symptoms of heart failure. He should know that to be eligible she should not have symptoms of low blood pressure, as her body needs to have a good chance of safely withstanding the blood pressure drop that can accompany heart failure medicines. He should know that her kidneys would have had to be stable before the drugs were started in a trial, and that in a trial her kidney function would be monitored assiduously and her drug doses adjusted, and that in the trials, although many did well, many patients were unable to tolerate the drugs – for them the drugs had to be discontinued. He should know that in one large trial the researchers could exclude any patient they considered 'unreliable'; in another, potential participants were excluded if they had any other condition that suggested they would not live another five years. He should know, therefore, that he is extrapolating data produced in carefully selected groups of people, mainly men, mainly in their sixties, data produced in controlled conditions, and he is applying it to someone a great deal more vulnerable. Pearl is eighty-three. She does not have symptoms of heart failure or at least is not troubled by them. She weighs just under eight stone. Her kidneys are dicey and her blood pressure, prior to the new medicines, was already low and is now even lower. She has had two hip fractures in three months. Pearl may have fallen over for many reasons, not least the dementia that she has had for several years and which is affecting the parts of her brain that control movement and balance as well as those that store memory, but her low blood pressure may well have contributed to her falls.

More important than any of this, that cardiologist should know something about Pearl. He should know what she wants.

I ring Ron.

'I've met your lovely wife, Ron,' I say.

'My Pearl?' he asks. 'How's she doing?'

I say she is looking pretty good, all things considered, but I can see she's been through a lot, and Ron agrees.

'She's skin and bones,' Ron tells me. 'I've had a job to get her to eat this twelve-month.'

I ask Ron whether Pearl gets breathless.

'Not so as I'd notice,' says Ron. 'She hasn't said – but she doesn't move much, mind.'

'Why's that?' I wonder, and Ron says he thinks that before the broken hips it was her back that's been playing her up for years and her balance has been bad.

'She's not what she was,' says Ron, and he adds, 'To tell the truth, doctor, she doesn't always rightly know who I am.'

'I'm sorry, Ron. You must have been married a while?'

'Coming up sixty year,' says Ron, and there's a pause and I can hear Ron rummaging and he blows his nose.

'What's up next, doc, then? Is she coming home?'

I explain about Pearl's heart, that it's not as strong as it was, and I say that Pearl has been started on some new medicines but I'm not sure they're right for her and she's on quite a few already.

Ron says, 'Well, doctor, I know I shouldn't say it, but it's the one thing we argue about, is her tablets.'

I say that must be hard for him, and Ron sighs.

'She's set against them, doctor. She don't like the big

ones. She don't like the little ones. I mush 'em up in her porridge but she spits 'em out.'

Ron and I make a plan. We stop the heart failure medicines. If at some point Pearl gets breathless, with fluid on her lungs, her GP might start a water tablet to help her breathe more easily, but she hasn't needed that so far. We stop the osteoporosis treatment, a weekly tablet, because Pearl struggles to take it and it may be contributing to her loss of appetite – we agree that I'll arrange for Pearl to have a one-off osteoporosis injection, zoledronic acid, before she leaves hospital. Its effect to reduce the risk of a further fracture will last several years – longer, I suspect, than Pearl. We'll continue the painkillers, simple paracetamol, because Pearl doesn't usually mind those, and laxatives if she needs them. Ron has a trick: mixing her Laxido powder with water and a drop of ginger wine. 'Just a drop, doctor.'

'You're doing all the right things, Ron,' I say.

'I know I in't got her much longer,' he tells me.

We talk about what will make Pearl smile when she comes home, which is the girls, her granddaughters, coming round to show her the wedding pictures and the baby.

So I was angry then and I remain angry now that no one had taken the time to understand Pearl or to speak with Ron. I am angry that we have not learned the lessons over thousands of years, since the time of Hippocrates, that doctors habitually overestimate the effectiveness of many medications and underestimate their side effects. I am angry that too often we present our medicines on a silver platter and that we do not take time to explore and explain, and that we leave someone like Ron feeling that if he fails to persuade Pearl to take her medicines she will drop dead.

It's not only the patients who are offered medications on a salver; I am angry that we doctors allow ourselves to be presented with new drugs on an even bigger platter, a platter burnished by the pharmaceutical industry and garnished with endorsements by professional societies, not all of whom are transparent about their financial ties to the drug manufacturers. We lift new medications blithely from the pretty platter, medications that are accompanied by fanfares at international conferences and by sponsored webinars that iterate the benefits of the novel treatments while glossing over their limitations.

I am angry that it can be so hard to find time for a conversation because we do not have enough doctors, or nurses, in the UK – we really do not – and I am angry that sometimes we doctors do have time but don't use it for a conversation, because we don't recognise that it is important or because we don't have the facts at our fingertips and do not wish to be caught out, or even because we think we know it all and believe that our drug is so good that no conversation is needed. I am angry with myself that too often I have not shared a decision properly with my patient – that I have made assumptions or not listened properly.

I am angry that we do not acknowledge uncertainty, and I realise now that this is the key to a better approach to this conflict between specialists with a patient caught in the middle. The behaviour of doctors is inevitably influenced by the patients we meet. Cardiologists look after those who have deteriorating heart failure, and they meet people, grey and breathless, whose heart failure medicines have been delayed or stopped, and the disappointment those cardiologists feel, that their patient was denied that treatment, is real. Geriatricians, on the other hand, see those who have falls and fractures or kidney problems or other upsets attributable to their medicines and feel aggrieved that harm has been done. Working together to understand one another's perspective will help, and we are beginning to do this. But more important than doctors understanding one another is that all of us should understand the patient's perspective, their goals and wishes.

So here is a message to my eighty-year-old self – to me the patient not the doctor – a message to any of us:

You, dear eighty-year-old, have accumulated knowledge and experience. We all have. You have values by which you abide, things you want to achieve and things you want to avoid. You can share these with your medical team – you can be honest. You can ask about your treatment – what are its benefits, what are its risks? You can share the decisions. And you can do this for yourself or for someone you love who cannot speak for themselves. The doctor will bring her pharmaceutical knowledge or knowledge about tests or scans or operations, but we will each bring our own knowledge, about what matters to us.

In some ways I do not know whether we made the right decisions, Ron and I, for Pearl, because I will never know what would have happened if we had made a different plan. It may be that had she been persuaded to take the heart failure medicines she might not have run into trouble with side effects after all and she might have lived longer or avoided an admission with heart failure. Or the heart failure tablets may have made things worse and she'd have returned to hospital with a new and different problem. Or the tablets may have helped her heart, while the rest of Pearl – her mind, her bones and joints and muscles – continued to fall gently apart and she'd have died of something else anyway. But, overall, none of these things mattered. What mattered was that Ron felt we had made a good plan, one that was right for the woman he had loved for sixty years, and that it was what she would have wanted had she been able to speak for herself. What mattered was that we shared that decision and Ron knew that he did not need to feel bad about her medicines and that he and Pearl did not have to argue every day. Instead he could sit and talk about runner beans and the cat they used to have and the grandson taking his first steps, with his wife, his precious Pearl.

4. Risk and Reward

It's a miserable morning, and the rain has been hammering down as I've driven to a town fifteen miles from the hospital. I've come over the high road, with views for miles on a good day, but right now grey cloud fills the valleys and there's more cloud above – the rain is falling from one cloud to another and there's water streaming down the lanes. I've wound round behind the big Tesco and found a place to park; it's on a yellow line but I'm not blocking anyone and I leave a note on the dashboard for the parking warden, grab my rucksack and head to Wesley's house. There's a bird table on the tiny patch of grass outside, and a pyracantha with orange berries by the front door, sparrows sheltering in it.

The door isn't locked and I see Janet in the kitchen – she's rustling in a cupboard – and in the front room I find Lexi, one of the trainee Advanced Clinical Practitioners, and here is Wes, sitting on a settee, 1960s Ercol-style with wooden arms and a brown tweedy fabric, bang on trend again six decades later. Wes has a blanket of pink crocheted squares over his knees and there's oxygen tubing running to his nose, and he is shivering and looks mortally ill. Sick enough to die.

Lexi finishes taking Wes's blood pressure and she clambers up from the floor, saying, 'Eighty-eight on fifty, pulse one twenty.' She picks up her laptop to log these details – it's on the double bed that has been brought downstairs and now fills the rest of the room. Wes can just see past the foot of the bed to the TV, and there's a three-bar heater and a glass-fronted cabinet along the other wall containing models of steam engines – not trains but tractors and threshing machines, black enamel, tall funnels.

I say, 'Hello, Wes. I'm sorry you're feeling so rotten.'

Wes scrunches his face up to show that, yes, he does indeed feel rotten, and I glance at the oxygen saturation monitor Lexi has applied to his finger. The monitor's not picking up any signal, the screen is blank, so I clamp it to my own finger instead, while I feel Wes's pulse, and his hand is clammy and white. The oximeter is showing 99% on my finger, so the machine is working, but Wes's body isn't.

I say, 'Excuse me, Wes, just going to have a feel of your nose.'

It's a proper old man's nose, crazed with tiny capillaries, and it is icy.

'What's the plan?' I ask Lexi and Wes, and he looks at her and raises his eyebrows and uses his head to point at me, to indicate to Lexi, 'Go on, I'm too knackered. You tell her.'

So Lexi tells me, 'Wes doesn't want to go into hospital again.'

I watch Wes breathe, snatching in air then letting it out in a stream through lips held almost together, and his feet on the floor are dusky blue and bare because his slippers won't go on. His legs are pale marble and swollen. I press Wes's thigh through his pyjamas, the underside where his leg meets the settee, and my fingers leave an imprint, deep and doughy.

Lexi says, 'He's got a horrible cough, haven't you, Wes? And you haven't had a wee since yesterday and you had a temperature last night but now you've gone a bit cold instead.'

Wes looks at the rug, beaten down by the litany of his body's failures. He knows he's on the losing side. He shakes his head.

There is guidance to tell Lexi and me what to do in this situation. Wes's heart isn't working properly, and he also meets the criteria for consideration of sepsis. Sepsis isn't just having an infection, and it isn't even signs of the body responding normally and effectively to infection – having a temperature and a fast heartbeat when we have the flu isn't sepsis. Sepsis is a condition that occurs when an infection becomes overwhelming and the body's immune and blood-clotting systems are in overdrive, and sepsis with shock is a life-threatening illness characterised by low blood pressure that persists even when we have been given plenty of fluid and by organs shutting down. Sepsis can cause death in people of any age (although it is uncommon in younger people) and the more quickly treatment is started the more we improve someone's chance of survival, so guidelines from NICE, The National Institute for Health and Care Excellence, are there *to ensure that all people with sepsis due to any cause are recognised and initial treatment initiated before definitive treatment on other specific pathways is instituted.*

The guidance is unequivocal: *Refer all people with suspected sepsis outside acute hospital settings for emergency medical care by the most appropriate means of transport (usually 999 ambulance) if they meet any high-risk criteria.*

And Wes does meet high-risk criteria, with his non-existent production of urine, his sagging blood pressure and his undetectable oxygen level. Lexi has totted up Wes's ratings on a National Early Warning Score, NEWS, also designed to highlight deterioration and to demand a speedy response from those who can intervene. A score of seven or more mandates an *immediate assessment by an emergency team with critical care competencies, and continuous monitoring of vital signs.* Wes's score is thirteen.

'OK, Lexi,' I say, 'what's he had so far?'

Lexi smiles at Wes and shows me; he's had a cup of tea and two amoxycillin antibiotic capsules and a couple of paracetamol for the aches. She's helped him take his usual morning tablets and has given him a double dose of his water pills half an hour ago, and Janet is in the kitchen making more tea.

I have met Wes before, on the ward a couple of

months back. He's been in and out of hospital this year with his shaky heart and infections and his kidney function wandering off. I know he was a cowhand and travelled from farm to farm as a younger man, taking his family with him as jobs arose, to milk cows and trim hooves, to apply balms for mastitis and treat calves for scour, and the first time he came into hospital – he'd never been there before, Janet had had their babies at home – he was jovial, and Wes watched the goings-on of the ward with interest and struck up a friendship with Josiah, one of the Health Care Assistants from the Philippines, because Wes's father had been called Josiah and was born in 1899 when the old queen was still on the throne. 'No, not the *Queen*, not Elizabeth; she were Queen Victoria. Did you ever hear of her, Josiah?' Then Wes had been discharged back home and come in again a month or so later to a different ward, and the second time he looked sadder, disappointed that all the rolling up of sleeves for a vial of blood to be taken and the tablets and the X-rays and the being weighed every day and the peeing in a bottle and the nurses decanting that urine into a jug to measure the amount – all that activity seemed to Wes to have come to nothing very much, because here he was back in hospital, and he missed Janet and was worried about her, with her memory not as sharp as it used to be. That second time he'd waited a long time for a care team to become available, for a carer who could help him to dress and another carer at lunchtime who would get a hot meal on the table for him and Janet. During that long wait in hospital Wes's bed and chair were at the end of the little bay, no window unless you counted looking round the corner to see through the door of a side room to a glimmer of daylight from the window there and a red brick wall beyond. At night his dreams were of home, and the strip light flickered all day.

I'm not surprised by what Wes has said about not going back into hospital, and I'm proud of Lexi because, although she has some years of experience as a nurse, she is still a trainee in her current role as an Advanced Clinical Practitioner in Frailty. Lexi's in the first year of a three-year course that will combine university study days with on-the-job learning, as well as some late nights sorting out her portfolio and writing up the records of what she has learned while her children are asleep and her partner's on night shift. I'm proud because she has heard Wes's wishes and she could have done what that NICE guidance says must happen for *all people with suspected sepsis* and called an ambulance to get him to hospital by the quickest possible means, but she hasn't because Lexi knows that *all people* does not mean *all people*, and specifically it does not mean Wes.

Dr Shelagh O'Riordan is a community geriatrician and a professional adviser to the community health services team at NHS England. She knows what she is doing. For fourteen years my friend Shelagh worked as a hospital geriatrician and she saw how rapidly older people could deteriorate, especially those with frailty or dementia, when taken away from their familiar environment. She saw that for many people even the best run hospital may not be a place of safety, because the little bookshelf and the fringed table lamp are inexplicably missing and sleep doesn't come, or the toilet is distant and the chair that would usually be there, just there, to catch hold of, is not there; or there is a blood pressure check in the night, a cuff tight on an arm, strange voices, and the morning comes too soon, with its pappy toast and a fiddly plastic pot of plastic jam, too difficult for exhausted hands and an unrested mind.

In 2017 Shelagh left her job to lead a Hospital at Home service, working with GPs and other community teams to offer real alternatives to emergency admission. The pandemic brought more demand for their work; for many older people the idea of going to hospital had taken on a new and horrible dimension, of separation from family, no visitors, masked strangers. Hospitals were under pressure and the debates about access and resources were heated and frightening, but for Shelagh avoiding admission for her patients did not mean denying them treatment. Her team extended their reach. Care home staff were happy to learn to look after a drip of intravenous fluid for those who had become dehydrated through gastroenteritis. The Hospital at Home team worked with carers and families to explain the alarming behaviour of people who had delirium – sudden confusion caused by an infection or a metabolic upset or the wrong pill – and to treat, support and reassure until peace might be restored. It turned out that many conditions usually treated in hospital could instead be addressed quickly and effectively in a patient's own home or care home. And Shelagh and her colleagues grew muscles – their kit bags got heavier and heavier. They began using blood-testing equipment that could give reliable results in a patient's sitting room. Their cars became mini-pharmacies, with a careful selection of the medicines found in a hospital ward drug cupboard.

Can it possibly be safe to keep people – frail, sick people who would usually go to hospital – at home instead? The answer is yes. For the right patients, who may yet be very unwell, services like Shelagh's have been evaluated in proper randomised trials, which show that those who have been treated at home have done at least as well as those admitted to hospital. The voices of patients and their families or carers provide an encouraging refrain: 'Mum gets on much better in her own home' and 'I'm happier sleeping in my own bed'.

But Wes is so ill. Lexi has popped into the kitchen to help Janet with the tea, and I crouch next to him. He's closed his eyes and I think about what we should do. Our Hospital at Home team is new. We don't yet have IV antibiotics in our kit bags; Lexi and I might be able to get some but it's going to take a while, driving around. I listen to Wes's heart – it's banging along, irregular and fast, and there's little air moving in and out of his lungs, which are waterlogged. Lexi's done what she can – the extra water tablet was a good move despite his low blood pressure, but I know the treatment that Wes is getting here isn't the same as he'd be getting in hospital, where we could give some of his medicines directly into a vein, and I also know that, with Wes this sick, hospital treatment may not work either, and he is likely to die there, maybe in that bed in the corner with no sight of the sky. And Lexi and I can't stay with Wes much longer; we have other people to see, and so Wes will be on his own, with Janet, until a carer pops in at lunchtime, and then Lexi might visit briefly again this afternoon and then there'll be the long night.

'Wes?'

He opens his eyes.

'I can see you're really ill, you know that.'

He nods.

'And we're trying to make you better, but I'm worried you might be going to die.'

Wes closes his eyes again, tips his head sideways, acknowledging this.

'And we could get you back to hospital . . .'

Wes's eyes fly open – he catches hold of my wrist and now he speaks: 'I don't want it; I'll bide here with Janet.'

There's a tension growing, as medical treatments advance. We are offered more and more – screening and tests and treatments – and much of what we are offered is welcome and has value. But increasingly, and most especially for older people, some of what is on offer may make us uneasy. We may think, *Do I want this? Will it help?* The tension comes from a desire to get things right in an increasingly complicated world, where attempts are made to simplify complex situations by providing algorithms and guidelines, steps to be followed. The guidelines are well meaning – there's an undeniable desire to improve care – but their application can too easily become rigid and unforgiving.

'They're guidelines, not tramlines,' says Jonathan Underhill. He's a pharmacist who works with NICE, and he's right. Every piece of the UK's NICE guidance is prefaced by a statement describing the responsibilities of the reader, who is *expected to take this guideline fully into account, alongside the individual needs, preferences and values of their patients.* And the statement continues (underlines my own): *It is not mandatory to apply the recommendations, and the guideline does not override the responsibility to make decisions appropriate to the circumstances of the individual, in consultation with them and their families and carers or guardian.*

It can be difficult making decisions, as a professional alone in a care home at two in the morning, or on a Sunday afternoon with concerned neighbours hovering at the door. That young doctor or paramedic or nurse may be listening to their patient but is worried – might there be repercussions if this patient does badly? Will a family say he was too ill, did not understand his choices? Why did you let him down? Perhaps the safer thing (safer for me, the professional, who must take responsibility for my actions) would be to call an ambulance and follow the pathway. It would certainly be easier.

I step into the back porch to ring Wes and Janet's daughter Lorraine, who is miles away in Evesham, and our conversation is frank. Lorraine can't come because her husband has MS, and her brother's in Australia, but she knows her dad well; this is the right plan that he has made, and she'll call the neighbours and see if they might drop in. Then we talk about how Janet will cope if Wes dies when they're on their own, because some hours may pass before someone else arrives to make breakfast or to help Wes with his medicines.

Lorraine is pragmatic. 'I think Mum will ring me. She might not, but better it happens at home. She'd want to be with him.' There's a sigh. 'It's a risk worth taking,' she says.

Lorraine has named one of the great barriers that stands in the way when someone older is unwell. We do not like risk. None of us likes risk – at least not when it concerns someone who we love or for whom we have undertaken to look out, our eighty-year-old neighbour up a stepladder with his Christmas lights or our mother in the Emergency Department with a shocking line of staples across her scalp and her hair matted with blood. We do not like it when she says, 'They're very nice and all that, but I would rather go home.'

Professionals are also uncomfortable with risk. But too often we all find it difficult to see where the risk lies. Sometimes we forget that Virgil was right two thousand years ago when he observed that our remedy may be worse than the disease. I watch our doctors in training – good, careful young doctors – anxiously reading the long list of observations and blood results for each patient, as they diligently note the results which are out of line and prescribe corrective medication – potassium supplements perhaps or an increase in insulin or an extra blood pressure tablet – because they perceive that without intervention something calamitous will happen. But that perception is wrong. The golden fruit of perfection that is now dangled in front of us is a snare and a delusion. We are seeing risk in the wrong place.

The risk is not that Wes will die. The risk is that Wes will die in hospital after a great many interventions that did not have value to him, that he will die without the three-bar heater and the threshing-machine models and without Janet. The risk is that Wes's care will be dictated by an algorithm that does not see the whole picture. The risk is that Wes will be pushed down cold clinical pathways and that as we tread heavily down those pathways we tread on his dreams.

*

I think of Shelagh O'Riordan's advice, when we were setting up our local Hospital at Home service. For many people remaining at home poses no extra risk – they might need specialist treatment which can now be provided in their own living room, but they do not benefit from the panoply of activity that comes with admission. But for others there's a balance – they may be alone for much of the time and our emergency services are stretched and a call for help may not be answered for many hours.

'You'll need to hold your nerve,' Shelagh told me. 'There's risk, and you need to share the risks with the patient to allow them to make the right decision for their own situation. You need to put your patients first.'

There's risk in every decision we make regarding health. I think of my colleague Peter's office with his paperwork and bike parts. I can picture the notice Sellotaped above his desk.

The science of medicine, says Peter's notice, *is knowing what to do. The art of medicine is knowing when not to do it.*

I think of the work of Don Berwick, kindly and wise, who led the Institute for Healthcare Improvement in the United States for nineteen years, and was invited in 2013 to review patient safety in the NHS, and I remember his message, clear and unequivocal:

'Engage, empower and hear patients and carers throughout the entire system and at all times.'

There is risk, but when we tread softly, when we listen

and hear, there's also reward. As patients too, when we can express our wishes, and when we are able to make sense of what is on offer and can choose what is right for ourselves or for someone we know and love, there is reward. Time and again there is reward.

Janet has come back into the sitting room, a cup of tea in each hand, and Lexi follows, her arms outstretched behind Janet, just in case, but Janet makes it to the little upright chair by the settee, where when sitting her knee almost touches Wes's. I've taken some of his blood, which will have to go back with me to the hospital, as we don't have testing equipment yet, and I hold his tea while he settles himself more comfortably and the sats monitor back on his finger is picking up a signal now. It's eighty-seven, eighty-eight, so still not good but better. In hospital the monitor would be shouting in alarm, but here it is peaceful and Wes's pulse has slowed down, though not much. I'm worried about how to explain things to Janet, but Lexi has already done it in the kitchen and tells me, 'Janet knows Wes might die but he's happier here at home.'

Janet's eyes well up as she nods, and I say, 'I bet you've been married a while, Janet – where did you meet this handsome fellow?'

Janet looks momentarily panicky. She can't remember.

Wes says, 'Tell 'em about Weymouth then.'

And Janet's face is all bright now, as she tells us, 'My

dad was a cowhand too and he only got the one day off each year, and my family went to Weymouth, and there was a big shop there with an upstairs, and I went up there and had a look around, but I didn't buy anything, and then I was going to come back down and I slid, didn't I, Wesley, down the . . .'

She's lost the word and Janet looks at Wes and he finishes the story.

'You slid down the banister and right into my arms.'

5. Ageing Without Children

Cecil is very unwell, and I'm trying to work out whether we should be trying to get him back to his residential home for this last stage of his life and whether the home will be able to manage his symptoms, because residential homes in the UK, unlike nursing homes, are staffed by people who know a great deal about care but are not usually qualified nurses, and they may need some extra support to look after one of their residents who is dying, just as a family would who are looking after someone dying in their own home. I'm also not clear what Cecil's view would be about dying in hospital or back in his care home and he's unable to tell me, and anyway he's critically ill and no one has yet called his next of kin.

Olga is surprised when she answers the phone.

'Oh, I'm not his next of kin,' she says. 'I don't think he has a next of kin.'

So I ask how Olga knows Cecil and she says, 'Well, I met him in the library.' Then she explains that she does some volunteering there, showing people how to work the computers ('I'm retired, you see, so I have some time').

'He asked me for help. He wanted to make a will.'

Olga has an accent, German I think, and she says 'vill' not 'will'. Her voice is rich and warm. 'So I said I could help him and it took a long time in the end; we had to have cups of tea and come back another day.'

There's a pause. I explain that Cecil is comfortable but also very sick – that he is dying – and I hear Olga pull a paper hanky from a box and blow her nose.

She says, 'It turned out he was a very nice man. He had a lot of money and he wanted to do a good thing with it and he was like me: he did not have family. So we maked a list, the charities for children and one for the refugees and one for the little hetch-hocks.'

Olga makes a small noise, an 'oof', as she thinks about Cecil and his closeness to death, and I say I'm sorry that I'm bringing sad news.

We talk about the plans for him to return to the residential home, and Olga says she does not think he would want any fuss and that he liked that home and would prefer to get back to stay there – he had moved in soon after making his will; she had visited him there, and the staff liked him too.

'Olga, I'm writing a form to explain the plan for Cecil, and I am going to write your name here on Cecil's form, where the next of kin bit is, and I am going to write that you are his friend. Is that OK?'

I hear a rustle, and Olga says, 'Friend . . . yes, maybe I am his friend.'

*

'Next of kin is a big issue for older people without children,' explains Kirsty Woodard. 'If we are in that situation, we can be asked who our next of kin is and we might think of a cousin or a niece or nephew, and we might not have seen them for years, but we still think that's who we should put down. We can all get very hung up on that blood relative thing.'

Kirsty's right. For many people who do not have children – indeed for some who do – it may not be a blood relative who is best placed to speak for us when we are unable to speak for ourselves. Kirsty encourages people who are ageing without children to think about nominating others who might represent their views, who might know their wishes better.

Kirsty has worked with older people for over thirty years, starting as an advocate working for what was then Age Concern shortly after leaving university. She is now the Ageing Well lead at Voluntary Action North Somerset, a programme bringing voluntary and community services together, and I met her after a talk I had given in Weston-super-Mare, when she and a colleague gently upbraided me.

Kirsty held up a finger as she posed a question. 'You said several times how important it is for older people to discuss their wishes and plans with their family. What happens if you don't have a family?'

Kirsty's colleague explained. 'I'm in my sixties and my mum is ninety-four and in a care home, so she can't speak for me, and I'm an only child and I have no children.'

I suddenly realised what I should have realised before, that this is not a rare situation. Many, many people do not have close relatives upon whom to call when things get difficult.

Kirsty founded a charity, Ageing Without Children (AWOC), which supports and campaigns for those who have never been parents. This accounts for over one million of the twelve million people aged sixty-five years and older in the UK. AWOC also represents those who have been parents but who now find themselves without children, perhaps by being estranged or bereaved. Being childless is a positive choice for many, but, whatever the circumstances, ageing without children may bring anxiety and fears, and not without reason.

A few weeks after the talk in Weston, I spoke with Kirsty on the phone and she described how the intersection between her work with older people and her own situation fell into sudden clarity when she was listening to a friend whose mother, previously independent, had suddenly become unwell and needed lots of help.

'My friend was juggling her job and home life at the same time as trying to find carers for her mum, spending hours on the phone to agencies and going to discharge planning meetings at the hospital and having to be at her mum's house for deliveries of equipment that then didn't arrive on time. My friend said, "God knows what she'd do if I wasn't here," and I realised that as I don't have children – I wasn't able to – I would be in exactly that situation.'

People who do not have children are more likely to move prematurely into residential care and there is also a link with life expectancy, with studies suggesting that people who have children (including adoptive parents) live longer than those who do not. Some of this may be to do with the reasons that someone did not become a parent – for example, people with learning or other disabilities constitute some of those ageing without children, and those conditions themselves may lead to a lower life expectancy – but, as the AWOC team report, *it is also clear that the informal care provided by many adult children to their parents as they age provides not only practical support but also contributes a strong preventative element in terms of continued independence, well-being and emotional support.*

More than 90% of unpaid care is delivered by family members, and as Kirsty tells me: 'There's an assumption hard baked into health and care systems that when the going gets tough, family support will be present.'

I think of Sylvia, who had descended into dementia with great charm, and how she made wobbly trips to the ward kitchen, where she would fill her pockets with small packs of custard creams that she then graciously offered to the therapists and medical students who came to her bedside. Sylvia needed for various reasons to move into a care home and had agreed with this plan, and Tariq

the social worker had made some enquiries and estab-
lished that Sylvia had plenty of money to pay for her
care – she had saved diligently in her years as a civil
servant – so she was classified as a 'self-funder'. At this
point the involvement of a social worker should end and
her family should take on the job of finding a suitable
residential home, but Sylvia had no family, none at all,
and a hiatus ensued because Tariq had many other tasks
on his list and advocacy for Sylvia was not a priority.

The number of people who are ageing without children is increasing. 'It's been difficult to get numbers,'
Kirsty explains. 'Being childless isn't a "protected char-
acteristic" like gender or ethnicity and it's not recorded
on census data.' But the data is there – of women born
in 1946, only 9% did not ever have children. Of women
born in the sixties, one in five is childless, and by 2030
two million of the UK's older population will not be
in a position to look to their own children for support.

I mention to Kirsty that I see nieces – and occasionally nephews – step up, and that I find that
relationship particularly touching, but Kirsty is wary of
any sentimentality.

'What is clear is that family sizes are falling. So as well
as maybe not having children, our extended family may
be more limited.'

Kirsty's own family is a case in point.

'My mum had three daughters,' she says. 'Only one of
us has children, and, in fact, she has only one.'

It's too easy for those who come from sprawling families to overlook the pressures that may coalesce around people whose family networks have become pruned from one generation to the next, and as I listen to Kirsty I think of Andrea, who I met at a friend's birthday party. It became apparent that she had been providing unstinting and stoical support to eight parents – her mother and stepfather, her father and stepmother, and her husband's parents and step-parents too – and Andrea was describing this situation to me, talking quickly to list them all, when she said, 'We got rid of one of them recently.' She caught herself, saying, 'Sorry, that came out wrong, but you know what I mean.' And I do.

I read an article by Jenny Collieson, one of Kirsty's colleagues at AWOC. Jenny describes the experience of people ageing without children in York during the pandemic, captured in a report by the charity. *Daily life during Covid made them [. . .] more aware of the potential fragility of their personal support networks and their invisibility in the media coverage of the pandemic.*

Jenny writes about *the dominant narrative focussed on family separation*, and I think back to images of older people mouthing messages to children and grand-children through windows, the hugs delivered via Heath Robinson style body-gloves made of plastic sheeting in a back garden.

77

I meet Denise on my ward, who tells me, 'I didn't belong in anyone's bubble.'

Jenny's article continues: *The media did not address the realities of life for many older people ageing without family support. Their stories did not feature.*

I can see that this is true in my own reporting from the front line of geriatric medicine and remains true well beyond the dramas of the pandemic. Relationships feature so heavily in my work – families that are loving or furious, warm or cold, respectful, demeaning, supportive, unrealistic or sometimes plain bonkers – and it's often important to work out how an older person's life fits with those around them. It's too easy not to notice when a relationship doesn't exist at all.

There are of course many positive aspects of life without children. Alongside my patient Denise's realisation of her vulnerability and her exclusion from others' bubbles, she has a lively attitude to her own situation. She's eighty-two and runs her fingers through her hair, which is mauve and has several tiny strands of polychromatic thread woven into it, miniature rainbows that catch the light.

'I don't have to worry about children,' she says. 'I only have to worry about me. And I've had far more money than I'd have had if I'd had children. I've done loads of travelling and been places I couldn't have gone otherwise.'

Denise has done some sensible things.

'I've sorted out my will and my LPAs,' she says,

speaking of the Lasting Powers of Attorney that we can choose to bestow on someone else who will speak for us should we become unable to speak for ourselves.

'Initially I asked my friend Polly to be my LPA and I would be hers, but then we realised that wasn't going to work because we're both quite old and one of us would hop the twig first or we'd both go dotty together, so that was no good, and we each got a solicitor. It cost a bit but it's been worth it for the peace of mind.'

I talk with David Satchell, who is a member of the Association of Lifetime Lawyers, originally known as Solicitors for the Elderly, a group of qualified lawyers who spend at least half their time working with older and vulnerable clients. He is a proper advocate. He takes time to ensure he knows the wishes of his client before they both sign the forms that give him Power of Attorney and his documentation in those forms is meticulous. I'm also aware that when the chips are down he is willing to spend considerable time representing his clients' interests, whether that means weighing up a decision about surgical treatment or persuading a ward discharge team to find the care needed to allow his client to stay in her own home, when that client had made it clear to him some years previously that staying in her own home would outweigh any other consideration. David's not going to sit in her house waiting for a commode to be delivered – there are limits – but he does ensure his client's voice is heard.

Denise has also sorted out her advance care plan and has lodged this with her GP. ('I've said "not for resus", nothing too heroic. I don't want to hang around on a ventilator.') Yet even Denise's resolute practicality wavers in the face of the possibility of dementia.

'That's the big one, isn't it?' she says. 'I might not even know I've got it; I've got no bossy daughter saying, "You're repeating yourself."'

The prospect of developing dementia with no close family is difficult to contemplate, is a major concern for many and is an area where those who provide health and social care can improve their processes.

'One thing I'd suggest,' says Kirsty, 'is that any social or healthcare organisation has a look at their policies, and wherever it says "family", try taking out that word and see if the policy still works.'

I try out Kirsty's advice and three clicks take me to the 'Policy for Protecting Patients Who Walk About' written by a team at a district general hospital not far away. People in hospital who are confused may often walk without clear purpose or direction, and in general this is something to be encouraged, given that sitting in hospital causes muscles to melt away at an alarming rate, but such wandering can create problems. Sometimes walking about poses risks to infection control, or a person may leave the hospital altogether, and sometimes walking suggests distress that can be alleviated by knowledge of that person's usual behaviour. (Do they need the toilet? Do they need reassurance about a lost pet or a missing handbag, even if the pet or handbag is neither corporeal nor lost?) Therefore the policy suggests several actions, the first of which is *Give families or carers the 'This is Me' document to complete; ask for a recent photo*, the latter being an insurance in case that person does indeed leave the building, because we can give that photo to the police or others who might help to track them down. I can see immediately what Kirsty means about policies. She doesn't mean that references to families should be taken out – when families exist, their involvement is essential, but our policies need to consider what happens when they aren't there.

. I wonder whether Denise's courageous pragmatism would run also to some future-proofing, to adding some important details about herself to a document – that she is a vegetarian, for example, can't stand radio stations with traffic news and loves the smell of freesias – and I wonder whether she might gather some photos too – not just of herself as she is now to inform some future search party, but also of herself as she was, on the top of Machu Picchu with a bandana and a rucksack, or standing on the bonnet of a Land Rover with binoculars, scratching a bite on her elbow, sand dunes rolling to the horizon. Families become the repository of personality and memory for someone who has dementia, and I have often seen how one tiny detail can catch the eye of someone who is a carer, rushing from this person to the next – a pocket set of paint blocks with a spiral-bound watercolour pad, a book studded with Post-it notes, a black-and-white photo of a young woman in a sturdy panelled swimming costume, tossing her curls – and suddenly this person is not someone who needs their face and hands wiping, their cardigan putting back on the right way out, but rather a *person*, with a life and a story, and at that moment care stops being a series of transactions and becomes care.

There's another group of older people for whom children are not going to provide the informal support upon which so much depends. I recognise Graham's name on the admission list – I met him only ten days ago with the same problems, breathlessness and chest pain, and we did a whole lot of tests that didn't come up with anything much, before his symptoms improved and he went home. Graham is seventy-eight; he has a bit of COPD (chronic obstructive pulmonary disease), old-fashioned bronchitis and emphysema, from a previous smoking habit, even though he kicked that years ago. He gets out of breath on the stairs and he's carrying some extra weight too, his shirt buttons straining. But his oxygen levels are OK and the sheen on his skin isn't caused by a heart attack or a clot on the lung or an infection. Graham takes a pull on his inhaler but it's not helping. He's not wheezy this time and he wasn't last time either; the salbutamol in the inhaler is just giving him the shakes now.

I sit on the bed beside his chair and listen to how he

cannot sleep, gets up in the night and makes a cup of tea. I say, 'That sounds frightening, Graham. Do you ever feel a bit scared?'

He looks at me and nods, his lips pressed, and I ask, 'Is there anyone at home with you?'

'Just Helen and the lad.'

'Tell me about your lad,' I say.

Graham says, 'He's a good boy. He's no trouble really, but he can't . . . he . . .'

Graham puts his inhaler back on the bedside table, and looks away from me, out of the window of the ward, but he sees nothing there to relieve his worry. He looks down and closes his eyes, and his hands are not shaking just from the salbutamol.

For older people who are parents of those with disabilities, children now adults who have always been dependent on their parents, the prospect of being unable to continue in that role may be almost unbearable, with uncertainty about what will happen next and who will continue the care. Who will understand Graham's lad when Graham is gone, and when Helen goes too? Who will know when he needs a pat on the arm, a smile? Who will make sure his West Ham shirt is washed again, notice that his big grey sock is on wrong, with the heel on top? Who will tell him, 'Goodnight, sleep tight' and 'See you later, alligator. Bring me a crocodile sandwich and make it snappy'?

I do not have a ready solution for Graham's anguish.

What he and I can do is acknowledge its presence and identify it as the cause of his symptoms – it is making him unwell. I can write a discharge summary for his GP and copy the summary to the learning disability team with whom Graham and Helen have had no contact for many years ('The lad is no trouble'), so that they may start a conversation in which the unspeakable can become spoken, which is who will love their child, their fifty-year-old child, when they are gone?

Yet even with help and planning, even with the best safety net in place for his lad, I know that Graham will be racked with worry. It is too easy to provide platitudes.

Kirsty Woodard has heard it from people who are getting older without children. 'Someone may confess a fear of losing their independence, and another person will say, "Oh, my kids are just going to put me in a home and forget about me," and that's not fair, because firstly it's unlikely to be true, but also it's shutting down the conversation.'

It's important that we are heard when we are worried about our own vulnerability or the vulnerability of someone who will be left behind when we are gone – a wife who has dementia, a child who cannot care for themselves. There are no easy answers, but sharing that anxiety, telling someone else, allows us to find allies.

We can write our plans, put our own personal frameworks in place, but when the chips are down, when we are vulnerable and alone, we need advocacy. We need people to speak for us collectively and as individuals.

And while we need to be clear-eyed about cost, this does not need to be an unaffordable exercise. Advocacy for Sylvia, stuck in a medical ward while everyone argued about whose job it was to find her a care home, would have been cost-effective as well as kind. It does not cost money to show sensitivity to a childless woman in a care home on Mothering Sunday, perhaps to say, 'I can see this might be a sad day for you.' And time and again when I hear the voice of my patient and can listen to their wishes, even when those wishes are transmitted through someone else who is speaking for them, we can move away from interventions, scans and blood tests and days or weeks in hospital and focus instead on care.

Those who do not have family are the most vulnerable. I think of Jeannie, called by the wrong name the whole time she was in hospital, but unable to recall her own name until a visitor recognised her because they had worked together; and of Marty, whose dentures were lost, with no way to retrieve them from the laundry and no one to take on the role of getting a new pair, and of Joachim, who only needed the window open and the scent of lime blossom drifting in.

I am writing up notes at the ward desk. In the bay I can see Freda, who was a teacher and is now alone, and has forgotten her past pupils and the companions of the staffroom. She is sitting by her bed and has a book in her hands, and even from here I can see that it is upside down – Freda is contented with the feel of the paper, and she turns a page, but Kristie, a new nurse who is sharp and focused on process, takes the book from her, saying to Paul the Health Care Assistant, 'Well, she's obviously not *reading* it.' Paul puts the book back in Freda's hands, and with this quiet action Paul becomes an advocate.

I think about the people I have met, who have been ageing without children and whose numbers are growing. I think about kinship, our notion that blood is thicker than water, and I think of the many people who care for their older parent through a sense of obligation rather than love, and conversely of those who care for a stranger for love not obligation. Sometimes I wonder if there's enough love to go round, and I realise that as the structure of our society changes, as the steel ties of kinship become fewer and attenuated, we can choose, together, to build up other supports, of friendship, advocacy and community. We can strengthen these supports by example, as Paul did, and by experience and by explanation. I know that even Kristie, with her good skills, her eye for a detail on a drug chart and her orderly handover of tasks to the night team, given a cup of tea and a moment of reflection (a moment perhaps to think how she would wish to be treated herself), would want to put that book back into Freda's hands and would comprehend its comfort.

I think of Gerry sitting beside his bed in B Bay, and

his merry smile with dimples and his bright eyes. I know he lives alone and I ask what he did for a living when he was younger.

He says, 'Ooh, I was in the shows.' Then he lifts his hands and flutters them, a quick ta-da, and he says, 'And then I did costumes – braid and sequins. Lovely life really.'

Gerry has been coughing and lost so much weight, and I must give him his scan results and explain that the tumour is big and has spread to his ribs, and I must also explain that we will ask the cancer team to see him, but I know ('I am so sorry, Gerry') that they will not have a treatment that can cure this cancer.

He rubs the crease between his eyebrows a couple of times while he looks along the ward, thinking, then he turns to me and he puts his smile back on, a smaller, less certain version of his smile.

'Luckily,' says Gerry, 'I do not have anyone to care for.'

Gerry does not have anyone to care for. But we have all undertaken, in the unspoken and precious contract underpinning our society, that we will care for Gerry. That contract is being tested now, more thoroughly than it has ever been, at least in our lifetimes, and is too often found wanting. There is fear in the air, and I read essays by older colleagues – retired GPs and professors of medicine – who now have first-hand experience, who have seen, alongside gestures of dizzying kindness, bad things happen to their spouses and friends, have watched as compassion has seemed to leach away, washed out by process and fatigue and busyness, diluted to invisibility by painful misunderstandings between cultures and generations. Yet we can change the picture.

Here are our values. We value dignity. We value social cohesion and intergenerational understanding. We value listening and being heard, and companionship and kindness. We value joy and laughter. We value the lives of others, including those who are vulnerable. And there are practical ways in which we can demonstrate those values. We can do it at a governmental level, tackling the low pay and poor working conditions which erode compassion, and by making changes to our society to improve education, environment and opportunity to iron out the imbalances that affect health from the start to the end of life. We can recognise that wealth goes beyond the material, that looking out for someone else can bring unmeasured, unexpected treasure. And we can demonstrate our values in health and social care, and in our own lives, in the myriad tiny interactions of every day, by listening, by learning and by understanding what matters most to those with whom we share our world.

We can and we will.

6. Choice

A long time ago, one Sunday evening, my husband had taken our two young children up for their bath and I was doing the washing-up when the phone rang. I dried my hands and was surprised when Robert introduced himself. I was not expecting a call from a hospital colleague, an obstetrician I had not yet met – the paths of geriatricians and obstetricians don't often cross – but I knew his name because it was on my own notes, as I was pregnant once more. My tiny baby was coming to life inside me and I loved that baby, who was no longer than my thumb. I put the ketchup back in the fridge while Robert talked, and he explained that he had found it a difficult decision to know whether to ring me and had sought advice from others, but in the end he felt it was better I should have the option to know what he now knew. I dried a glass, and my movements became slower as he spoke, and I sat down at the kitchen table with crumbs and wrinkled peas around me and I thought, *I do not know what to do.*

The situation was this. In those days women were offered two blood tests in early pregnancy – one tested for the risk of a group of problems in the baby called neural tube defects, which range from mild spina bifida through to very severe conditions like anenceph-aly, where the baby's brain is so underdeveloped they cannot survive more than a few days after birth. The other blood test was to assess the risk of Down's syn-drome. My husband and I had decided, as we had with my previous pregnancies, to have the test for neural tube defects, because if after further scans it was clear that our baby was to face a short life of great suffering, we might choose instead a termination. But we had opted not to test for Down's syndrome because we would have that baby anyway. That's not the decision everyone would make, but it was ours, and we were happy with it – until Robert explained that the lab had done both tests by mistake and he had the result of the Down's test, and he felt he had a duty, a duty of candour, to offer me that result.

I did not know what to do.

'You're not going on a waiting list,' says Jude firmly while she types her notes. 'You're going on a preparation list.'

Kojo leans away from her a little because he can sense change coming, and none of us likes change. His partner Teresa smooths a hand through her hair – lilac and pink streaks – and smiles in satisfaction. It is time her man made some improvements to his lifestyle, but Jude's next question is directed at her.

'Do you smoke too?' And Teresa admits that she

does – not like Kojo, much less – and Jude says, 'Well, that makes it easier, because you both have to stop smoking.'

Kojo and Teresa look at one another. There is work to be done.

Kojo has been kept busy in this clinic, this appointment with the POPS service – Perioperative Medicine for Older People having Surgery – at Guy's and St Thomas's NHS Foundation Trust. The team here provides a comprehensive assessment of every person over sixty-five in whom major surgery is being considered. Today Kojo has already answered thirty questions fired at him by a nurse. He has recognised pictures of a rhino, a lion, a camel. He has joined numbers and letters in a logical order, has copied a picture of a cube. He has repeated the words 'red', 'daisy', 'face', 'velvet' and 'church', and recalled several of these words some minutes later. He has taken seven away from one hundred, and seven again away from the answer, and again, and again, until his palms have sweated. Kojo has identified the similarity between a train and a bicycle and has thought quickly of more than eleven words starting with the letter F. He has drawn a clock and has set the hands at ten past eleven. Kojo scored twenty-eight out of thirty, and the nurse congratulated him, and Teresa squeezed his hand.

The questions continued. Teresa has sniffed – she is less pleased with Kojo's performance on the Nottingham

Extended Activities of Daily Living Scale, which Kojo
has been given to complete between other assessments.
Did you do your own housework? it asks, and Kojo has ticked
'yes', and 'yes' also to *Did you wash small items of clothing?*
Teresa has leaned over to look and said, 'You did not.'
And Kojo replied, 'Yes, but I could have if you hadn't
done it all,' which sounds like a criticism, that Teresa's
selfish hogging of domestic duties has caused Kojo to
fail a test, but Teresa has pointed out that the question is not whether he *could* do the tasks but whether
he *did* do them in the last few weeks. She has tapped
the page and whispered, 'You gotta be honest,' so Kojo
is honest, and has anyway gained plenty of points for
making hot snacks, reading the newspaper and walking
across uneven ground. He has also completed a Timed
Up and Go test, and a Hospital Anxiety and Depression
score. He's blown into a spirometer, been weighed and
measured, opened his mouth for swabs and again for an
assessment of the space behind his tongue into which
an anaesthetist would pass a breathing tube. His medications have been listed and someone has recorded the
layout of his home.

Now Kojo and Teresa are sitting next to one another
in the clinic of Dr Jude Partridge, a geriatrician.

'It's no good the partner sitting opposite,' Jude tells
me afterwards. 'Then I can't see the eye-rolls, the body
language. And for a procedure as big as this, they need
to be in it together.' The process through which Kojo

has been moving this morning is a Comprehensive Geriatric Assessment (CGA). Its value has been proven already: older people who undergo such an assessment in acute geriatric wards are more likely to be alive and in their own homes a year later, with a better functioning brain, than patients receiving ordinary medical care. And we know that when older people are being offered major surgery, this careful comprehensive assessment improves the chances of a successful outcome.

An hour ago, I watched as Mr Prakash Saha ('I'm PK, good to meet you') outlined Kojo's choices. PK laid out a sheet of A4 clinic paper and took a pen from the top pocket of his suit. He's young but he's a London teaching hospital vascular surgeon and he looks the part. In black ink PK drew Kojo's aorta, a chunky tube running from the top of the page to bifurcate near the bottom, and he neatly sketched in the bulge in that aorta that was detected on a routine ultrasound scan, a national screening programme for aortic aneurysm, at Kojo's local hospital a few weeks ago.

'Here is the aneurysm,' said PK. 'It's five point seven centimetres wide now. We can leave it alone and it may cause no harm but there's about a five per cent chance it will rupture –' PK looked at Kojo's face and held his gaze – 'which means it would burst and that's a serious situation because without surgery very quickly you cannot survive.'

Kojo and Teresa nodded. They were told this when

the first scan was done. Later, they describe to me how everything has felt different these last few weeks. Kojo has been dreaming of Ghana, of peppery soup, kids shouting. Teresa has found herself crying on the bus on the way home from work; she wiped her eyes with her hand, and her hand on her trousers, and stroked the fuzzy velvet of the empty seat beside her. Everything has felt precious.

PK added some key features to his drawing – the renal arteries that come off to supply the kidneys – and he showed Kojo how the aneurysm was abutting those renal arteries. 'Sit up please, sir,' and Kojo sat up straight, as PK held the piece of paper against Kojo's purple stripey shirt. And it was a clever thing to do because Teresa and I could see just where his abdominal aorta ran, from the bottom of his chest to the top of his flies, and Kojo looked down and could picture it too.

'The position of your aneurysm is very close to the kidney arteries, and that limits our options,' PK explained. 'We can do the open repair. We go in through your tummy and we can see the aneurysm and all the arteries that come off that aorta, and we can "open stitch" a graft into place. The alternative is called endovascular aneurysm repair (EVAR), where we go in through an artery in your leg and we get the graft into place from the inside. But for you, because the aneurysm is long, we can't do the simple EVAR surgery where we just put a simple tube up through the artery in your leg into the aorta.

Instead we'd have to get a special graft made for you, with exactly the right measurements. It has little windows in it where each of your important branch arteries come off, like these ones to your kidneys. We can still put it in through the leg artery, but it's a good bit more fiddly to get it exactly into place.' He pointed at the drawing, showing how the graft would fit. 'Getting it made for you takes a bit of time. It's made to measure in Australia.'

Kojo and Teresa looked at one another. Teresa raised her eyebrows and Kojo tipped his head, a surprised smile. He's being cared for. His life has value.

PK went on. 'You'll want to know about complications.'

There was another tiny movement of Kojo's head. I don't think he wanted to know about complications at all, but Teresa leaned forward and put her hand on that of her man and rested it there while PK continued.

'The risks are low, but they are serious. So even if the risk is only one in one hundred, if you are that one, that's serious for you. For this operation there's about a three per cent risk of death – three in one hundred people will die having this operation. There's also a risk of a chest infection or strain on the heart, kidney failure or a clot on the leg or the lung. There's a small risk of needing a bag for your bowels.'

Teresa sat back and took a deep breath.

PK continued. 'So if you're having an op, the choice is between the open op or the keyhole sort, and we don't really know which is better. The open one is obviously a bigger operation, so the risks at the time of surgery are a bit higher, but it may overall be a better operation because it lasts longer and we're less likely to have to go back in.'

Teresa blinked. One operation feels like enough; she hadn't thought of two.

Kojo took the piece of paper from PK and looked at it, frowning at PK's neat shading of that 3D bulge in his abdomen. He slid his hand on to his tummy, feeling for an answer.

'We will write all this down for you,' said PK. 'There's a lot to take in.'

When I read the research paper by Jude Partridge and her colleagues – an evaluation of this comprehensive assessment of older people who are considering major vascular surgery – everything made sense. For years, like everyone in my specialty, I had been asked to see patients on the surgical wards after they had had an operation but were doing badly. It felt as if that was traditionally when a geriatrician would be called in – after it had all gone wrong. These patients had not behaved as they and their doctors had expected. They were now confused or ill or not eating or too weak to stand, and there was no baseline, nothing to say in detail what that person was like before they had had a massive operation. We'd have to search for clues, warning signs, things that could have been mended before that person went through a procedure that would challenge every ounce of their physical and mental strength. And sometimes I'd look at someone very frail, who had probably just been hanging on and was now falling apart, and I'd wonder why anyone had thought that an operation was a good idea.

Jude tells me how she and her colleagues made the case for their service. 'The message to the surgeons was, we are aiming to get your patients out of hospital faster, a reduced length of stay with fewer complications. And that went down well; we weren't saying, "You can't do that operation." We were mostly saying, "If you're going to do this op, there are things we can do in advance that will make it go better." And sometimes we might suggest not doing the operation at all.'

Kojo has had his session with the surgeon PK. The operation itself has been explained, but Kojo is not expected to decide right now. The team want him to have all the information he needs. Now Jude explains to Kojo and Teresa more about their options.

'We don't operate on everyone,' she says. 'We wouldn't even think of operating if you were, say, three hundred years old.' She smiles and Kojo nods, relieved. He's sixty-eight.

'And we wouldn't operate if you were dying of something else,' Jude continues.

Kojo nods again.

Jude frames a question for both doctor and patient to consider. 'And what if we leave it alone?'

She pauses. Leaving it alone is an option.

Kojo tips his head – this is information he needs: the likelihood of the aneurysm bursting.

Jude explains. 'Well, in 2015 a paper looked at rupture risk of patients with an aneurysm like yours, between five and six centimetres, that weren't operated on for one reason or another, and there was a three and a half per cent risk of rupturing in that year. So that's more than ninety-six in one hundred people *not* having a burst aneurysm.'

Kojo takes that in, but Jude continues. 'But then each year you haven't had an operation, you still have that risk.'

Jude then explains what would happen if the aneurysm ruptures. 'There's no blood to see,' she explains. 'It's on the inside, so you might get a bad pain in your back or your tummy or you might just collapse. If you got to hospital quickly, we might be able to do an emergency operation, but your chances of survival are a lot lower with an emergency op. And some of our patients have a different plan; they don't want any operation, planned or emergency, and they're clear they just want to be kept comfortable. And we can do that – it's a pretty quick way to go.'

Kojo rubs the back of his head. He's hearing a lot of stuff today.

Jude has a clear face, honest and sympathetic. 'I'm not telling you what to do, but if you are going to have an operation, we want to make sure it goes as well as possible.'

Kojo and Teresa nod. That's a positive thing to hold on to.

'Here's the plan. If we're operating, you're going to be waiting for a while, especially if we go for the complex EVAR because of getting your graft made and sent over. And we're going to use that time to get you as fit as possible.'

Jude lays down the rules. 'You stop smoking – both of you.' She nods at Teresa. 'Then you have a much better chance of coming through this operation well. And you reduce your risk of the aneurysm bursting anyway.'

Jude glances at Kojo's paperwork, and asks, 'How much do you drink?'

Kojo shifts in his plastic chair and says, 'A bit more since I retired. A whisky and Coke . . .'

Jude holds up her finger and thumb stretched wide apart. 'Just one? How big?'

He smiles and wags his finger at her. 'No, no, just a little one, but also a Guinness.'

Teresa says, 'Two,' and Kojo concedes – two pints of Guinness.

Jude says, 'Well, that's too much, and before this op there's going to be no booze in the house; it's having a toxic effect on your brain and it's not doing your bone marrow any good. I can see that on your blood test. And exercise?'

Teresa and Kojo look taken aback.

'I been taking it easy since they said about the aneurysm,' says Kojo.

Jude reassures him. 'Exercise is fine. More than fine; it's good. In studies we've put plenty of people with aneurysms on those exercise bikes and they're fine – in fact, they do better. Exercise won't make it burst. You can start getting fitter for this operation, OK? You're going to get walking a bit further and faster every day, and you can get some nicotine products, gum or patches from your doctor for free to help with the smoking.'

Later, I find Kojo and Teresa. They're waiting for a final set of blood tests before they leave. Teresa is tucking information leaflets into her handbag – among them an explanation of the delirium that can arise after a major operation. I've read the leaflet – it's thoughtful and clear. It includes quotes from families who have watched this common condition evolve:

After her hip operation my mother became very confused and aggressive. She kept pulling out her drip and shouting at the nurses. It was a shock as she is usually so polite.

My father became very confused. He was sleepy at times and agitated and restless at other times.

The leaflet explains that delirium usually resolves, but not always. It explains what patients can do to reduce its risk. There is space for the patient to record routines that are important to them and activities that might prove reassuring should reality evaporate and bed curtains become cell walls, familiar faces now malign and horrid. The leaflet is both honest and terrifying.

I ask Kojo and Teresa how they feel after this long day.

'It's very thorough,' says Kojo.

Teresa adds, 'It is scary, but I am glad they have told us everything.'

Kojo rubs his forehead, rests his hand once more on his stripey shirt. He can feel the pulsation of the aneurysm. He looks tired and afraid.

'We like the "prehab" plan,' says Teresa. 'We knew about rehab after, but we hadn't thought of doing rehab before the op to get him fitter. He's gonna be an Olympian.'

She squeezes Kojo's biceps, and his hand leaves his stomach and he flexes his arms and makes his eyes pop at Teresa, and suddenly they laugh — it's a relief really, and a challenge, and all of a sudden there's hope and people on their side and life to be grabbed.

But then Teresa puts her hands together, her fingers on her lips for a moment before she speaks. 'It's like we hadn't really thought about this. We thought they'd found the aneurysm and now they're going to fix it, and it was like they'll tell us what to do. But now I guess we know a lot more is down to him . . .' She looks at Kojo. 'It's like we have a part in this. Like, things we do, me and Kojo, they'll make a difference.'

I nod and Teresa looks down at the leaflets sticking out of her bag.

'I mean, I'm a social worker. I kind of know this stuff about responsibility, owning your own bad decisions, but it's different when . . . well, they made it clear, didn't they? We've got to make changes; it's our choice.'

Kojo joins in. 'I want to have the operation, and I want it to turn out good.'

He opens his hands. His smile is broad.

After the clinic I talk with Dom, who is a clinical nurse specialist in the POPS service. She recognises that this assessment is hard work for her patients. Many are considerably older than Kojo and have multiple problems.

'They do get tired,' says Dom. 'Some even nod off.'

Dom is aware that the clinic brings disappointment for some. Her patients are given information they might rather not have. They are suffering, maybe from a grating hip or a knee, and an operation has been proposed that would provide relief from that pain, and now here is a nurse talking about a decline in cognition or in function due to the operation, rather than the recovery, new life, that previously seemed to be on offer. But it's about making the right decision.

'I watch my patients when we give them good information,' says Dom, 'and sometimes they say, "Oh well," and "Now I come to think about it," and some people decide not to go ahead. We can focus on other ways to help them, sorting out their pain relief, looking at social prescribing. How else we can make their lives better.'

In their original study Jude and her team showed that their CGA picked up far more issues than were detected in the standard preoperative clinic. They also demonstrated that tackling these ahead of planned surgery paid off. For a few patients in the trial the CGA process resulted in a decision not to operate at all. For those who went ahead the results were spectacular. The team had hoped to reduce the number of days participants had to stay in hospital by 25%, but the figure dropped by 40%. The rate of post-operative confusion was halved. The CGA patients were less likely to develop infections. Their heart rhythms remained steadier, their kidneys deteriorated less and they were less likely to wind up in the intensive care unit.

But what of those who cannot become fit enough for an operation?

Jude outlines the situation. 'For some people, it's clear they should be having surgery. For others it's equally clear they should not.'

I've watched her talking with Iryna, who has attended with her mother. Vera's foot has been a dusky purple for months now. It aches and the pulses that should be palpable under the soft skin behind Vera's ankle and between the tendons of her toes are absent. Perhaps a bypass could be done, a grafted vessel to resupply blood to that foot. But Vera's also breathless; her heart is stiff and does not fill or squeeze properly. Iryna no longer fills her cup right to the top when she makes tea for her mother, as Vera does not have the strength to hold a full cup to her lips, and Vera has not left her wheelchair during the assessments this afternoon – no weight could be recorded, no Timed Up and Go test. A nurse had begun a Montreal Cognitive Assessment, with Iryna translating, but the nurse quickly became aware of Vera's fatigue, her anxious glances towards her daughter, who reached to steady her mother's hand as Vera drew the outline of a clock and placed a hesitant *12* outside the wavering circle she had drawn, before Vera stopped, putting the pen down, defeated, and the nurse reassured her that there was no need to answer more questions.

Jude explains gently to Iryna that an operation would cause Vera more harm than good, which Iryna conveys to her mother, but Vera frowns, looking from Iryna to Jude, searching for understanding, and I watch as Vera leans towards her daughter, who tenderly pushes her mother's black headscarf back behind her ear, the better for her to hear, and Vera's tired head is tilted to listen again. Iryna says, '*Operatzie ni potribna – bez operatzii,*' and moves her hand horizontally, palm down, to cut off that option.

Vera's face clears; she has understood there is to be no operation and she looks at Jude and nods, smiling. Such relief.

The conversation moves on to medicines for Vera's

pain and to making plans for her inevitable death, not just yet but soon, and to making that death as good as possible.

'And sometimes,' says Jude, 'it's a difficult decision whether or not to go ahead with an operation. Sometimes we need to give ourselves more time, gather more information.'

I think back to that time when I sat at the kitchen table, when Robert the obstetrician knew the result of the blood test I had decided not to have, about the baby that was not yet a baby but my baby still. I knew immediately that there must be a problem – he surely would not have rung had the result been reassuring. And I remember how the rational decision my husband and I had made, not to have that test, now seemed less obviously correct. I began to think of the implications for our existing children if they had a sibling with disabilities for whom they would remain responsible when we were gone, and I thought of my baby who might have other conditions associated with Down's syndrome, like heart problems. I remember how quickly I became uncertain and tearful. I knew that if the test was positive – a high risk for Down's – the next step would be an amniocentesis, a needle through my abdomen to take fluid from around the fetus, to confirm or exclude the diagnosis, and I knew that, whether or not my baby had Down's syndrome, the amniocentesis carried a risk of causing a miscarriage – a minor op for me, a major one for my baby – and my tears became hotter, my thoughts more confused.

I recall how carefully Robert spoke when we met him in clinic to discuss the unwanted test. Rationally I should have refused to be given the result, but I could not do that. Robert put figures on the risk, because one person's idea of high risk is not the same as another's, and he explained the risks of amniocentesis and wrote them neatly in ink for me to take away and look at. I remember how kindly he explained alternatives – that we could avoid the amniocentesis but have a more detailed scan of our baby at a later stage, so that if she did have Down's syndrome and had associated problems, we would be prepared, and could make plans for a more complicated time after her birth than just coming home with a new baby.

I think of Kojo and Teresa, and how the information they were given would help them to make a decision that was right for them, how this meant not only that they felt confident in the decision but also strengthened their resolve to play their part in making things go well. I think of Vera, and how Jude could see that an operation might restore blood to her foot but would overwhelm her heart and her mind, and would make her life worse, not better, or even shorten it.

I think of older people and my future older self. How might I come to a good decision about surgery when my own body is the subject of debate? What is helpful to know when we are older and are making decisions for ourselves or on behalf of someone we love?

I suspect that my future self will have her own views and may not be shy in stating them ('Gobby,' volunteers my dear husband), but I have been a patient before, more than once, and I know how quickly I can become disempowered. I know how rational thought can be banished by uncertainty and fear. I know I have been so unsettled that I haven't been able to hear my doctor's voice. I know I have felt unable to trust myself to make the right decision, and have needed time, information written out and numbers to read and contemplate.

It's helpful to know that there is choice; an offer can always be declined. It's helpful to know that we can ask questions, and that we deserve honest answers, even if the answer is 'I don't know'. It's helpful to know that some outcomes are down to our own behaviour, that we can often make ourselves a little fitter while awaiting surgery and doing so will materially improve our chances of success. To know that we don't need to be Olympians, yet small changes make a difference, like stopping smoking even just weeks before an operation. It's helpful to be realistic about the implications for driving or shopping. It's helpful to know that big operations hurt, and that we need to be prepared to work through pain after, say, a hip or a knee replacement and it will resolve.

As with decisions about medications, a framework

named BRAN is helpful, which encourages us to weigh up Benefits, Risks and Alternatives, and to discover what might happen if we do Nothing. But this doesn't work for everyone. Some of us find it overwhelming. We might prefer a more paternalistic approach. Some of us know what we want and will wave away offers of treatment, or conversely will grab such offers with both hands, ignoring the small print. Others will gather information, ponder, conclude. But many of us don't want to make our own decisions. We may frown and sigh and say, 'I don't know, doctor. What do you think?' That's a reasonable response; our doctors have training, knowledge and experience that we do not, and we need to trust them to guide us when we make our decisions or to make decisions for us when we feel unable. However, when considering surgery, the answer a patient gets to that question might be quite different, depending on the doctor they ask and the background and experience of that doctor.

I was told once of a test you can use with medical students to work out whether they are likely to become a surgeon or a physician. You show them a chest X-ray with an obvious tumour – a large white lump in the middle of a lung – and all the nascent physicians suck their breath in – they see bad news – and all the surgeons breathe out – whoa, I could get at that. It's a cliché of course that surgeons are gung-ho and physicians are cautious, but there's truth in it, and these attitudes can bring conflict. We're always going on about team-work, which is great when we're all on the same team, but too often physicians and surgeons may find them-selves opposing one another. Although both teams will claim that our goal is better care, in the worst cases our patients discover that they have become a human foot-ball passed uncomfortably between players who seem to be working against one another rather than together. GPs may be pulled in too as unwilling referees. It doesn't have to be like that.

The POPS model of teamworking (a team which includes the patient) and comprehensive assessment is currently being extended and unsurprisingly is prov-ing its worth in other areas. Doctors with expertise in specific conditions such as heart failure or cancer are discovering that older patients do better if their treat-ment and care are shared with geriatricians, who have the experience needed to see beyond the immediate prob-lem and can identify conditions that might be fixed in order to make treatment more successful, or which may render the proposed approach ineffective or dangerous. And sometimes geriatricians and their teams are better able to hear a voice saying quietly that that treatment is simply unwanted.

'When I'm eighty,' says my friend Linda, 'I'm going to be pliant and genial.'

I snort into my wine glass because she so is not, and I don't want her to be. I want Linda to have her own opinions. I want her voice to be heard. Linda deserves – we all deserve – a great team who will explain her choices, who have the skills and time to identify and treat conditions that are worth treating, who will work together to offer her the best chance to benefit while being honest about the limits of their offer. Linda deserves a team who will listen to her, and to each patient, so that together they can make a good choice.

7. News

My dad had a tweed suit and a gold pocket watch. At
any one time he also had at least three dogs with varying
levels of nonchalant delinquency and a small grey Mini
van, and he had converted the back of this van into a
tiny kennel with smelly straw into which his dogs leaped
enthusiastically, and their breath condensed on the metal
roof of the Mini and dripped on to us as we sat on the
wheel hubs between the dogs and the front seats on
the way to school. There were two dents in the grey
anodised fascia in front of the passenger seat, where
Mum's knees had met the shelf when they had crashed
into someone's car on the way back from voting, but
no one was much hurt and Mum and Dad said that no
one should know how you voted because voting was
secret and private and you didn't have to tell anyone, but
we knew that they voted for the Alliance Party because
Dad's face was on their posters and we were allowed left-
over Ritz crackers when they hosted cheese-and-wine
evenings to raise money to help people come together
in peace and stop putting bombs under cars.

Dad had brought Mum to Northern Ireland in the
sixties, to live first in Belfast, then moving a few years

later to our house in County Tyrone, where she later claimed the only reliable water supply arrived through the roof. An architectural almanac described it as 'an endearing jumble'; it had battlements and a pointless tower in which jackdaws nested, and a billiard room and a cavernous space called the theatre, full of old bikes and handy planks, and it had one bathroom, which was extremely cold and smelled of paraffin, and the 'jumble' bit was apparent to all visitors but the 'endearing' aspect was lost on some.

Dad had a carpentry workshop with a blade sharpener and you could turn the handle till it spun and sparks flew from a chisel held to its gritty surface, and he always had Fruit & Nut chocolate in the glovebox of the Mini, and he had two wards, one of which was in the General Hospital, which held long-stay patients downstairs in rows, and the other was at the County Hospital, up on the hill. The General also housed the maternity unit where I had been born, and we would visit the old people's ward on Christmas Day (Dad leaning to whisper something into an old man's ear and straightening his green tissue-paper crown) and then we would run upstairs to see if there were any Christmas babies, and the midwife who was always on duty would say, 'Lucy, I brought you into the world. You have *changed*,' which I found funny and mortifying in equal measure. In the County Hospital Dad had persuaded the authorities to build another ward, a whole unit, bright and airy with bays and single rooms and a day room and rails for rehab, and he had a ward sister, Rose, who knew everything worth knowing about older people, and Dad pretended to be annoyed when someone bought the ward a colour television to say thank you for their care, because now no one would want to go home and going home was the whole point of Ward 12G. G for Geriatrics.

When I was eleven, my parents had decided I should continue my education in England, but they didn't have enough money for boarding school, so I was enrolled in a girls' day school in London, where I was interested to find Jewish girls, Muslim girls, a Quaker and some atheists at desks alongside mine, but I was astonished to find also girls who were Roman Catholic, because even though I had been on peace marches and my parents had campaigned for the healing of our divided community and for non-sectarian policies, it had not occurred to me that in other parts of the UK Catholics and Protestants might be educated in the same classroom. That was an early lesson in the insidious nature of prejudice.

My mother and I lived in my grandparents' tall and thin house for a year while she rekindled the career in oph-thalmology which had largely been on hold while she had three children, and she attended Moorfields Eye Hospital by day, and studied anatomy books by night, tracing the course of the nerves of the orbit through tiny foramina in a skull that sat on her desk. The next

September, Mum passed her Surgical Fellowship exams and returned to Northern Ireland, and I went to live with some cousins. I had met them once at a Save the Children Fund Christmas fair in Kensington Town Hall, but they were very distant cousins and it was kind of them to take me in on a two-year trial period which eventually extended to five years, over which time they became a generous and loving second family to me. My cousin Isa went to a neighbouring school and we played cards and invented a game of tennis with complicated rules that involved knocking a ball against a wall in the car park next door, but Sundays could seem very long in London and I missed home. When we got back for the holidays, my sister and brother and I would pull on our wellies and go up to the moorland behind the house to shake a bucket of nuts for our muddy ponies, and we'd lead them down to the stable and smell the fur behind their ears.

One London Sunday when I was thirteen, Isa and I were staying next door with her granny, because her parents were away on a business trip. We had done our homework and the day stretched ahead, when Isa's granny announced that my aunt would be visiting that afternoon. This was a welcome idea, as I loved Aunt Gillie, my mum's sister, with her long batik skirts and red hair, darker red than Mum's, and her joyful disregard for rules. Gillie had an older son, my cousin Mike, whose father was a communist and lived in Cuba in order to advise Fidel Castro on his economic policy, and her other son was my baby cousin Shamba, whose dad Bunny was from the West Indies. Gillie was the leader of a nursery school in north London that was attended by children from many different backgrounds, including at that time a number who had fled Vietnam with their families in small boats after the fall of Saigon, and I was looking forward to hearing how they were getting on, for Gillie had described how damaged these tiny children had been by their terrible ordeals and how maybe play and laughter would help their recovery.

When Gillie arrived that afternoon, she and I were ushered into Isa's granny's drawing room, and Isa and her granny went off somewhere and we sat on the sofa facing one another. I asked about the boat children and Gillie said they were doing well. And then she said that she was sorry but she had come with some bad news, and she was silent for a moment while those words dropped into the space between us, and she said again she was sorry but the news was very sad, and there was another long pause before she said that there had been an accident. I said, 'Who?' and she said, 'I'm afraid it is your daddy,' and I could feel my insides go hollow, the blood flowing backwards in my wrists, and I said, 'How bad was the accident?' and she said, 'A very bad accident,' and I asked, 'Is he badly hurt?' and she did not reply but looked at me with kind round eyes through her thick specs, and I said, 'Is he dead?' and she nodded and gathered me into her arms.

Years later at medical school, we were given lessons in how to share bad news, and I realised then that Gillie, my dear aunt who had had no training at all, no lessons in sharing bad news, had delivered a masterclass when she told me about the death of my father. She had prepared the space she needed. She had warned Isa's granny why she was coming but had asked her not to breathe a word, and Isa's granny had respected that request. Gillie had ensured that we were in a quiet place and would not be disturbed. She had used silence over and over again. She had given me a warning, telling me that she had come with bad news, and she had given me time to absorb that message. She had handed over the information in such measured amounts that eventually I knew what she was going to say.

Over the years I have often witnessed the delivery of bad news, and seen it done well and done badly. I have shared such news myself now countless times – news of loss, disability or illness that cannot be cured – and have not always done it as well as my aunt did in 1979. I have realised also that the sharing of bad news is not only the preserve of those who work in healthcare but is something that any of us may need to do at any time. We may need to share news with our friends, parents, children or partners, or with students, colleagues or even strangers, about the terminal illness of someone we know or the death of a pet, of separation, a move to a different continent, or a job lost, an exam failed, a landscape irrevocably destroyed.

Sometimes we deliver news badly because we are not thinking and do not take a moment to consider the meaning of this news to its recipient, which may mean we do not even recognise that the news is bad. I think of Pádraig, one of many Irishmen who lived in north London when I was a young doctor. They worked on building sites, these country men, as labourers and hod carriers, as brickies and at the controls of hydraulic diggers, and one of them told me my favourite Irish joke, which involves an English site foreman who is 'sick of thick Paddies', who interviews Pat for a job.

Pat is doing pretty well and the foreman says, 'OK, Pat, if you get this next question right, you can have the job . . . Now, what is the difference between a girder and a joist?'

And Pat says, 'Well, sor, I tink that is straightforward, for Goethe wrote *Faust* and Joyce wrote *Ulysses*.'

Pádraig had come to the Emergency Department with weakness down his left side; he was just about able to walk but his arm and leg were unreliable and I had identified that as well as the weakness the sensation in his left limbs was altered – he seemed on first inspection to have normal responses, could feel the brush of a cotton wool wisp and the sharpness of a pin when I tested one hand at a time, but with his eyes closed and the cotton wool touching both his left and right hand at once, he could identify the sensation only on the right, and the same happened when I ran my finger along his calves. Pádraig could detect sensation on each side when stroked separately, but when both calves were touched at the same time he did not detect sensation on the left. This is a condition called sensory inattention, which accompanies the weakness that occurs in some strokes, and it indicates that a larger part of the brain has been damaged than if there is weakness alone. I had been studying for postgraduate exams and had predicted from my careful examination exactly where the damage might be seen on Pádraig's CT brain scan, and, sure enough, there was a blur on his scan, a patch of brain starved of oxygen in the territory supplied by his right middle cerebral artery, so I was satisfied by my analysis.

I went to see Pádraig as he lay waiting for his results, his tired head with grey lambchop whiskers on the pillow, and I told him brightly that the scan had showed that he had indeed had a stroke, and I was about to tell him that the damage was just where I had thought it would be, when I saw that Pádraig had closed his eyes and turned his face away from me. I curled up inside. I had not for a moment considered the implications of this diagnosis for Pádraig – for a wiry man in his late fifties, working, carrying bricks to send money home to Cork. I had not thought about no work, no pay, a long road to an uncertain recovery, the cost of the treatment, can I drive, will there be another stroke, is my life ended?

I knew many of these would be questions I couldn't answer there and then, but I could have paused and thought about Pádraig: his life and this diagnosis and the meeting point of those two things, and I could have shared my information more circumspectly and with more consideration and kindness.

Sometimes in order to share bad news well we need to remember that what may be routine to us, an everyday sadness, may be unforeseen and horrible to someone whose world does not ordinarily involve such news. I have received bad news given gently by a nurse whose work encompassed the need to convey unexpected loss frequently, regarding a tiny fetus with a future, already named – I was so sure she would be a girl – a baby who would sleep in the pram in which her siblings had slept before under the green trees. The nurse who was carrying out the routine scan said only, 'I'm sorry, Lucy.' (She used my name and a pause.) 'I'm so sorry there is no heartbeat here.' (Clear is kind.) Then she did not say anything else for a while, and held my hand.

I have received bad news delivered clumsily in a phone call, rushed and shocking, by someone I love, who needed to tell me, some years after the death of my father, that my aunt, compassionate Aunt Gillie, had died suddenly too. Sometimes we are made so uncomfortable by the burden of the bad news we are carrying, we feel a need to dispose of it, to hand it over as quickly as we can, but there is rarely a need for bad news to be delivered immediately and we may need to hold that burden for a while, sometimes for a few long seconds or some minutes, sometimes a day or more, until we have prepared the recipient to take it into their own hands.

In other situations we may choose not to share bad news at all, and that is very often unkind. We may be hampered by anxiety about causing upset and we may be silenced by defensiveness, a feeling that we may be found out or found wanting – perhaps the treatment that we proposed has not worked and we find it hard to admit our limitations, to withdraw the hope that we ourselves had offered.

We are silenced too by a desire (often denied) to protect ourselves from an emotional connection that may cause us distress. That instinct for self-preservation is not to be dismissed lightly, as such moments of connection can act as a conduit for sadness, and sadness flowing too freely from one person to another may fill us up and leave no space for joy, beauty, hope. For several years when we were unable to recruit specialists in stroke medicine, I looked after our stroke patients myself and I learned to watch for those moments of profound connection and realised that, most often, the leat that held such emotion upstream would be opened by a moment of physical contact – my patient's hair had fallen across her face and I would smooth it with my thumb, or I would help a farmer's clumsy foot back into a worn slipper, and my patient's sadness would flow into me, and I could feel my own resources being drowned by empathic distress. I learned to visualise a Harry Potter wand, energy streaming to deflect that sadness, to send it to the ground to dissipate. Or I could imagine a silver teapot with a handle that could become too hot when the pot is filled with boiling water, but there are rings at its top and bottom made of old ivory or bone or Bakelite that prevent the transmission of heat into the handle and so it remains useful, performing its function even when the pot is too hot to touch.

There are other things that help in the sharing of bad news, and I watched long ago as a surgeon – my first boss Harvey Ross, with his smooth brown head, dancing brown eyes, and hands, such hands – explained to his patient the results of her scan. First he introduced himself, apologised for the delay and the wait for the scan to be reported, then Harvey said, 'You must have been worrying. How have you been this last few weeks?' And his patient Anna told him that her weight loss had continued and that the ache here – her hand on her waist below her ribs – had not gone and might be worse. He asked her so carefully whether she had been told what the scan might show or whether she had her own ideas, and Anna put her lips together and screwed her eyes shut, then opened them and said, 'I think this will be cancer.' Harvey nodded slowly, at which point it was clear that her understanding and his had now met in the same place and they could journey onwards together.

I read the words of Kathryn Mannix, a palliative care physician, in her book *Listen*, in which she describes a nurse coming alongside a woman at a moment of searing and unbelievable new grief; her husband is dead of a heart attack and she has been told but cannot accept it. The nurse Dorothy acknowledges her grief.

'This is very shocking, my love. Very shocking.'

She uses gentle questions: Did you know he had a bad heart? Were you worrying about him?

Kathryn Mannix describes what she saw as a young doctor and how Dorothy's questioning and listening allowed the bereft woman to start to make sense of the senseless, as she tells Dorothy 'the story so far'. When I read this phrase I recognise it so vehemently that Dr Mannix's book actually falls out of my hands.

Kathryn's phrase captures so much more than what we are taught in medical school about taking a history – algorithmic questions with answers that narrow down the options logically. When did the pain start? Suddenly or slowly? Where is the pain? Is it sharp, dull, coming in waves? Algorithmic questions that do not say: I can see you miss your wife very much. Questions that do not ask: might there be something of which you are afraid? Algorithms that do not offer: tell me more about the noises from next door. Tell me what makes you happy, what causes you to smile. Questions that cannot detect loneliness, poverty, jealousy, the sister whose cancer was missed. Questions that do not allow for the telling of a story.

A great deal of the work we do with older people involves making nuanced decisions. Algorithmic medicine does not work for people with complex medical problems, and I realise that the need to know enough of 'the story so far' perfectly pinpoints the process by which we may together – a patient, and those who know, love or care for them, and a clinician – come to a shared understanding, of wishes and values and what matters most, a place where we can stand alongside one another to make the plan a good one that may bring resolution and confidence.

And when we have bad news to impart, it is wise and kind again to find that shared place, to come alongside someone as far as we are able, and we can find that place by pausing and considering how that news will be received and taking a moment to understand the story so far. We must do the work to bring the person affected to the right place, where they will be as prepared as well as possible to allow that information to come into their lives.

One could say, what difference does it make? The news is the news. The manner of its delivery does not change the facts. Despite my aunt's care that Sunday afternoon in 1979, my shoulders began to hunch and drop, as I tried to shrug the information she had brought off my back, and my body would not stop doing that for some time, and even now when I look back I find my shoulders are up around my ears again. But I also remember each detail of Gillie's powerful kindness. I know that it helped then and has helped me for decades afterwards that she shared what she knew with such tenderness.

8. Brought Back

It's a Tuesday afternoon, and I've returned to the head and neck ward to see Diana, who is one of our medical outliers – a medical patient in a surgical ward, because there are not enough medical beds; there never are enough medical beds. Diana was on the point of going home but has suddenly become seriously unwell. The young doctor covering that outlier ward is Saamir, one of a cohort of doctors who have joined our hospital recently and are new to the NHS, and he and I have talked about his experience in Pakistan, then in Qatar, and I know that Saamir's training has been good but that he is overwhelmed by a profusion of bureaucratic tasks and that he has been granted log-in details for only half the IT systems he needs. He's assessed Diana and taken the right blood tests, but his radiology access isn't working so he can't request the scan that will help us work out what's going on, so I open the system and request the scan myself instead. I check Saamir's plan, which is a sensible one, and he and I agree that I'll call Diana's family while he gets on to the overstretched IT department again to get his passwords sorted out. I'm about to pick up the phone – I'm casting around for Diana's

next of kin details because they're not in the folder –
when I look up because a man is standing near me and
he wants to ask me something.

'I'm sorry, Dr Pollock,' he says, 'but when you have a
minute, please can I talk to you about Mum?'

The man inclines his head sideways and I follow the
direction of his eyes to the corner by the window, where
Sally is sitting watching the sky.

Sally has been here a few weeks. She fell at home, no
one's sure why, and broke her pelvis, and it was a while
before she was found because she had a pendant alarm
but did not use it. Her son Drew was worried when
she didn't answer his daily check-in phone call, and he
rang the neighbours, who went round and spotted Sally
on the floor. Drew had given them a key to Sally's house
a year ago, after she had a fall in the garden, so they let
themselves in and put a pillow under her head, called
an ambulance and sat with Sally, even though she told
them she would be fine waiting on the floor. While they
were waiting, those neighbours looked around and realised that things were not as good in Sally's house as
they had assumed. There was mouldy food in the fridge
and no milk, there were paper bags full of medicines
that Sally had not taken, the light bulb had blown on
the staircase, and paperwork was piled up on the table
and the sideboard – notification of a gas price rise, a
reminder about an unpaid house insurance policy, bro-
chures inviting Sally to take a cruise on the Danube,

replace her windows, buy a pressure washer. For Sally was diagnosed with dementia three years ago and was then discharged from the memory service, because it is short-staffed and only provides a diagnostic service. That service has indeed given Sally and her sons a diagnosis but has not told them what to do with that diagnosis, so they have been muddling along, and Drew and his brother have done some sensible things like sorting out Lasting Powers of Attorney for their mum and setting up the pendant alarm, and Drew has been doing her repeat prescriptions and her weekly shop online, so who knows why there was no milk because it was on the order and there should have been plenty. But Drew lives in Leicester and his brother's in Huddersfield, and it's been hard for them to get to see Sally with the long journey and then the COVID rules.

'Nice to meet you, Drew,' I say, and I explain that I need to make a call, and then we can talk. He goes to chat with his mum, and while I'm waiting for Diana's nephew to answer – I found the number in the therapist's notes – I can see Drew taking some clothes out of a suitcase for Sally and folding them into her bedside cupboard for her to wear tomorrow, and he puts her coat on the back of her chair and takes out a framed photo from the suitcase and props it on her bedside table. Sally leans back in her chair and closes her eyes; she's tired, with all the fuss and the plans.

I phone Diana's nephew and explain that she is very

unwell – sick enough to die – and while we are talking I see a message on my phone reminding me that there's a meeting at three about the new Hospital at Home service to discuss how to get the right medicines to patients in their own home when they are sick and alone and on the other side of the county, and I'm on duty this evening so I need to be on the AMU by quarter to five, and I've already had a message that we are two junior doctors short for tonight's shifts. I'm also supposed to have looked at a complaint that has arisen in one of the community hospitals, for which the deadline was yesterday and the complaint is long, suffused with anger and misunderstandings, and the patient was not one I have met, so it will take longer to figure out what has happened and find a path to resolution. In addition, I have signed my clinic letters but received an email reminder that I haven't yet 'outcomed' my patients from last week, which drives me nuts because the electronic process for this is protracted and counterintuitive but must be done, as it's the only way the admin teams know whether I'm planning to see the patient again and within what sort of time frame, or whether I have discharged them or referred them to another team. So it's important but why does it have to be so difficult, and anyway who let someone get away with making up the verb 'to outcome'? So by the time I have been gentle with Diana's nephew and talked about uncertainty and about what her wishes would be (he professes to have no idea) and whether he should visit (yes, if he is able) I am quite cross, and I know I need also to check that Saamir is OK and that he has been shown how to generate an electronic discharge summary, because Sally is going to need one.

But Drew is waiting and I've been told he is driving Sally up to Leicester tomorrow, for she has agreed to move into a residential home which Drew has found for her. This plan eludes her at intervals through each day, and she sits watching the busyness of the ward and asks from time to time whether she should be getting a bus back home.

Drew is neat in a lambswool jumper and proper shoes, and he has brought his mum a folder from the residential home, with pictures of a table laid for tea, a gentleman laughing with a young carer, a bird bath with a coal tit splashing in it. He gives it to Sally, who holds it uncertainly, looking around for somewhere to put it – it must belong to somebody, someone else.

'We know you'll like it there, Mum,' Drew says. 'Have a look while I'm talking to the doctor.'

Drew and I walk over to the computer so that I can open the prescribing system to show him his mother's medicines – the ones we've stopped because they weren't doing any good, and the ones we've stopped because she didn't like them, and the new ones we've started – a calcium and vitamin D supplement and a plan for a six-monthly injection to help bind calcium into her bones, to reduce, a little, Sally's risk of having another fracture.

Then I say, 'Drew, I wanted to check another thing. Your mum has a Treatment Escalation Plan –'

Drew interrupts me and puts his hand up and smiles. 'Yes!' he says. 'My brother and I have spoken about that and we want Mum to be resuscitated.'

I look at him and for a moment it feels like a scene in a science fiction film, where there are parallel universes and a shimmering sheet of plasma divides the characters in each. Drew's reality and my reality are utterly, impossibly different.

Drew has seen the look on my face and tries to re-assure me.

'If you'd asked me a few weeks ago,' he says, 'when everything was in a state, I'd have said no, but she's so much better now, with the company here, and she's eating –' which is true, Sally has put on weight – 'and she looks happier, more interested, and we think she'll have a good time in the home. It's nice and she might have, I don't know, ten more years.'

He glances across to where Sally is sitting, the residential home brochure folded on her lap. He looks at me and I cannot disguise my expression. I have leaned back a little, as if I have walked into a scene I do not wish to witness. I know that Drew senses my emotion. He clasps his hands. He is negotiating, wants to gain my approval. 'She's only got one life.'

And at this point the shimmer disappears. Drew and I are in the same place, standing on the head and neck

ward, and I have a choice. Drew's round face is purposeful, earnest and kind, and he is doing his best by
his mum, and I am in a hurry and late for my meeting,
so I smile too and say, 'That's OK, Drew, I understand.
Maybe it's something you can think about again when
your mum's settled in.'

I wish him luck with the journey and I walk away, and
I never quite forgive myself.

Around ten years ago, the UK's Resuscitation Council
started collecting data about outcomes of resus attempts
in hospital. Their results are published annually as the
National Cardiac Arrest Audit, to which almost all UK
hospitals contribute. The audit team look at where each
cardiac arrest has taken place, how quickly help was
provided and what treatments were given. They look
at how effective the treatments have been – vigorous
chest compressions, oxygen by mask or by tube into the
lungs, and electric shocks to try to persuade a quivering heart back into a coordinated rhythm (only for
some – in others the heart is at a standstill and shocks
cannot help). The team collect data on whether each
patient's heart started beating again and whether they
survived a further day but died later, or whether they survived long enough to leave hospital.

Overall, resus teams in hospital manage to restart
the heart in about half of those to whom they are
called. Of these another half die while still in hospital.

Around a quarter survive long enough to leave hospital. Predictably, however, older people who have had a cardiac arrest are less likely to survive than young people – their heart is less likely to return to a normal rhythm, and of those few who do survive the initial cardiac arrest, a higher proportion do not live much longer, maybe a few days. Many subsequently die, not of a heart rhythm problem, but rather of the other illnesses that have brought them into hospital in the first place – pneumonia, say, or kidney disease, cancer or frailty due to the burden of multiple conditions added together. Resuscitation isn't a treatment for ordinary dying.

The statistics for those who have a resus attempt outside the hospital – at home, on the street, in the office or the pub – are less good. Fewer than one in ten survive when resuscitation is attempted, and again the outcomes are worse in older people.

But there are survivors. Older people can survive a cardiac arrest, so why am I looking at Drew with such concern, when he states his intention that his mum should be resuscitated?

Ella and Camilla came to see me. They had been qualified for a year and bounced into the office in pretty spring dresses with pockets and flat shoes for busy jobs.

'We'd like to talk about resus,' they said, pulling swivel chairs from the desks of my colleagues, wriggling them closer to mine between the piles of patient notes that my colleague Simon would work his way through, dictating clinic letters at the weekend, every weekend. I'd done a teaching session the previous week for the Foundation Years doctors, including Ella and Camilla, about how to talk about resuscitation with older people and their families, a delicate subject fraught with mis-understanding and fear. We had discussed opening phrases, the importance of explaining the treatments that are already happening. We had discussed how to judge whether a patient would be able to understand and weigh up the options – the assessment of cap-acity – and we had talked about when and how to involve a family, friend or carer instead, in order to work out what a patient's wishes would be if they have become unable to speak for themselves. We'd talked about how to explain futility, how to take the burden of guilt away from a daughter-in-law or grandson who may fear he is being asked to make a decision, being made to judge whether someone will live or die, when, in fact, for older people with several illnesses the decision is often a med-ical one and already made, and the doctor's job is to explain gently and honestly why a resuscitation attempt should not take place because it cannot work, it will not restore life and has no role in ordinary dying.

The young doctors in the teaching session had described what they had learned already about how to read signals and hear hidden messages, how to anticipate hopes and fears. We had talked about my experience that most older people do not want a resus attempt and are relieved to have had the conversation and to get their views recorded. The trainees had told me of their frustration, the difficulty of finding records that would tell them that their patient had already discussed this topic and had a good plan in place but it was invisible, buried in old hospital notes or in an inaccessible GP record. And finally I had shown them some of the data from our own hospital for the outcomes of cardiac arrest. We had talked about those who had survived and left hospital and returned home, alive again.

Now in my office, a week later, Ella said, 'The thing is, we want to know what happened next. I mean, after someone leaves hospital.'

Camilla continued, saying, 'And for the others, the ones who you get back when you do the crash call, but afterwards you have to walk away, go back to the ward, and you don't know what happened after that. Did they make it home?'

Ella looked at Camilla and me. 'We did a really sad one the other day on AMU – and he was just a wee old man, and we did get him back, he went to intensive care, but I looked him up and he died yesterday. And I was thinking about his ribs . . .' They both shifted on the swivel chairs and Ella's lovely brown eyes looked down and away across Simon's patients' notes on the floor, and Camilla's lovely blue eyes looked up to the corner of the ceiling, and I knew that Ella was not saying he was 'just a wee old man', but rather that she saw that he was an individual, a person, and that he was vulnerable, and Ella and Camilla were not sure that they had done the right thing by their patient and knew they had caused him harm.

So the three of us did a project. We contacted the resus officer who collects data for all our cardiac arrest calls and we went through his spreadsheet to identify all the forty-seven patients over the age of eighty who had received a resuscitation attempt in our hospital in the previous two years. We requested their notes. Of the forty-seven older people in whom resus had been attempted, five had survived to leave hospital. Another two had come through the initial resuscitation attempt but had died during their admission. In the other forty the resuscitation attempt had made no difference – these people had been dead when the resuscitation attempt began, and remained so.

We sought advice from the research ethics team, who were happy for us to go ahead, and then we wrote some very careful letters.

We wrote to each surviving patient, or to the families of those who had survived the resus attempt but subsequently had died, asking if there was anything they would like to tell us about their experience. We enclosed stamped envelopes for replies, but also offered a telephone call or a face-to-face meeting. And here I must speak gently, my reader, for we listened to some stories and they were sad or brave or both.

In one case a man had been resuscitated and only afterwards had the team found the DNAR form in his notes, recording his wish not to have a resus attempt. He had died a year later of lung cancer. The next person was a woman who had spent fifty days in hospital after her resuscitation and further time in a community hospital and had finally moved into care. Her daughter rang me after receiving our letter to talk about her mother. 'In the space of an hour her whole life changed . . . She wishes she hadn't been brought back.'

Arlene rang me herself. She had a bright voice and greeted me cheerfully. Arlene already had some medical problems and was eighty-four when she collapsed at home. Later, she had a cardiac arrest while in the CT scanner in the Emergency Department. Her heart had gone into ventricular fibrillation, an uncoordinated quivering that does not allow the heart to pump, and the team acted quickly. Arlene's heart was back in a normal rhythm after two minutes of chest compressions and one shock. A few days later her team had discussed resuscitation decisions with Arlene and her family, and she had been clear that she would not want another CPR attempt, even though the first had been so evidently successful. Arlene's voice, over a year later, was firm.

'I worry all the time, Dr Pollock. I am a worrier. I get frightened . . . I know I shouldn't say it because I am lucky; they worked on me and I had the helicopter and everything but they shouldn't have . . . I'm hurting all over. My husband and me, we have talked it over, we wouldn't want to be resussed like that.'

And Tina described her father-in-law's last days: a resuscitation attempt shortly after admission, a spell in intensive care during which it became clear that he would not wake again, her regret that resus had not been discussed. Tina told us, 'If they had asked him, I don't think it's what he would have wanted.'

A son rang to talk about his dad, and of his gratitude for the care, and of how well informed the family had felt between his father's cardiac arrest and his death seven days later. He continued, 'He would never have wanted to survive not independent. He wouldn't have wanted you to bring him back to be like that. He was waiting for God. Dignity was his number-one priority; not being a burden was number two.'

The son explained that he wished he had been prompted to talk with his father about his views and wished that his father had been offered a chance to make a different plan before his heart stopped. But another man wrote to us from Lincolnshire – his wife had had a cardiac arrest while on holiday. His letter thanked the ward for their 'wonderful hospitality', adding, 'Luckily my wife pulled through.'

Our study was small. Of our seven patients and their families five told us of their experience, of whom four expressed regret, feeling that they or their relative would have made a different decision had they been given the opportunity. Older people can survive a cardiac arrest, especially if they are truly well, independent and active ahead of some sudden unheralded cardiac event. They can survive and have a good quality of life thereafter, but the great majority do not, and some survive with a considerable change in their circumstances, becoming dependent when they had previously been looking after themselves, capable and resourceful. And the words that were used, by Arlene and Tina and the others in our study, are words I have heard plenty of times before and since: words of gratitude for the care, alongside words of regret, expressed cautiously and politely, but regret nonetheless.

As we get older, we deserve good conversations about important treatments. Our eighty-year-old selves, now and in the future, deserve honesty, clarity, kindness. We need to be able to learn from the experiences of others and we need courage to hear what we need to know so that we can make sound decisions for ourselves and contribute to the right decisions on behalf of those whom we love.

I think often of Drew and Sally. I could have done things differently that afternoon on the head and neck ward. I could have made time out of no time, sat with them together, and gently, carefully explored Sally's wishes, because even though she may not have had capacity to understand and weigh up details, someone who lacks capacity to make a specific decision may still have an opinion. That opinion is important and needs to be heard. My experience tells me that most older people, my patients in their eighties and nineties, do not want to have a resuscitation attempt, especially once they become aware of the likely outcomes. Or if Sally was not able to do that – if she was looking around, distractable, thinking about her paper hanky or a crumb on the table, unable to focus on disturbing questions about hearts stopping or breathing machines – I could have taken the time to talk with Drew. I would have chosen my words very carefully because Drew would need to know that I value his mum's life, that I understand that someone living with dementia in a care home may yet have a life that is contented and happy, that has value. He must not feel I am withholding something from her, something to which she should be entitled. I do not want to make him frightened or force him to contemplate a scenario that is ugly and traumatic, and yet I would want him to be aware that the future is less bright than he hopes for Sally. Dementia in those in their eighties progresses more rapidly than it does in younger people and the average life expectancy of someone moving into residential care is not the ten years for which he expressed hope but rather around two years (in nursing homes it is one) – not because the care is poor but because the conditions causing that person to need care tend to be progressive and fatal. I would want Drew and his brother to think very carefully, because this decision is not about what they would want, but what Sally would want if she had all the information and was able to speak for herself. And I would want him to be aware of the ramifications of the request that he and his brother have made on behalf of their mother.

I've thought about Drew's reasoning and wondered what sort of situation he had anticipated in which a resuscitation attempt might take place for Sally. We always declare hope for a peaceful death in old age for those we love. Sometimes when someone like Drew says, 'She's only got one life,' there is a subtext, which is 'I've only got one mum,' and there is hidden anguish, a grief that anticipates loss before it has happened, and it is unbearable and cannot be expressed.

If he had to, if Drew was compelled to envisage Sally's ending, I suspect that he would hope his dear mother might die peacefully in her sleep one night – not just yet but at some point. I wonder whether he realises that his wish for a resuscitation attempt means that the carers in the home, upon finding her still, chilly and peaceful one morning, all life having departed, will have to start chest compressions, call 999, and continue their efforts until a paramedic arrives or until a senior nurse or doctor on the phone re-evaluates the situation and permits them to stop.

But my concern is that more likely Drew and his brother may have based their request on wrong information, on a misplaced optimism about outcomes, an impression that resuscitation is a simple clean process. Even the phrase he used ('We want Mum to be resuscitated') suggests that Drew thought that our attempt would be successful, rather than just that, an attempt. Or perhaps Drew felt guilty, felt that agreeing to a DNAR for his mum who is unable to speak for herself would be giving up. Yet surely Drew would want someone to sit with his mum at her ending if he cannot be there, and to talk gently to her, tell her she has done so well, tell her that she is loved. This is not giving up. It is letting go. Giving up is wrong. At the right moment it is kind to let go.

You can read Ella and Camilla's study here: https://academic.oup.com/pmj/article/96/1134/186/6842802

9. Honest and True

'Oh my God, you wouldn't believe it,' says Suze. My phone is propped between the pen jar and the bowl of things that don't have a better home – plastic collar stiffeners, mystery keys, a phone charger that doesn't work as well as the other one – and I chop onions as my sister-in-law recounts the events of their weekend.

'We had to get to the christening – you know, Abbie and Will. I'm a godmother and it's miles away and we're late because – oh everything. Sasha had tipped her breakfast down herself, and one of the dogs had run off, and I forgot to give Oli his pill and you know what he's like with travel sickness so *his* breakfast came up on the A1, and then there was this massive jam, a cow on the road. I mean, not what you need. So we're getting later and later and we find the church and we're about twenty minutes late by now. They'll have started the service. So Josh says, "You go on in. I'll park and bring the kids." So I run in in my floaty dress and I've got a present for the baby and I'm trotting up the aisle saying, "I'm so sorry, so sorry," and I get to the top and, oh, Luce, I'm standing there and there isn't a font – there's an urn. And they're all looking at me, and this little lady is there in her black coat, and you could see she'd been crying. She put her hand on my arm and, Luce, she was so sweet; she gave me the loveliest smile and she said, "I think you're in the wrong church, dear. This is a departure, not an arrival."'

Harry Erland is in the middle bed of three in a bay on the AMU. I can see him from the desk. His dark hair is streaked with grey, and he's thin, so thin; there's a socket of deep shade between his cheekbone and his jaw. His eyes are shut and oxygen is flowing through soft prongs tucked into his nostrils. He is very still.

I look at the notes from the Emergency Department, neat curly writing despite haste. *HPC*, it reads, History of Presenting Complaint, *cough, drowsy*, and there's a little circle, then $E+D$, meaning not eating and drinking, and then *BG*, background, *dementia, recurrent pneumonia, last DC 6/52*, which means Harry was last sent home from hospital six weeks ago. There is a short list of medications, nothing that causes me to wince, and then the examination findings: *dry, crackles R>L.*

She (from the curves of the writing I assume the Emergency Department doctor is female) has found that Harry's breath sounds are crackly, more so on the right than the left, and I have already listened to those crackles, my stethoscope bridging two ribs at a time, a deep runnel between them, and Harry impassive, awake perhaps but with no interest in my activities.

The Emergency Department notes continue: *Pneumonia, ?aspiration. Plan, bloods CXR Abx ivi, admit medics.*

Things have moved fast. Harry's blood results are on the system already; that doctor was right: he's dehydrated, his kidneys are foundering. And his chest X-ray has been done too, and the whole picture is crooked because Harry could not sit straight in the bed despite being propped up, and the X-ray shows his jaw hanging in front of the top of his left lung, as his head had slumped, despite the radiographer's command to 'Lift your chin, deep breath and hold,' which Harry could not hear, understand, carry out or perhaps all three. There is hazy pneumonia at the bottom of Harry's right lung, and the X-ray from his last admission looks much the same. The antibiotics have been given, they're there on the electronic prescribing record, and there's a bag of fluid running into Harry's vein, the plastic line disappearing under the thin blue blanket.

The Emergency Department doctor's instructions have been carried out speedily and efficiently. Her diagnosis of pneumonia is correct. The treatment plan is logical. And she is wise to speculate that Harry may be aspirating, with tea or crumbs or custard getting into his lungs. The muscles that I can see, those of his limbs and between each rib, are wasted, which means that the muscles I can't see will be wasted too, muscles that should control his swallowing, to ensure that only air goes to lungs and that food and drink are sent safely to the stomach. It's a common problem in those who have become very weak for any reason; they cough and splutter and have recurrent lung infections. And each time Harry has pneumonia, he becomes weaker and more likely to develop another infection. He is on a sad slide: steep periods of decline punctuated by increasingly brief spells of relative respite, spells when the trajectory of his life might be less dramatic – some weeks at home, perhaps a little colour in his cheeks, a smile – but the trajectory is nonetheless downward.

There is one further entry in his Emergency Department notes: *SH, lives w wife.* Social history. The only information I have that is personal to Harry is that he lives with his wife.

I ring Mrs Erland, introduce myself, and explain that I am a doctor from the hospital.

'Harry's comfortable, Mrs Erland, I can see him from here, and it's not an emergency, but it would be good to have a chat. Is that OK?'

She sounds distressed, flustered. 'I'm so sorry I couldn't come; they wouldn't let me come in the ambulance. I'm on my own and I didn't know how long he'd be in the A and E – I can come tomorrow. Our neighbour will bring me. I'll bring his slippers.'

I listen and affirm that tomorrow is a good plan, as it's late now anyway, and I check that her name is Iris and whether she minds if I call her that. Then I say, 'Iris, Harry's been in hospital a lot. I can see that you must have been having a difficult time.'

'Oh, doctor, it's been difficult, you are right. It's hard for him; he doesn't know where he is, and the nurses don't know him. I mean, of course they can't; they're all different each time, but it is hard . . .'

I ask, 'What did Harry do for a living, when he was a younger man?'

There's a pause before Iris replies. 'Oh! History. I mean, he was an academic really, medieval history.'

'That's a nice job. I bet he liked it,' I say.

'He loved it – never really stopped, until the dementia.'

I look at Harry and then I look at the computer screen. His admissions to hospital are listed: a couple last year, a hip fracture, an infection. Then this year Harry was in hospital for most of April and a bit of May, some of July and again in September, every time infections and falls, and now it's November.

'Iris, do you mind if we talk a bit more?' I say. 'Are you able to sit down?'

I can hear her move at the other end of the phone and a kitchen chair is pulled closer. There's a rustle as Iris sits, a puff of breath, and she says, 'That's better.'

I feel bad. I should have made sure she was comfortable earlier.

'I'm sorry to be ringing late when it's dark, but it's so helpful to know a bit more about Harry – I can see he must have lost a bit of weight.'

'Oh, doctor, the weight has dropped off him. He never was a big man but there's nothing to him now.

And the falls, I'm always listening out, because he'll be on the floor, but that hasn't been so much recently; he doesn't really stand up now unless I'm with him . . . I mean, now he . . . well, he sleeps a lot.'

'Iris, what does Harry still like? What makes him smile?'

There's a long silence.

'I'm not sure really, maybe watching the birds. It's difficult to tell, because, you know, he doesn't speak.'

'How long has he not been speaking?'

Iris thinks. 'Maybe since Christmas? It happened slowly. I'm not sure.'

'I'm sorry, that must be very lonely for you.' I continue, 'Iris, I want to have a think about what we are doing, because I want to do the right thing by your lovely husband, and I'm not sure that what we are doing is the right thing.'

There's a sigh and she says, 'Well, he would not want to live like this.'

I wait and she continues.

'Last year he told me, he said –' There's another pause, and when she speaks again Iris's voice is very quiet. 'He said, "If I could, I would just walk into the hills and not be found."'

I look up at the strip light on the ceiling and close my eyes for a moment. 'Iris, I'm sorry, that is very sad.'

We sit, Iris and I, and say nothing, and I think about the hills, which can be seen from the top of the hospital's multi-storey car park, hills that were mauve in the pale light this morning, and I say, 'I think perhaps we could make a different plan.'

I thank her for telling me about Harry and I explain that he has pneumonia again – Iris is not sure it ever went away because he had a terrible cough when he came home last time.

'Iris, antibiotics might make a difference, and we could try different ones in case the infection is resistant, but I'm not sure that's the right thing to do. I wonder if maybe this is the right time to stop the antibiotics and concentrate on keeping Harry comfortable, because actually I think he is very close to the end . . . Iris, I think Harry might be going to die quite soon whatever we do.'

There's a silence, then Iris says quietly, 'Yes, I know it's going to happen.'

So I say, 'I have a feeling, listening to what you've told me about Harry, that he would prefer that we stop the treatments that are trying to keep him alive and we keep him comfortable instead.'

'Exactly that, just keep him comfortable. I know that's what he would want.'

I explain that, even though we are stopping active treatment, I cannot be sure that Harry will die just yet, because death doesn't always arrive when we think death is going to arrive, and Iris agrees, yes, she knows that, they thought Harry might die last time and he didn't. I'm writing in Harry's notes as I speak with Iris, the phone tucked between my ear and shoulder. I write a new plan: stop antibiotics, give intravenous or subcutaneous fluids only if thirsty and unable to drink. I write, *EoLC* – end-of-life care – and I'm looking at the labels on the slim tower of drawers next to the desk to find the End of Life form that will remind me to ask the nurses to stop checking Harry's blood pressure and pulse, because those numbers have no relevance now. The End of Life form will also give me guidance on the doses and formulations of drugs Harry may need if he has any signs of suffering, and will remind me to check that Harry's spiritual needs have been met, and Iris's. While I am pulling open drawers to find the right form, I hear Iris say, 'Thank you, doctor, I am glad we had that conversation – and I know you won't tell anyone; no one else needs to know.' And my heart turns over.

A few years ago I asked a group of GPs attending a training day, what is the single most common cause of death in England and Wales. They sat up and pulled their heads back, chins tucked in, surprised, I think, to be asked that question, with an unease that this was something we don't really think about, together with a feeling that the answer was obvious. When I asked for suggestions, a man in the front row confidently stated 'ischaemic heart disease, heart attacks', but his neighbour suggested stroke, while a younger woman behind him looked worried and asked whether it was lung cancer, and they were all wrong and none offered the correct answer, which is dementia.

Dementia became the commonest cause of death in England and Wales in 2015. For women it has been the commonest cause of death since 2011. For some very grim months in 2020 and 2021, COVID-19 took the top spot and was the leading cause of death in both those years, but dementia has now reasserted its dominance and will continue to do so. Globally dementia has risen from the seventeenth leading cause of death in 1990 to the seventh in 2019. And this means we need to do some work, as individuals, as friends and families, as healthcare workers and social care workers, and as a society – and we need to do it now. Dying with dementia can be difficult, and we can make it better.

When Iris confesses her confidence that I will not share our plan, that 'no one else needs to know', I realise that Iris, who loves her husband and cares for him day after day, who redoes his buttons when he has buttoned them off-kilter, and tucks in his shirt and listens for his breathing in the night, thinks that she and I have done something wrong. She thinks we have done something for which we may get in trouble, something that is against my code of practice or is shameful, unethical or perhaps even illegal. I had been about to put the phone down, leaving a woman who has loved her husband for fifty-eight years to sit alone in an empty house believing she has done something bad. I must stop looking for the right form in the filing cabinet. I must put down my pen and instead spend a little time explaining gently and clearly to Iris that what we have done, the plan that she and I have made, is far from wrong. It is exactly right.

Why have we got ourselves into such a muddle, into a situation in which Iris feels that the conversation we have had, full of love and honesty, should be a secret? We have confused ourselves with debates about euthanasia, which is deliberately killing someone to relieve suffering and that is illegal in the UK, and assisted dying, which is helping someone to kill themselves that is also illegal in the UK. The arguments continue. As I write, a public consultation in England has just ended, with the results due in the next few months. The views are ever more polarised with heartbreaking stories of unrelieved suffering, of longing for autonomy and dignity, and there are promises that there will be checks for coercion. And yet coercion can be subtle and can apply not just to an individual, because the attitude of a whole society can quietly shift, and there is a valid concern that if assisted dying is permitted there will be many who will come to feel that they should make arrangements to have their lives ended when they are not only terminally ill but also perhaps feel lonely or unloved, or are disabled and need help, or fear that they are a burden, physically, emotionally or financially to their families or friends. And the argument has been sharpened now by the fact that our resources are so stretched, and the provision of care and the palliation of symptoms sometimes does not happen as quickly as it should. Sometimes it does not happen at all, and Alistair Heather writes in the Scottish newspaper *The Courier* of *a real fear that bringing in assisted dying would act as a pressure release valve for failing services, with those suffering choosing a speedy death rather than an uncertain and painful wait for care.* I read Prue Leith's experience of the death of her brother, who suffered dreadfully at his end with cancer because his doctors refused to increase his painkillers – she felt they were fearful of prosecution for hastening his death – and I feel sad when I read her words, for surely the cure for such a deficiency in palliative care is better palliative care, rather than enabling people to kill themselves. I remember standing outside a hospital in London many years ago, when I was still a young doctor in training to be a geriatrician, and I thought about assisted dying, and realised that an ethical question – perhaps the biggest ethical question, with life and death at its heart – might all too easily become an economic one. I can sense even now the chilling feeling that years ago made me pull my coat round me, because whatever one's views on assisted dying, the conflation of economics and ethics – well, for me that represents a pathway to hell.

Let us put assisted dying aside for a moment, and think about *unassisted* dying, which is how the majority of people die now and which is likely to be how most of us will die for the foreseeable future, whatever the outcome of our national deliberations. There is, right now, a pressing need for clarity and honesty. I respect those who campaign for assisted dying. Their work is dignified and considered, and often springs from harrowing personal experience. However, their campaigns inadvertently perpetuate a myth that doctors are compelled to keep people alive. Quotes are used, in the literature of the Dignity in Dying campaign, from relatives of those who have asked not to continue treatment: *And she said, 'Can't you just give me something to kill me now?' And this oncologist just laughed and said, 'No we can't, we've got to keep you going.'*

Even though the oncologist is not permitted to procure death, the second part of his reply was wrong: it is simply not true that doctors must 'keep you going'. Another campaigner writes of trying to talk with his GP, *They're basically just trying to say, 'Look, you do realise you're talking to somebody that's sworn an oath to keep people alive?'* Again this perception is wrong. No doctor has sworn an oath to keep people alive without consideration of the wishes of each of those people or the consequences for them. Many doctors do not swear an oath at all; in some medical schools a variation of the Hippocratic oath is used, and sometimes such oaths declare *the utmost respect for human life*, but having respect for human life is not the same as prolonging it at all costs. Journalist Alice Thomson writes in *The Times*: *I do not want to die covered in tubes [. . .] and medicated in order to postpone death.* Alice does not need to die like that. None of us needs to die like that.

The General Medical Council's guidance on the subject is clear. In its document 'Treatment and Care Towards the End of Life' the GMC carefully defines the population to whom the guidance applies.

> Patients are 'approaching the end of life' when they are likely to die within the next 12 months. This includes patients whose death is imminent (expected within a few hours or days) and those with:
> (a) advanced, progressive, incurable conditions
> (b) general frailty and co-existing conditions that mean they are expected to die within 12 months
> (c) existing conditions if they are at risk of dying from a sudden acute crisis in their condition
> (d) life-threatening acute conditions caused by sudden catastrophic events.

The guidance also applies to extremely premature babies whose prospects for survival are known to be very poor, and to patients who are diagnosed as being in a persistent vegetative state, who may be stable but for whom a decision to withdraw treatment will lead to their death.

The GMC guidance states that *decisions concerning potentially life-prolonging treatment must not be motivated by a desire to bring about the patient's death, and must start from a presumption in favour of prolonging life. This presumption will normally require you to take all reasonable steps to prolong a patient's life.*

Sometimes it feels as if doctors, and maybe their patients, have stopped reading right there, with that clear, safe message, but the guidance continues: *However, there is no absolute obligation to prolong life irrespective of the consequences for the patient, and irrespective of the patient's views, if they are known or can be found out.*

I must scrutinise my thoughts when caring for Harry and others like him, and I must wonder if the decision that I am discussing with Iris is *motivated by a desire to bring about the patient's death*. I review this question and am clear. Iris and I are considering the consequences of potentially life-prolonging treatment for a man who is coming to the end of his life, who has suffered and wishes to suffer no longer. There is a difference between being motivated to bring about a death and being motivated to allow someone to die when we know his views.

We make these decisions all the time. A young woman, a mother with children, talks with her oncologist and decides not to continue cancer chemotherapy when that treatment no longer offers her a quality of life she values, is not making enough difference to the things that matter most to her, her time at home with her family. Sidney is seventy-eight and elects to cease his thrice-weekly trips to dialysis after several discussions with his renal team, and he brings cakes and a plastic keg of mouth-puckering home-made cider to his last dialysis session, where he knows the team so well; he has known them for years, and there are tears and hugs, and everyone respects his decision. But this courageous young mum with cancer, and Sidney, full of winks and laughter, have made their own decisions. They have sought and been given information and weighed up their options. For people who have dementia that has reached a stage at which they cannot participate in such discussions, for people like Harry, the door to making their own decision has closed.

Even just twenty years ago heart attacks and cancer were the commonest causes of death, and heart disease remains just ahead of dementia in terms of death for men. But in December 2022 more than one in every ten deaths in England and Wales were due to dementia, and the picture is similar in Scotland and Northern Ireland. Some of the increase is due to changes in the way death is counted – in the past a death due to pneumonia was counted as just that, but now if that person had a diagnosis of dementia, doctors are encouraged to record dementia on the certificate alongside that final illness of pneumonia, as we recognise that it was the underlying dementia that brought about the weakness and frailty that caused that person to succumb to an infection. So there has been a change in recording, and the rules vary from country to country, hampering international comparisons. Globally we are better at treating the old killers, the quick killers – heart disease, stroke and cancer – but we are living longer, and dementia is a disease of old age (it became the leading cause of death in people over the age of eighty long before it became the overall leading cause of death). So whichever way we look at it, all over the world more people are dying because they have dementia, and that number will continue to grow.

This presents us with sad and difficult decisions, which are always more difficult when the person to whom the decision applies is unable to tell us their wishes. I listen to Shauna, whose mum Annie had dementia for many years. After her husband died Annie lived alone and kept neat lists to guard against the erosion of her mind, like groynes running from a beach into the sea, but her lists got lost and Shauna and her brother arranged more support, daily carers to help Annie with shopping and cleaning, and later Annie moved in with Shauna's family. The eldest two children were away at university, the twins were completing their A-levels, and Annie would be doing pretty well one day, surprised but happy to find herself staying with her daughter again, but on another day she might be restless, uneasy, packing her bags and searching for a letter, an appointment, saying to Shauna, 'You've taken my letter. Where have you put it?' And those events escalated, with Annie coming into the kitchen at breakfast with her coat, saying, 'I'm ready to go now,' and Shauna would explain that the shopping trip would be on Thursday, not today, and Annie would be frustrated or petulant for a while before settling with a cup of tea and the television, while Shauna worked from home, joining board meetings on Zoom – strategy, finances, some thorny problem in HR, one ear listening always for her mum. A year later, Shauna would be woken in the small hours by noise from the kitchen and find cupboard doors open and a saucepan on the gas ring, hot and empty. Then there was a fall, a broken wrist and another fall – no breaks this time, but: 'Oh, Mum, your face. You look like you've gone ten rounds with Mike Tyson' – then a chest infection, three weeks in hospital and a urine infection, another fall, district nurses to dress the gash on Annie's leg and problems with continence, which Annie initially tried to hide but latterly she became insouciant and the shape of her face had changed, part of its structure missing or the light in her eyes.

Shauna and I walk as we talk, and she looks away from me, at hedges, at primroses by the edge of the muddy path, and she says of her mum, 'The thing is, the doctors offer you the option to stop, like maybe we don't treat the next big infection, and you think, *Oh, thank goodness, that's the right thing. Now is the moment I think Mum would want to stop*, and then you think, *Well, is that just me saying that? Because I'm so tired and I've been doing this for years now, and I just want it to be, you know, over* . . . So then I'm feeling guilty. It should be about Mum not me, and how do I decide? And I think Mum smiled at me last week. There's still a glimmer there.'

Shauna walks on in silence for a moment. 'You can't win. I feel guilty that I want to keep Mum alive only because if I don't keep her alive I'll feel guilty.'

I ask Shauna whether it would help to think back to what her mum was like years ago, before her dad died, and what decisions Annie would have made for herself.

Shauna smiles, shaking her head. 'We've thought of that, and she'd be horrified. She'd say, "Let me go . . ." But she's not the same person now; it's still difficult.'

It can be hard to find our way to the decision that feels right on behalf of someone else, and sometimes we talk of guilt, but even when that word is unspoken I can often detect it. I know that Iris was weighed down by this in our conversation about Harry, who has been through so much, and maybe, in fact, her concern is not about the legalities of stopping treatment for Harry – maybe she knows that we are allowed to withdraw those antibiotics – but it is guilt that makes her want to keep this plan a secret, a fear that she will be judged by family, friends or neighbours, and, perhaps most of all, that she will be judged by herself and find herself guilty. Guilty of giving up.

There can be other forces at play too. Eileen Mawer is unwell and no guidance has arrived with her from her care home as to her wishes regarding serious medical treatment, although there is a long document full of cut-and-paste platitudes telling me that Eileen *should be encouraged to maintain her hydration* and *requires assistance with personal care.*

I phone her son, who sounds bleary.

'It's one in the morning,' he explains. 'I'm in Hong Kong.'

I hear him swing his legs out of bed, as I explain the situation, the decisions we are making, and that I would like to feel confident that our actions are aligned with what his mother would wish for herself.

There's an impatient sound, a huff of breath, and he says, 'Oh, she's had enough. Could you just let her go?'

I wonder but cannot ask what it is that Eileen has had enough of – life or his attention or his inheritance? – and I am casting around for some questions that might tactfully shine light on this situation, but Mrs Mawer's son says, 'Look, I've got to go. I've got an important meeting tomorrow. You do what you think is right.'

I phone the home, and the deputy manager says, 'Eileen? She's a cheery lady – no trouble to anybody.'

So for now we continue the antibiotics, the blood tests and X-rays, and I do not know whether I am doing the right thing, because of that dissonance between the views of her son and those of the carers who see her each day. The next day Eileen is rosier and has a smile for Zlata who is offering her a cup of tea, yet she looks around the ward uncertainly, lost, and we will need to explore and resolve that dissonance to make a better plan for her, for when she is next unwell.

How can we manage this better? We can start with conversations. While we are able we can talk to those close to us, our family or friends, and ensure they know our views. We can write them down – an informal letter of wishes, or a formal, legally binding Advance Decision to Refuse Treatment, an ADRT, and we can do either of these without recourse to doctors or lawyers, but we must ensure that in the case of an ADRT our document follows certain principles and is signed, dated and witnessed, and if the ADRT includes the refusal of life-prolonging treatment, we must write explicitly that we understand that such a refusal may shorten our lives.

In addition, or instead, we can choose to appoint formal attorneys to speak for us when we are unable to speak for ourselves, but we need to be aware that such Lasting Powers of Attorney for Health and Wellbeing can be less useful than they look in an emergency, as doctors are duty bound to check the validity of such a document and most of us do not carry a certified copy around with us, ready to whisk out at three in the morning, and in the case of life-prolonging treatment again we must explicitly give permission to our attorney to refuse that on our behalf.

Most people do not have an LPA, and when we are making decisions about treatment medical teams fall back on choosing a course of action that is in the best interests of their patient, and for this they need to have some idea of their patient's values and wishes.

The most helpful thing any of us can do, when we are getting older or if we have some condition that might cause us suddenly or gradually to lose our ability to speak for ourselves, is to create an advance care plan (ACP), which will capture what is important to us and can also include decisions about treatments such as resuscitation attempts and being ventilated by machine on intensive care. Advance care plans, sometimes called Treatment Escalation Plans (TEPs), exist in different formats across the UK and in many other countries, and it is wise to use the format that is in common use locally and will be recognised and respected by medical teams.

For many older people an advance care plan may include a statement about whether they wish to be treated in hospital at all, because for some people, even though they may be very frail, life-prolonging treatment is wished for and welcomed, yet for others such intervention is devoutly to be avoided. And if the latter is the case, it's no good writing a plan that says, *hospital treatment only if necessary* or *would prefer to avoid hospital treatment*, because that is true for all of us – neither you nor I would fancy 'unnecessary' hospital treatment. In addition, paramedics, GPs and others working in the community try very hard not to admit people to hospital if their treatment can be provided elsewhere. Woolly statements can give emergency teams some hint of the level of risk we might be happy to accept (a paramedic may be more readily persuaded to administer an oral antibiotic and leave the patient in their care home, rather than transferring them to the Emergency Department if the plan includes a sentence about preferring to avoid hospital), but if we truly wish to avoid admission, our plan needs to be explicit and it needs to state that we would prefer not to have any hospital treatment, *even if our condition is life threatening.*

Advance care plans are not immutable; they can be changed, and they evolve as situations develop, and we can change our minds about the contents of our own plans, but for those who have dementia the opportunity to participate in such planning has often been missed. It therefore falls to those who are close to them to gather up what they know or can surmise of that person's wishes, and to weigh up the options that are open to them and to work with their medical team to come to a conclusion about what would be in that person's best interests as far as medical treatment is concerned. Those decisions require courage, and they require us to examine our motives and to be honest, and to be true to the person for whom we care.

I would like Iris to set guilt aside. She has heard Harry's voice, knows his views and has helped his medical team to hear his voice too. She has been his advocate. Iris does not need to feel guilty. I would like her instead to feel proud, that she has done the right thing by her husband. I would like her to know — I would like anyone who is in Iris's position to know — that when we know someone well, and when we know what they would wish for themselves, it is not a wicked thing to love that person and at the same time to wish they would die.

10. Social Prescribing

TBP – the presenting symptom is written on the front of her Accident and Emergency card. I am in Newham Hospital in east London. It is 1992. I read out her name, Meena Bibi, and a man stands and looks behind him at a young woman who is putting the lid on a baby's bottle. She tucks the bottle into a fabric bag and stands, her left arm curved round the baby against her chest. She shrugs the bag on to her shoulder and takes the hand of a solemn-faced toddler. Her husband walks in front of her to the cubicle. I smile and hold out my hands as she prepares to get on to the couch, but she casts her eyes down and gives the baby to her husband.

I ask what the problem is. Her husband translates and Meena Bibi starts speaking in a language I do not understand. Her slim hands fly up and down, her fingers tapping her forehead, her cheeks, then she spreads her fingers across her chest, and moves them now to her abdomen, pressing her fingertips here, and here, and here, and back to her chest, she is talking and talking, but her husband tells me only, 'She is saying she has pain.'

I nod and ask some more questions and I listen to her chest and heart and press on her abdomen ('Deep breath, and again please, deep breath') and I explain the tests that we will do – some blood and urine tests, a chest X-ray – and although I do not say this I know that these tests will not elucidate the cause of her symptoms nor alleviate them. Her symptoms are not a manifestation of asthma or a kidney infection or liver disease or anything else for which I may have a useful treatment. My contribution is spurious, pathetic in the face of her suffering – I may not even be calling her by the correct name, as it is unclear whether 'Bibi' is really her surname or is an honorific title. She bears no stigmata of illness or physical abuse. Meena Bibi's symptoms have some other meaning entirely and the triage nurses are aware of this too, but they are also complicit, having nothing else to offer.

TBP, they write on the cards of Meena Bibi and many other young women. Total Body Pain.

'My clients do not need yoga lessons,' says Gay firmly. Her face is full of optimism and energy, but her words are serious. Gay Palmer is a social prescribing link worker in Southwark in inner-city London, and she is speaking at an event at the King's Fund at which the concept of social prescribing is being introduced to journalists with an interest in healthcare. Gay looks around the room and continues, 'My people perish for lack of knowledge.'

The audience has heard already from Professor Tony

Avery, the National Clinical Director for Prescribing, who has talked about how we might use conventional medicines more safely and effectively. He has spoken of the vital role of medicines but has also pointed out that the prescribing of a pill is not always the right solution. There may be different and better ways to respond to situations that manifest as illness.

Gay's clients have already visited their doctor once, and then again, and again, with headaches, chest pain, backache; with addiction and obesity; with depression, anger, anxiety, despair. The pills do not work, and nor do the different pills or the stronger ones. Gay listens and asks some careful questions and makes her own diagnoses. She explains how she and others work with those referred by their GP. At least one in five consultations in primary care are driven by problems that are rooted in social issues rather than medical ones. The audience at the King's Fund has been told of alternative approaches – of referrals to walking groups and Chronic Pain Cafés, of help to find employment, of swimming lessons and choirs. They have listened to descriptions of training programmes and complementary therapies, of gardening groups, of aromatherapy and indeed of yoga.

Gay continues, 'My clients mostly need help with money and with housing. It might be just sorting out direct debits, which sounds simple, but look at Terry. His mental health had spiralled down, he was in chaos, overwhelmed and suicidal. And once he has some degree of control that gives him the security he needs.'

She knows she can't sort out every problem. 'If someone's on a housing list, we can't just make that happen, but we might be able to put in something they can do that makes them feel better while they wait.'

Gay describes how important it is to understand what is really troubling the people she sees. 'If my client thinks he is losing his home, he won't attend an exercise class. You have to prioritise.'

Matt Day tackles housing and finances too. Like Gay he is a social prescribing link worker, and in a small town in Somerset he takes me to visit Delia, who was falling over 'Oh, all the time' in her upstairs flat with its uneven floors and dark corners.

'Terrible vertigo. I still get it. I wish they could fix it, but what can you expect at eighty-seven? At least I don't fall over as much – this place is better, don't you think? Matt helped me find it.'

Delia looks around her sitting room. It's no bigger than a family car. One wall is a library: history, biography, art, botany, architecture. The other walls are jammed with black-and-white photos of rubber trees, pontoon bridges over thick rivers and women in white dresses squinting into the sun. There's a tiny neat kitchen, a bathroom and a bedroom. There's a postage-stamp garden with a rotary washing line above pots of early daffodils.

'And now you're helping Cheryl with her housing application,' Matt prompts, and Delia nods at her huge computer screen and concedes that she has led Cheryl through the council website, showing her how to fill in the questionnaire that will rank Cheryl's specific need for new accommodation alongside that of every other applicant.

'It might even work,' says Delia.

'We're trying to set up a time banking system,' says Matt, and I look blank so he explains. 'It's a sort of reciprocal volunteering. You know, someone looks after your cat, and they earn a time credit and they can spend that in the future, when they need a little help with something else.'

As we walk from Delia's to visit Steph Upton-Pittaway, Matt says, 'The thing is, most people want to help. We want to be useful. Then some say, "But what can I do?" Some people lack confidence, but everyone can do something.'

Matt leads me along the high street, past a chemist and the charity shops. We take a short cut through the foyer of Waitrose and he continues, 'Cheryl's life is complicated, she doesn't have access to the internet, but she can get herself to Delia's. Delia can't get out of the house easily but she's a whizz online. And she's very patient.'

At the community centre we meet Steph. Alongside several other roles, she is a money detector. She scans national and local news, scrutinises press releases from

NHS England, and applies for every grant she can find, from large sums from the National Lottery to smaller ones from local charities, and an annual grant from the town council. She approaches local businesses and supermarkets for donations and raffle prizes.

'The electricity bills are huge now and this building is ageing,' she says.

I follow her gaze to the top of the high windows, where the damp will come in if it's given half a chance, but Steph is not going to give the damp half a chance. Thirty people, mostly in their eighties and nineties I guess, are having lunch in the hall, and a young woman is singing 'Puppet on a String'. The lunch-goers are segregated as naturally and decisively as the participants at a school dance – a posse of bewhiskered men sit along the back table, some with a bottle of beer. There's a bar in the foyer.

'We have private events too,' says Steph, 'parties, wedding receptions; it brings some cash in.'

There's a twice-weekly memory group. Twelve people with dementia, five volunteers, one paid member of staff.

'Who is it for?' I ask, and Steph tips her head and smiles a beautiful soft smile.

'Well, the people who come love it, they want to come each week, but we know it's one hundred per cent for the carer – they can meet a friend for coffee, get their hair done, just have some time to themselves.'

The community centre is in constant use. There are Lullababy music classes for babies and toddlers. There are health visitor clinics and two carer support groups. On Tuesday there's Rugby Tots and yoga, Wednesday is Pilates, Thursday is t'ai chi and conversational French. There are lessons from two different dance companies and acting classes and short mat bowls. We could join a drop-in session, should we wish to learn to knit, play chess or wrangle a smartphone or tablet. There's a gardening club and brass band rehearsals and the meetings of U3A and the Rotary Club and Alcoholics Anonymous.

I look at the picture board of the trustees of the centre.

'One's five years older than me,' says Steph, who looks very young. 'The next up is Helen, she's seventy-two.' She points to each picture. 'I love the trustees. They have loads of energy. And experience. Tom is the vice-chair.'

Steph taps Tom's photo. 'He's ninety-three.'

In the afternoon Matt and I visit a day centre to which he refers some of his clients. We're leaning on the fence of a small enclosure, beyond which is a pond, a bare hedge, then fields folding across one another into the distance.

'What makes them therapy pigs?' I ask Nigel Bell, who has set up and runs this service, but I don't really need to ask. Two black pigs are standing snout to snout in deep mud. There is a rich smell and the pigs are amiably grunting at one another. It is all very therapeutic.

'Well,' says Nigel, rubbing his hands against the cold, 'you can watch them, smell them, listen to them, rub their backs. And if you're coming here and you're a bit shy, you can slow down and talk to the animals on the way in; it's not like you have to burst through a door into a group of people.'

Nigel, like Steph, has developed a sensitive nose for money. He seeks out the cash needed to sustain the ARK at Egwood just as surely as his pigs rootle in the earth. Grants for helping care leavers and grants for building the confidence and skills of those who are not in training, education or employment. Duke of Edinburgh's Award money that comes with kids excluded from school, bank transfers from people with long-term disabilities or mental health problems, who choose to spend their Personal Independence Payment here. Private donations and grants from charities and the council. The eclectic sources of funding reflect the diversity of the attendees.

Nigel explains the criteria on which clients are accepted. 'I don't go shopping exclusively with middle-aged, middle-class men, and I don't think anyone should have to attend a day-care centre on that basis either,' he says. 'Our age range is five to eighty-eight.'

We walk past the herb patch and the open-sided

dining area with benches, the kitchen where Maebh and Jo are stacking clean plates into cupboards. There's a wood burner glowing in a huge polytunnel, trays of seedlings that will soon be transplanted into crumbly dark soil. The centre is largely self-sufficient in fruit and vegetables; a sideline in cut flowers generates the funds for next year's seeds. Near the wood burner, four people are playing cards at a table made of an old door, and later there's another wood-burner in a wheel-less bus, where a young man in a snazzy deerstalker hat inspects my face for a little longer than is comfortable before demanding, 'Who are you and why are you here?'

I introduce myself and say I am visiting to learn and am enjoying it very much, and I ask who is he and what he is doing here, and he tells me he is Robert, announcing, 'Today I have been cooking for the old people in the village hall.'

As Nigel and I walk to the woodland area, he explains. 'Obviously we provide lunch here each day for everyone on the site, and anyone can contribute to getting that lunch on the table. We also make lunch every Tuesday down the road, for the village senior citizens' group, and again various people join in to make sure that happens. We have attendees and a few paid staff and a lot of volunteers. And then we have "therapeutic volunteers", people like Robert, who need to be here. He's been with us a couple of years and he's really come on. He can talk to people and got up the confidence to have his own flat. And Robert's great at keeping records of who has come to lunch – he gets everyone to pay up.'

Among the beech trees, Nigel shows me the logs, carving tools and foot-operated lathe, and a low laid-back chair made of slim hazel poles from which one can watch the stars. 'This is Woody Simon's domain,' he says.

Simon teaches young adults to use the sharp tools safely and has done so for years, an encore career after a lifetime in the manufacturing industry – night shifts and whining machinery.

Nigel describes how several of the volunteers found themselves adrift in retirement, unmoored from the structure of work. 'Some people get lost and lonely.'

He alludes to the need for purpose that we all share. Some of the staff were originally referred themselves at a time of need and found a place of sanctuary here – an ark – and have contributed even as they healed and recovered.

It is a recurrent theme, that those who have faced adversity themselves are often the first to extend a hand to others. I read a Christmas bulletin from Sara Thakkar, Chief Executive of the Camphill Village Trust, whose communities help people with learning and other disabilities to experience lives full of opportunity. Sara describes Kindness Crews, groups of *community members who are getting out in the local area to support other people – and gaining skills and confidence at the same time.*

Aimee, one of the Camphill residents, has been helping run a coffee morning for older people. Aimee says,

'I leave my anxiety at the door! When I arrive at the hall I focus on the people and their needs, to bring them warmth and joy, and for a few hours I forget about my own issues.'

Nigel knows this too. 'Everyone is here for a reason,' he says. 'But we don't need to talk about it. Here everyone can be themselves.'

It's 2023 and I am back in the East End of London. I walk from the Tube; this is still a difficult place in which to live. Litter blows round my ankles, there is angry anti-vax graffiti in the underpass, and traffic hurtles along the A12 towards the Blackwall Tunnel. There's a tang of diesel. My phone's out of battery so I get slightly lost – there is no mention of a health centre on the signs, just BROMLEY BY BOW CENTRE, and there is no NHS logo, but there's a café and a park and a winter-flowering cherry. But I am in the right place and am greeted by Sam Everington, a GP who has worked in this area for decades. I tell him that I remember admiring one of his lectures when I was a junior doctor at Mile End Hospital.

'Back then,' he says, 'everyone thought I was just a sandal-wearing bearded hippy.' I must point out that, as I recall, he *was* a sandal-wearing bearded hippy, but now he is Professor Sir Sam Everington, and the approach he and his team pioneered – healthcare embedded in a community, interventions that take account of the fact that around 70% of health outcomes are driven not by genes or even by health systems but by socio-economic factors – is an approach that is becoming increasingly mainstream and attracting international attention. A group of Singaporean government officials are visiting the centre. I sit behind them on a pew in a church that also serves as lecture hall, playschool, craft centre, concert venue, dance floor. We listen to Sam's colleague Dan Hopewell explaining that we currently spend less than 4% of our NHS budget on prevention and the rest on responding to problems that might have been averted. Why do we accept that poor people develop long-term health problems twenty years younger than the well-off? Dan talks of how people who are lonely tend to smoke more, and of how what we eat is influenced by what people around us eat. I think of my daughter, who returned from the supermarket in our Somerset town having noticed, 'Everyone's buying the same thing, Mum – four cans of Thatchers Gold and a chicken Kyiv.' The Singaporeans shift and smile. Paper magnolias decorate branches at the end of each pew.

Over coffee Sam outlines his philosophy. Health behaviours are largely dictated not by free will but by socio-economic and cultural factors. To improve the health of individuals we must look at our society – Sam tells me of the indigenous people of Alaska, who say that the health of their population today is inherited from behaviours that go back four generations. The Bromley by Bow Centre is not a health centre, although it provides the services of a normal GP surgery among its other functions. In fact, the GP surgery was a relatively late addition. The centre itself grew from a United Reformed Church with a dwindling congregation and a new young vicar, Andrew Mawson, who told Sam years later, 'I realised I could turn to drink, or write a thesis about poverty, or do something different.' A group of elderly members suggested that, rather than amalgamating or closing altogether, their church could open its buildings for the community. A children's nursery was joined by a dance school, a community café, a series of art studios and workshops. Buildings were adapted and added, and the adjoining park was leased for thirty years for a pound from the local council, who were relieved to be rid of the responsibility.

Now the centre offers advice and help with training, computer skills and grant applications to get a new business off the ground. It has provided the kindling for over eighty social enterprise businesses, a high proportion of which have thrived. There are English lessons for speakers of other languages and advice on how to reduce food and fuel bills. There are multiple creative activities and volunteering opportunities. The three-acre park is maintained by the local community – here anyone can lie on the grass while the sun warms their eyelids. Support is a theme, but so are development, new skills, resilience. It's not about handouts – there's a recurrent pride in helping people into employment.

I ask Sam what makes a perfect social prescribing link worker, and he switches into full flow. 'They like people. They're emotionally intelligent, they have skills of persuasion and negotiation, they know when to be a fixer and when to be a motivational coach and when to just listen. They have huge local knowledge.' Sam describes how that local knowledge turns into targeted projects. The Bangladeshi women's walking group precisely meets a specific need for companionship, fresh air and exercise.

It doesn't always work. I have read evaluations of social prescribing interventions that have fallen flat, websites that suggest solutions, phone lines that direct those in distress to other services. I tell Sam that I'm uncomfortable with 'signposting', and he rolls his eyes.

'Exactly – too often signposting really means, "I don't want to hear about your problem. I'm going to pass you on to someone else." The key to the link workers is the time they take to understand someone's situation. Making a website doesn't usually help.'

Link workers also need time to help people get started on a new route.

'It's no good telling people they should go to this or that exercise class,' says Leanne, who works in Newcastle. 'The first time you may have to take them. It's time-consuming.'

It's also clearly rewarding.

'I love my job. I *love* my job,' says Laura, a link worker in Devon.

In Bow, Shahanaz echoes this. 'I love my job . . . I know I'm making a big difference to people's lives by supporting them during challenging times.'

Does social prescribing work? On the train home from London I read evaluations by the Bromley by Bow Centre team and the National Academy for Social Prescribing. I read the report of the College of Medicine and Integrated Health, co-produced with the Social Prescribing Network. I click on every reference I can find. The volume of papers is dizzying, and not all of them are helpful. In one project, encouraging older people to visit museums more frequently had a positive effect on their well-being, measured on a special scale of older people's well-being in museums. It's a lovely study but there is no suggestion that this will have had an impact on the participants' health or the frequency with which they visit their doctor. In another study, provision of a new heating system for those on low incomes and vulnerable to cold led to improvements in their environ-ment and lower fuel bills, but it may or may not have improved their mental well-being. I read a good paper showing that community health workers' targeting of patients' social needs and health behaviours was asso-ciated with improved diabetes control, which should translate into the avoidance of more serious illness, but those effects, of course, will be many years down the track – the researchers can't right now prove their intervention makes a difference to longer-term health.

Multiple small studies report a reduction in the number of times that a person needs to see the GP – even a reduction in the number of times they attend hospital Emergency Departments – but the numbers of patients involved in each study are modest, the magnitude of the effect varies wildly, and the interventions are disparate and ill-defined.

I find myself in a new world of 'grey literature' – reports from charities and non-governmental organisations, claims made in blogs and on websites. I am far from the security of the peer-reviewed scientific journals with which I am familiar. I think of the granular precision of randomised double-blind trials of conventional medicines, with their rigid inclusion and exclusion criteria, patients who are all being treated for the same condition, with the same drug in the same dose in the same formulation, and a control group treated with a placebo drug that looks identical to the trial one. I think of the care with which the patients in control groups in these conventional trials must be matched to those receiving the intervention, and of the well-defined end points that are to be measured and must be specified before the trial begins.

As my train heads west, I read further reviews of social prescribing that sound notes of caution, reviews that allude to the difficulty in collecting good data, the variety of overlapping roles – link workers, community support workers, village agents, health navigators.

I read of the risk of bias in reports written by those who understandably want to show that their work is worthwhile, and of the difficulties of reproducing a success story that may have hinged on the personal skills of one or two individuals. I read reviews that demand more and better evidence before social prescribing is promoted further.

The train divides in Salisbury – only the front four carriages will go where I want to go – and I have a crisis of confidence. Have I been admiring the emperor in his new clothes? I'm suddenly assailed by doubt. As the train clanks and thumps through the Wessex countryside, I lean on the dark window and think of what I have learned.

It was 1981. The church hall smelled of floorboards and baking, and at tables beneath the high windows people sat or stood and talked, their heads bent towards one another over projects. I was fifteen and had confided to my mother a plan to apply to study medicine, and Mum had spoken with the vicar's wife and now here I was, sweating with shyness. And here was Geraldine, who took my hand in her tiny soft hands and raised it to her lips, saying in her high voice, 'I love you, I love you, how lovely to meet you.' Her sky-blue eyes behind thick glasses searching my face, her sky-blue cardigan and a string of plastic beads to match. And here was coloured raffia and fuzzy felt and bright plastic pegs to arrange on a board in a pattern. And here was Stephen, who had

Down's syndrome, and he shifted from foot to foot in his big fawn corduroy trousers and check shirt, his hair neatly brushed down with Brylcreem. Stephen's mother gave me a biscuit cutter to stamp out frilled rounds of dough for scones, while Stephen showed me the box full of pine cones he had collected that morning from the damp earth below tall trees that grew between the grey hall and the grey rectory. And Sarah sat by the wall, against which she was knocking her head over and over. She was wearing a helmet, its surface scratched – I could see that it was not a new thing for Sarah to bang her head – and her long fingers writhed. A woman lifted Sarah's hand and stroked her palm in a pattern that I could not comprehend and led her out to the toilets. That hall in rural Northern Ireland was full of understanding and acceptance and of people finding a way through a difficult time, and each mother (they were all mothers) had known the loss of a child who might have brought friends home from school, might have grown up to be studious or a tearaway, to take over the farm or the pub, to run away to sea, to move to England or America and return in glory with money and fancy attitudes. But those futures had been imagined and set aside a long time ago, and the mothers of these children came together in the hall every week to share what they had learned instead about caring for a child, now an adult, who has a different future, and to give one another practical advice: to talk of wet trousers and washing machines and medication for epilepsy; of belligerence or fearfulness or nightmares; of sanitary towels for a young woman who cannot and will never understand the reason for a sanitary towel; and to listen and be heard, to share sadness and worries and what will happen next. And they also met to laugh and plan birthday presents and outings, fetes and holidays – and never (of course) to talk of love, except perhaps the love of God in a hymn or a Bible reading. But that hall glowed with love.

Many of the organisations to whom social prescribers turn have mission statements. I find myself drawn to their messages. I read of Age UK Camden, an organisation whose work on loneliness I have seen to be subtle, intelligent and profoundly effective. *Our values are important to us and are represented in everything we do. Our values are kindness, courage, hope and justice.* There is a powerful sense of fellowship. I come across the Camerados organisation, which has sprung out of a belief that *when we look out for others we are taken out of our own problems and given a strong purpose and a connection.* The Camerados talk of meeting *someone who looks out for you, and you for them.* Nigel's team at the ARK propound values of inclusivity and equality.

It strikes me that many of the organisations and activities involved in social prescribing are stepping into a space that was previously occupied by religious worship. The themes of equality and justice, of loving one's neighbour and offering hospitality to a stranger, of joy

in the marvels of the natural world – these are familiar facets of the world's great religions and traditions.
That overlap between traditional and modern does not
seem a bad thing to me – for many people the support structures of their lives still involve religion, but
increasing numbers are avowedly agnostic or atheist, or
are humanist or simply vague, unconcerned by talk of
philosophies, yet their secular values are strong. And
the practical structures are similar – those attending a
walking group or a community choir, like those attending a church, temple or mosque, can expect to find a
familiar group of fellow attendees each week. We will be
made welcome. The event will follow a format that initially may be new and strange, but which over time will
become reassuring, stable. There will be strangers who
may become friends. There will be serious talk but also
laughter and companionship, and in time we may find
that we are offering to someone new, someone who is
hovering uncertainly at the door, the kindness we were
offered ourselves.

There are problems that cannot be fixed by either conventional or social prescribing, and I listen sometimes
to the discussions in the complex care meetings about
Jason, a recidivist alcoholic, vile to his family and haught-
ily dismissive of every lifeline that is thrown his way,
and about Francine, a reclusive hoarder, her floorboards
rotting under her feet, as the conversations meander on

about mental capacity and safety and personal choice, and it's clear that the only way to fix the problems of both these people is to turn the clocks back – seventy-two years for Jason, seventy-eight for Francine – and since that is not an option, it would be better that we leave them as they are and maintain a level of contact that is humane but also respectful and realistic.

Many of our communities face huge challenges, from poverty, from racism and division, from relentless marketing by the sly producers of tobacco and ultra-high-processed food, from air pollution and crappy housing, from loneliness or disability, from rapacious development and the erosion of green spaces, from drug use and gang violence, and from the fragmentation of families and the loss of traditional sources of succour. Rural populations can suffer as much as urban ones. Yet our society is resilient. We have known what makes humans happier for thousands of years. In every community there are people with knowledge and skills who are ready and willing to help others. And a link worker can be exactly that – a link between someone in need and someone else who can help them.

As I was leaving the Bromley by Bow Centre, I passed an open reception area with a handful of desks with computers. There was an Asian lad with a sharp haircut frowning at a screen, his foot tapping. A woman with mad lilac hair and ten-hole Doc Martens was working her way through a pile of papers, glancing from screen to page, adding details to an application form. A young woman in the corner was wearing a pale green saree over a cream-coloured T-shirt and she looked up from the computer and I smiled at her. She smiled back and gave me a thumbs up.

If social prescribing means listening to people, understanding their life and then offering something that has value for that person, that will do for me. I have stopped worrying about whether social prescribing works. Of course it does.

11. Dark Places

It is February 2021. I have a day off and have been spreading sacks of manure on the vegetable patch. Our son has been sent home from university again. COVID numbers have picked up and the UK is in its third national lockdown. It's freezing and I retreat to the kitchen to make coffee but find my phone is ringing. It's Estelle, one of the complex care nurses. She is competent and forthright and does not ask for help unless she needs it.

'I'm so sorry, Lucy. We're a bit stuck here – it's just a bad situation.'

Estelle is ringing from a care home, Littlefield.

'I was worried about them,' she says. 'I knew they had some staff and residents positive, and today they've just not been answering the phone, so I came round.'

I've been to Littlefield before, a few years ago. It's single-storey, with long corridors, pictures by primary-school children on the walls, forty residents. It's a home that accepts people on social services rates alongside those whose houses have been sold to pay for their care; the margarine is spread thinly on the bread, but I remember how Jacqui the manager smiled as Shirley went past with her triangular fold-up walking frame, Lambert & Butlers poking out of the pocket of her grey fleece dressing gown. Jacqui stopped Shirley and adjusted the frame so that its strut clicked properly into place more safely and said, 'All right, Shirl, I'll hold the door,' as Shirley made her way out to the summer house, aka smoking shed.

But not today. Today Jacqui is off; she has COVID – she tested positive yesterday. The deputy manager is off. The activities coordinator is off. The assistants on the Willow unit are off, as are the two for Beech and for Oak. The cleaner has been off since Monday; her mum has COVID at home. The cook and his assistant are off. Someone reports that the assistant is in hospital; he's sick – has got it bad.

Estelle says, 'There's no one. I mean, the company are finding staff; they're sending people in from other homes. But no one knows anyone.'

And the residents?

'That's the thing. We don't know. None of us usually works here so no one knows what's normal for anyone.'

I text my husband and shout to my son that I'm going out. I park in the home's staff car park, which has plenty of spaces, and walk to the front door, where a motor-bike courier is swinging his leg off his bike. 'You going in?' he asks, and hands me a couple of envelopes.

In the foyer I gel my hands, pull a plastic gown from the roll, take a mask and wave it a couple of times to get rid of some of the factory smell. I put it on and some gloves, then I push open the door.

Estelle is in the office, and Alice is there too, a GP who I am very glad to see; she is quick and kind and sensible.

Alice looks up from her laptop at the desk. 'I've written a list of residents.' She hands me a photocopy. 'We've seen some. I've ticked them off.'

Estelle says, 'I'll see John Hughes in twenty-three. Back soon. Where's that oximeter?'

I look around the office. There's nowhere to put my bag. The floor is covered with boxes of masks, gloves, gel dispensers. There are two desks, some filing cabinets. Every surface is covered with paper. The pinboard has notices, and notices on top of notices, and others are Sellotaped to the walls next to the board. Messages, guidance, orders – from NHS England, from the infection prevention and control nurses, from social services. There are pieces of paper in the mouth of the printer; someone has pressed print but has been distracted, called away perhaps even as the machine has whirred. There are files and folders piled on the desks and a pizza box is wedged into a bin and there is a KFC bucket on the windowsill. And this is not right; this is not what that office looked like last time I was here, when Jacqui asked who I had come to see and pulled Ivy's file promptly out of the cabinet and handed it to me, all neat and complete, with a photo of Ivy and details of her preferences as regards tea or coffee. This office has gone wrong. Someone has been trying to keep it under control, but the paper tide has risen and flowed in through the front door and seeped out of the printer and all over the walls and the desks.

'Jacqui was sleeping here, because they didn't have enough staff,' Alice says. She indicates with her head the little sitting room by the front door, where there's a bunch of fake flowers in a pot and a sofa with a sleeping bag rumpled on it. Together this office and sitting room look like a place that has been left in a war after a realisation that the stronghold can no longer be defended – a sudden evacuation, everything left behind. There is a cup of coffee by the computer, a grey ring on the liquid's surface.

The envelopes are still in my hand.

'They'll be results,' says Alice, and takes them from me and pulls from each a handful of microbiology forms, flicking through them. 'Marie, positive. I thought so. Phillip, Janet Carter, Gwenda. Oh, and John Hughes. I'll tell Estelle. I've got a column for results on the list, see here, if you can add the positive ones and the date.'

The residents' names are listed in pods.

'Shall I do Willow?' I ask, then: 'Do we know who looks ill?'

Alice looks up. 'That's the problem. We don't know what anyone is usually like. I mean, it's residential not nursing, so most of them should be up and about, but who knows?'

'Does everyone have TEP forms?' I ask, meaning Treatment Escalation Plans.

'They should,' Alice says, 'but we think they're in this cupboard –' she pats it – 'and we don't have the key. I've looked in the drawers. Jacqui might have taken it home by mistake, but she's not answering her phone. Some of them have got TEPs on EMIS –' Alice is talking of the GP record – 'and I've got my laptop, so I can look them up. But I've only got access to the patients registered with our practice. Someone's gone round to Jacqui's to see if she knows where the key is.'

I get out my stethoscope, cleaning it with a disinfectant wipe (the tubing is cracking – everyone says the wipes aren't good for stethoscopes), and pick up an oximeter, and find my way to Willow, where there's a door open and a nurse in a neat navy uniform straightens up from where she has been bending over a small figure who is sitting in a chair. There are pictures of ballet dancers on the walls, and a figurine with pale skin and a pink tutu on the windowsill. There's a carer in a lilac uniform on the other side of the chair, holding a beaker of orange juice to the lips of the small woman, who is vacant, clammy.

'This is Doreen. We think she's probably having a hypo. Definitely diabetic,' says the nurse. 'There's gliclazide in her meds. And hello, I'm Claire, and this is Stacey. Stacey, you keep trying with the juice and I'll see where the glucometer is – we'll get a reading. Doctor, can you see the little lady opposite? I think she's Elaine maybe, Elsie? I don't think she's right.'

The room opposite is dark despite the daylight when I knock on the door, which is ajar, and there's no answer, so I turn on the light. There's a print of Exmoor on one wall, screwed on, the curtains are closed and there's a bed with a beige duvet. I look at the list: Willow 12 and Elma. Elma's curled up under the duvet and crinks her eye open when I put my hand on her arm, saying, 'Hello, Elma, it's the doctor here. My name is Dr Pollock. I'm sorry you're feeling poorly.'

She closes her eye again and turns her cheek further into the pillow. I do not know if Elma likes to be called Elma. I do not know if she usually speaks. I do not know if she usually climbs under her duvet at noon. I do not know if she laughs at the television, watches *I'm a Celebrity* or *This Farming Life*, likes Jaffa Cakes, hates cats, has a son, flirts with Daniel, the assistant, at teatime, says her prayers, was a teacher. I know nothing about her.

COVID in older people does not always cause the cough and fever that are its hallmarks in those younger, but it often does. As in younger people, the delicate air sacs of the lungs can become inflamed and puffy, filling with fluid so oxygen can't get to the fine capillaries that hold red blood cells waiting to be replenished. Those capillaries can become clogged up too with microscopic clots, and between the inflammation and the tiny clots, the lungs can't work and the oxygen level in the blood drops too low. But even without those respiratory effects, even with a normal oxygen level, older people with COVID can simply become unwell, not themselves, muddled or sleepy, and it seems to have a toxic effect on the brain, causing delirium, which comes as no surprise to geriatricians, because we recognise that all manner of infections in distant parts of the body can cause upset to the older brain. And similarly, because walking is a very cognitive skill – we need lots of brain power to keep us upright, one foot moving after another – older people who have COVID fall over more easily.

I check Elma's oxygen level, putting the oximeter on her finger and holding it in place, my hand on hers under the duvet. Her level is fine, and her lungs are clear and she doesn't seem to be in pain. I ask Claire to help me now that she's found the glucose meter for Doreen, who was indeed hypoglycaemic but who has now sipped enough orange juice and eaten a custard cream to become a different woman and is joking with Stacey. I take Doreen's gliclazide box and score through where it says *take two* and instead write *take one*, because her sugar level was low due to overtreatment of her diabetes, and I put a note on my list to remind me to let Alice know I've done that so that she can amend the GP record, to which I have no access.

Claire crosses the corridor and helps me to prop Elma up and offer her water, but the bed is soaked with urine and Elma already has a sore patch on her hip where she has been lying too still for too long. I need to talk to her son if there is one (why do I think she has a son?) and I need to find her escalation plan and work out whether Elma is someone who should be taken to hospital, where she will have blood tests to discern whether she has been flattened by COVID alone or whether there is some other reason for her to be under the duvet, drowsy and fading, something that needs more active treatment than just waiting. She may need hospital, where even if it is COVID alone, Elma can be given some fluid through a drip in a vein or even just under her skin on her back or tummy to stop her becoming dehydrated, because she's not going to drink, I can see that. There are those who are frail who die from COVID, not through its effects on the lungs, on breathing, but rather through its effect on the brain, a delirium that will most likely improve but while present is life threatening.

I'm aware there are teams in a few places in the UK who are doing this differently, who can do blood tests with instant results right there in the care home, teams who carry bags of IV fluid and antibiotics, and steroids and blood-thinner injections already made up and ready to give, and can snap their fingers for an oxygen con-centrator when it's needed, but we are not there yet – we have been focused on hospital treatment for COVID. But it may also be – if I can get hold of that son, or someone, anyone, who knows Elma – that she would not want any treatment at all in any place, that she has, in fact, reached the end of a long road, has bad dementia that has brought intractable suffering or a cancer that has spread or kidneys that no longer function, and maybe Elma has been waiting for a moment like this, when she can curl peacefully under a duvet and be comfortable, and be looked after by people who will wash her gently and brush her hair and apply soothing balm to her lips. I do not know, and she's not registered at Alice's practice, so Alice has no access to Elma's GP record and we can't find her son's number, if there is a son, so I call the hub to arrange for an ambulance for admission to hospital; they'll have to work it all out there.

Claire, meanwhile, has been on to head office and arranged some nursing beds to be delivered, with pressure mattresses for those who may stay in the home but need to be cared for in bed, and while I am on the phone I watch as Claire greets another carer who has knocked uncertainly at the door, a young guy with a ponytail who has been diverted from a home on the other side of town where he usually works, and she has shown him a trolley with jugs and cups, pointed him towards the kitchen, where he might find tea and biscuits to take to each resident in their room. Gloria has appeared too, from the nursing home where Claire is matron, and they bump elbows, and Claire says, 'I'm glad you're here.' Gloria has been set to answering call bells, and Claire has told her, 'Just find me if there's anything. I'll be down that corridor or in here.'

Then Claire and I are walking down the corridor to see Helene, and then Jack, and Jim, and another, and still more, each a person, when Claire, calm and competent, methodical, prioritising, suddenly stops and turns to me and takes hold of my shoulders. Standing in front of me, she looks into my eyes, and says, 'This is what ugly looks like.'

I nod and raise my eyebrows above my mask, then we walk on.

We spend the day assessing, deciding. I see Helene, who is coughing and feverish but cheerful, reading her copy of *People's Friend*, surrounded by photos of grandchildren and a wedding group with sturdy young men and dimpled bridesmaids. 'I'm good, doc, you go on,' she says and gives me a thumbs up.

I see Jack, who is so unsteady on his feet that he has fallen twice already today. His room is right at the end of the corridor, round the last corner, a room he's been given because he needs less scrutiny from staff – he is usually independent but has lived for some years now in the home, where his mental health problems, schizophrenia I guess, are understood and accepted, and the carers help him buy CDs online for his jazz collection and persuade him to let them cut his hair from time to time. Jack can barely stand now and is racked with coughing. He and I agree that hospital is the best place for him; we cannot keep him safe here. He feels rotten and wants to go in, and I call the hub again for another ambulance.

I see Jim, who is haggard, silent, thin and slumped in his chair. I ring his daughter, who last saw him through the window a few weeks ago but could not bear to return because Jim was beckoning her to come in, come round, but she was not permitted and could not explain this to him, the combination of his bewilderment and bad hearing making explanation impossible. She and I have a conversation about Jim, his previous work as a probation officer and his determination to make life better for others and his decline into dementia, worse since her mum died, and his gradual withdrawal into a world of few words. His daughter and I agree that Jim would not want to be admitted to hospital and should stay here. He is not in pain, we will find enough carers to look after him and he will, I think, die here, because although most older people who get COVID do not die of it, many do. Jim's oxygen level is low even though he's not breathless, and he's sleepy and has not been drinking, but when I hold a cup to his lips he turns his head away, not thirsty. A little later I take my phone to Jim's room and FaceTime his daughter and her sister, so they can see him. 'Hello, Dad,' they say, 'we love you. We love you,' before they turn their heads away from the camera so that he does not see their tears.

I work with Alice the GP and Estelle the nurse and Andy, another GP who has joined us – he should be vaccinating this afternoon, but they will just have to manage without him – and eventually we have seen all the residents and we have found the Treatment Escalation Plans. The cupboard key was on a hook, but many of the plans are incomplete or vague and do not give us the guidance we need, and in some it is not clear whether the plan has been discussed with the resident or those close to them, and in others the plan is unrealistic and includes a directive for intensive care even for someone who would not survive a trip to the seaside. I phone my son and ask him to come in because there's no cleaner, and he arrives in his crummy old Fiesta and I show him how to don mask, pinny and gloves and he cleans the communal areas and toilets, because few of the rooms here have ensuite bathrooms, and he wipes the hand-rails that run along the corridors with disinfectant. The residents should be isolated in their rooms, but Jeanette cannot do isolation – she is walking along the corridors on a private mission that she cannot explain and from which she cannot be deflected, and Phil is the same.

Late in the evening, after I have left, Estelle will sit with a woman who is dying. Estelle will find on her phone the audiobook that the woman has requested, and together they will listen to a gentle BBC voice reading the opening chapter of *Pride and Prejudice*.

On the way home I stop in a lay-by and stare at the headlights coming towards me and feel overwhelmed by guilt. I remember a care home in Spain. Early on in the pandemic there had been a news report of a home abandoned, the residents found dying and dead. At the time I talked in a meeting in our hospital, explaining to colleagues that so far, in Italy and in Spain, the majority of deaths had been in care home residents, and that care homes would need our support, even though we were already so busy seeing admissions, more than we could manage. Our hospital had ceased almost all planned surgery and given the beds in our handsome new surgical block, all single rooms, to the surging medical patients, people with coughs and fever. Even then, early on in our learning, we were detecting COVID in people who had been admitted with seemingly unrelated problems, falls and confusion, older people who had already spent days on open bays in other wards. We were moving those unexpectedly COVID-positive patients across to the single rooms, but it was too late; the other patients in the bay would test positive too.

I sat in the lay-by thinking of what had been done in this first year of the pandemic to help care homes – ever-changing advice on isolation, masks, visiting; residents kept for days or weeks in hospital, not permitted to return to the place they call home when they were still testing positive, long after their symptoms have gone, and we don't know whether this was the right thing to do, because those who are old and frail have immune systems that do not tidy up properly after an infection, which leaves fragments of virus lying on the lining of nose or throat, and we're not sure whether those bits of virus still might be infective or are harmless residues, like pieces of seaweed left on the beach after a storm.

I think of Dave and his team at social services, determined, pragmatic, working alongside an NHS team of nurses who check in twice weekly with each home manager or deputy, a welfare call, supporting them with equipment – sometimes these days you can't even get a thermometer, even Amazon has sold out – and sorting out shortages of masks, gloves and aprons, and resolving disputes with families about visiting restrictions or care standards. I think of the palliative teams who have helped with guidance about symptoms, set up a phone line, the right medicines provided quickly to relieve breathlessness or distress. I think of care home staff who have learned to carry out the verification of death in order to reduce visits from doctors or nurses who might introduce the virus to their home, and of GPs who are receiving mixed messages from NHS England and from each care home manager – should they visit, see the sick or stay away – and I think of carers who have themselves developed symptoms despite all precautions, have isolated themselves, driven miles to testing centres, never mind their low wage and the price of petrol, or who have made their coughing teenage children stay in their bedrooms for days on end, piling more misery on to miserable young lives. I think of families and residents who have had to accept separation, subsisting on a phone call, on 'I love you' mouthed through a window or a plexiglas barrier, no touch, no hug, no visit from the toddler and the new baby. I think of Jacqui's sleeping bag on the care home sofa. And all of it not enough.

The next day I attend a meeting online about the vaccination programme and I am angry because a care home up the road from this one had been visited by the vaccine team two weeks ago, so why not this one, the home where this has happened? The GP leading the programme tries to explain; she talks of the prioritisation being set centrally, the workforce, the training, the delivery and storage of the vaccine, the planning required to avoid wasting a dose, because the vaccine is new and needs special conditions, and I choose not to notice her pale face, the lines of worry and exhaustion, her eyes that close under my criticism, and I am rude. I am unforgivably rude. And later I sit in the lay-by again on the way home and I cry and cry.

Now, in 2022, I am visiting Littlefield again. I have looked up its website to find the phone number to check for a good time to visit, and the website has reviews from last week and last month, which catch my eye.

Mum absolutely loves it at Littlefield, and I feel very happy and relaxed knowing Mum is happy and being cared for. All the staff are amazing, they are very friendly and welcoming, as well as being very professional and caring.

My grandmother is very fond of each and every member of staff at Littlefield, so thank you for making her feel welcome.

Lovely home. My father was admitted for a month and he was well cared for and everyone was always lovely to him and us when we visited. He was clearly well looked after and there was always something on for him to do.

I looked at the photos on the website. Same dining room. Same garden. Same foyer.

The young staff particularly are great.

Just wanted to say how lovely it is to see my aunt so happy and well. She is now mixing with other residents and joining in activities.

Every time I visit I always hear the staff chatting with residents and having a laugh.

I drive to Littlefield and sit in my car under the trees for a moment looking at the entrance, then gather my bag and a plant I have brought and a card. There is a notice Sellotaped to the door, a blurry photo of a small dog.

MY NAME IS BASIL — I LIVE HERE, says the notice. PLEASE LET A MEMBER OF STAFF KNOW IF YOU DON'T WANT TO MEET ME.

There's another notice. MASKS ARE NO LONGER NEEDED IN LITTLEFIELD. YOU ARE WELCOME TO WEAR ONE IF YOU WISH.

I sit with Jacqui in the manager's office.

'I can talk about it now,' she says. 'Talking about it is my therapy, the doctor says.' Jacqui talks of how she got COVID in the queue for the vaccine, and when she rang the vaccine team to let them know, they said, 'You and everyone else – the whole queue got it.' She talks of moving into the home when the pandemic began, she and two other staff, and of sitting with those who were dying. She talks of playing a CD to Dot, which kept sticking on one song. Dot's daughter asked afterwards which song it was. It was a Beach Boys song and she told Jacqui, 'That's the one we chose for the funeral.' Jacqui talks of writing to Boris Johnson, who had claimed that all care home staff had been vaccinated when they hadn't, not yet, and she asked him, *What planet are you on, Boris?*

Jacqui pauses. There's a chap at the door of her office, leaning on a walking frame.

'What have you got, Marv?' she asks.

'Hospital letter, Jac,' Marv says, handing her the piece of paper. 'Eyes. Can you make the appointment?'

And Jacqui says, 'Yes, no problem.'

Marv adds, 'Not too early mind. I don't like early.'

Jacqui reassures him. 'I know you, Marv, you're not the early bird.'

Jacqui talks of watching the hearses and how her mask rode up whenever tears got behind it, and she says, 'We were in it together, and if we didn't joke, we would cry all day.' She talks of her recent sky dive and a sponsored silence (six hours!) and her bucket-list trip to Australia next year.

203

She says, 'I felt so guilty . . . I still feel guilty.' She says, 'I cried every day for a while.' She says, 'I would do it again if I had to.'

There is still no room on the floor of Jacqui's office. The boxes of masks and gloves have gone, but instead there is Basil in his bed and toys for Basil.

'Is he yours?' I ask.

Jacqui leans back and waves an arm. 'No, he's Mrs Gerald's. He came in with her. He's not going anywhere.'

I notice that the office is tidy; all the paperwork has been filed away, except an open folder on a table by Basil's bed. I read it.

Care plan, it says, and there is a photo of Basil, a chart for his food and fluid, and another chart titled, *walks*, and there are many different initials all down the page.

I say goodbye and go out to the car, and the sky is blue and there are great tits chinking at one another in the trees.

12. Lessons from a Pandemic

'I would do it again if I had to,' said Jacqui, as she glanced over her care home's staffing rota at the same time as talking to me.

Oh, Jacqui, I do not want you to have to do it again. None of us wants to do any of it again. What can we learn? What changes can we make?

'It was our darkest hour,' Jacqui told me, with Basil at her feet, 'but we're out the other side now.'

We have been through a terrible time – so much loss, loneliness, anger and fear. It would hardly be surprising if we decided, individually and together, that we don't want to think about it, that we want instead to embrace our freedom. We want to get through the security queue to have a pint in an airport pub some time before ten in the morning; buy tickets for a festival where we will be jammed up against others in a pulsating crowd of hot, happy humans. We want to take our kids to trampoline lessons or chess club or the skate park; to Center Parcs; to choose a kitten or buy a stick insect in a glass case. We want to make fairy cakes with grandchildren, get all liberal with the sprinkles, or learn to dance – a waltz, cheek to cheek; we want to volunteer, to run the Red

Cross plant stall, where we will write prices on labels, borrowing a pen from a stranger who might become a friend. And yet we will be doing ourselves a disservice if we do not stop for a moment to consider what has happened and what we might learn. The British Geriatrics Society (BGS) published a report in November 2022, describing ten lessons we might take from the COVID-19 pandemic. As I read it, I smile, recognising my own experience in each of its messages, and each lesson falls into place with a thud to create a wall that might stand between us and something ugly.

The 'Ten Lessons' report is introduced by Dr Jennifer Burns, whose tenure as BGS president coincided with the first two years of the pandemic. Jenny is firm about the bad things – she approached her suddenly redefined role with robust patience and good humour – and she cites particularly the situation in care homes and the lack of personal protective equipment (PPE) in the early days, but she notes that we must also remember the things that went well and recognise and build on them. Jenny's message calls for improvements in pandemic preparedness. She notes that this is unlikely to be our last pandemic and that the next is also likely disproportionately to affect older people. She calls also for improvements in the everyday running of systems that should support us when we need support.

Older people are the biggest users of health and social care services – and that is a good thing. It would be a sad world if children and young adults suffered the multiple conditions with which older people contend. This is not about distributing resources unfairly, allowing older people to soak up services that are then unavailable to the young. But, as Jenny observes, if our services work for older people they will work for everyone. And our services can work better. The lessons in the report are based on hard experience and thoughtful evaluation. We know what needs to be done.

The report is directed at governments and at health and social care organisations, but many of the lessons are ones we can consider as individuals, as families and as communities. What shall we change? How can we help?

Lesson 1

Treatment decisions should always be tailored to the individual patient – blanket decisions should never be applied to an entire patient group.

I think of the horrified responses – rightly horrified – when it became apparent that in some cases whole care homes, all their residents, had been subjected to blanket 'not for resuscitation' policies, and other home managers had been told that their residents should not be transferred to hospital for treatment whatever the circumstances. I remember a project our hospital's Clinical Ethics Committee was given early in the pandemic to plan the best use of limited resources and to consider the implications of one intensive care bed and two patients. The BGS guidance is clear on this, saying that *while for many older people with frailty, intensive treatment options are likely to cause more harm than good, these decisions should be made on an individual basis and no one should be denied access to any type of treatment based on age alone.*

But the need for individualised treatment decisions goes beyond avoiding blanket bans. Decisions about treatment, especially for someone who is frail and who has multiple conditions, often require analysis of the interplay between what might be effective and what is wanted, and too often doctors have a good idea of the former and know nothing of the latter. I recall the Treatment Escalation Plans at Littlefield, the scanty information for some of those residents, the equal frustration of knowing that Jack or Helene may have a good plan that was clear and applicable, but being unable to find it when it was needed. How hard it was to find out anything of the wishes of those residents once the situation had become urgent and frightening and their voice inaudible. Advance plans were important before the pandemic and they remain important now, because there are plenty of threats to the well-being of an older person beyond COVID. When we have a kind, honest conversation with each person or with their family or friends, or, best of all, everyone together, and especially when those conversations take place in better circumstances, with time to explore hopes and fears, then good plans can be made often surprisingly easily and with a sigh of relief.

Yet right now most escalation plans are created in exactly the type of situation they are designed to avoid: in an Emergency Department, or on a dark wet night in a care home or a bungalow with the paramedics' stretcher waiting in the doorway for a decision, to stay or to go. Advance care planning, including the creation of kind, articulate Treatment Escalation Plans that reflect the wishes of their owner, should be a right, not a burden, for all older people, and especially for those who have chronic conditions that can suddenly worsen and for those who live in care homes, whose views about treatment are better explored than assumed. This then is a lesson for all of us. Our advance care plans belong to us, and to the people we love and care about. We can say, right, this is a good moment. It's time to make a plan.

Lesson 2

There is a need to ensure that a balance is achieved between protecting care home residents from a virus that could be fatal for them and also protecting the human rights of individuals to see their families and loved ones.

The BGS report does not pull its punches. It describes how Amnesty International *found a raft of failings in the management of the virus in care homes. This included discharges of COVID-positive patients from hospitals into care homes, advice that personal protective equipment (PPE) was not necessary if residents and staff were not symptomatic, a failure to provide PPE, a failure to help care homes isolate infected residents and a failure to ensure regular testing of residents and staff.*

By March 2020, the day before lockdown measures came legally into force in the UK, the BGS team had issued guidance for care home staff, including, even at this early stage, the recognition that older people with COVID may not have typical symptoms, urging a level of caution, with isolation and testing to protect residents. The guidance provided practical advice about quarantine, recognising the dilemmas posed by residents who walk or who cannot be prevented from walking, like Jeanette and Phil at Littlefield, and it remains the most frequently downloaded resource the society has ever produced. Yet the guidance also acknowledges the terrible effects of isolation, the potentially lethal loss of connections and the sadness of lives that continued or ended without contact with the people who matter most, those who make our hearts sing. *Infection-control policies and procedures [. . .] limited residents' access to family support for many months and in some cases, residents were isolated in their rooms for weeks on end.*

I think of Candice, who came into hospital from her residential home and by the next day had COVID. Maybe she had it when she arrived or caught it in an Emergency Department cubicle or in X-ray, who knows? Candice spent days alone in a single room, the oximeter's monitor turned towards the window on to the ward corridor so that staff could see the readings without having to come in. Days with no visitors became weeks with no visitors, Candice testing positive again and again because her tired immune system could not clear the fragments of virus from her nose and throat, and she pulled her purple dressing gown round her shoulders because the window was open for ventilation and the room was cold, and looked at photos of her grandchildren on her phone, and she asked, 'Please may I go home?' Finally one day she was free after a negative test and returned to her care home, where no amount of reassurance would persuade the manager to change her view that Candice – Candice who has just had COVID, who is at last clear of COVID, Candice who cannot right now give COVID to anyone – must undergo a further two weeks of quarantine in her room with no visitors, because she has come back to the care home from the hospital and that is the rule. The report continues: *Rules on visiting in care homes changed regularly with many families and care home operators struggling to keep up with what was allowed and what was not. Many of the restrictions in care homes remained in place long after restrictions were lifted in the rest of society and many family members became frustrated at not being allowed to visit their loved ones face-to-face, even once both the visitor and the resident were vaccinated.*

Dr Clarissa Giebel and her team in Liverpool carried out a study mentioned in the 'Ten Lessons' report. They listened to care home staff and families of residents and acknowledged work by others confirming what was already obvious to those familiar with care homes, that isolation and loss of social connections were accelerating the decline of people with dementia. Giebel's team identified anger and frustration at delayed or inconsistent offers of face-to-face visits. They heard of the difficulties for care home staff in trying to interpret the guidance, together with frustration among families who were aware of variability in visiting arrangements between homes. Fear and disinformation were circulating regarding the vaccine and there were logistical difficulties in accessing vaccination. Direct quotes leap from the pages of Dr Giebel's report regarding fear for fertility, and scarce appointments at the end of long days and infrequent buses and *just lies* and *don't get me started*, and the heartfelt words of a wife: *I was going to see my husband in the pod but two carers that I spoke to who came in with him, they both declared that they weren't going to have the vaccine. So I'm sitting on the other side of the pod, thinking, Well, actually he's at greater risk on that side of the screen than he is with me.*

Dr Giebel's article highlights the lack of clear communication and support from 'decision makers' to care homes and from care homes to families. Her team looks for solutions – both care home staff and families were given advice, particularly about visiting, that was complicated and sometimes irrelevant and that often changed at short notice, and they were all trying to make sense of it. I think of the paperwork filling Jacqui's office in Littlefield and I know we can do better.

The article calls for better support for care homes regarding infection-control measures and demands access to PPE such as masks, gloves and aprons for care workers at parity with those working in the NHS. It calls for help for care homes in their communication with families – such communication would have been better had care home staff known what they were doing themselves. There's a call for better information about vaccination for all involved. And although there's an acknowledgement that there will be times when, as a last resort, a visit cannot happen because the risks are too high, that 'last resort' bar is placed as high as anyone can reach. The lesson is unequivocal: *Face-to-face visits are a human right.*

Lesson 3

Services should be available and adequately funded to provide patients with the most appropriate care in the best place for them. For some patients, this will be hospital. For others, it will not.

Ah, I love this lesson. I have been sitting up straight in class, ears pinned back, learning. I can see the application immediately. I can see Josephine in her little living room with its glass-fronted cabinet and pretty plates, suddenly confused because of a chest infection, and she needs to stay in her own home, where her niece has come to look after her. Her niece has placed a Z-bed on the floor next to Josephine's and the cat is curled up on it already. I can see Maurice, who will not leave Barbara's side; he has been in hospital three times in the last three months and has had enough, so we can put a cannula into one of his veins at home and give him the medicines for his failing heart that he would have had in hospital, which will help his breathing in this last stage of his life, because we all know that Maurice is likely getting to the end. We can visit him and do his blood tests and keep an eye on his kidneys, adjusting his medicines just as we would if he were on a ward, until the right moment comes to stop doing even that, and let Maurice have peace. I can see Elma, who I sent to hospital from her care home with COVID, but with other resources she could have had intravenous fluids right there in Littlefield, could, in fact, have had everything she was given in hospital, except for the unfamiliar faces, the noise, the sleepless nights and the long, long wait to be allowed back home. And this lesson, about the best place for care and the resources needed for that care, is also based on good solid experience; the teachers aren't just making it up. These Hospital at Home services for people who are frail have existed in some places for years before COVID and have been carefully evaluated, and we know that for many patients – even for those who may be very unwell indeed – hospital may not be the right place for them, and studies show that for the right patient the outcomes are as good or better (in terms of dying or needing more care) and the costs are the same or less, and the experience is much better for that patient than being in hospital. We need more choice and access to such services, for they bring relief.

Lesson 4

During a pandemic, particular attention should be paid to the risk of contracting the illness in patients admitted to hospital for unrelated illnesses and measures must be taken to prevent this happening.

That is a lesson for the government and for those who plan and fund our hospital estate, where we now have two beds in each single side room divided by a flimsy screen, and two extra beds in what was the dining and therapy area of our frailty unit, and another new bed in front of the nurses' station on every ward, where the water cooler and the comfortable chairs used to stand.

And our offices are cramped and shared, and our rest spaces likewise, and poorly ventilated, and it's hard for staff to maintain distance from one another, as well as from their patients. But we also need to take responsibility and to be aware of our own behaviours; some hospitals did better than others in terms of patients contracting COVID, and not all of that was down to single rooms and well-ventilated spaces. Clear guidance and the leadership and support to follow that guidance will have tipped the balance in many settings.

Lesson 5

Planning for the response to a pandemic should involve experts on the population most affected by the illness in question. These experts should be involved at the earliest possible stage.

I can understand the dismay with which the BGS realised that they were not represented at the Scientific Advisory Group for Emergencies (SAGE) for COVID, and they are right to describe that as a misstep. The society holds a great deal of expertise regarding the population most affected by this pandemic, which, at least in terms of illness and death, was older people. I wonder why they were omitted – after all, you'd include a paediatrician on a group tackling a disease that disproportionately caused the death of children. Perhaps this represents our collective blindness towards two facts: that older people are different from younger people, because they have complex problems and different goals (so there are different and better ways of delivering their care), and that they are also the same, because older people are people – they are the rest of us grown up and equally deserving of expertise.

Geriatricians are a modest bunch and few of them do private practice, and many drive clapped-out old cars of which they are perversely fond. The treatments they offer do not generally come with the backing of big pharma with international symposia and sponsored trials, and perhaps geriatricians have not made as much noise as they should about their skills and the science that underpins their work, and the fact that good care, good holistic care, costs less than bad care. That's changing, and geriatricians, GPs and those psychiatrists who specialise in older people are finding their voice to challenge static, ineffective systems and to champion new ways of doing things, not just in response to a grim pandemic but in response to the success story that is an ageing population. The voices are becoming stronger too of those professionals with whom we work – therapists, specialist nurses and many others who listen to and speak up for older people, people who work in social care or in charities, voluntary organisations, community projects and in housing, people who have visions for change, who can see how lives can be made better. And of course the real experts are older people themselves, who are growing in confidence to talk about getting older and all that it means. 'I have noticed,' says Joanie of the knitting group she set up twelve years ago, 'that we talk a lot more easily these days about things you used to brush under the carpet. I like that.'

Lesson 6

Clinical trials must include the populations most at risk and most likely to benefit from the treatments being tested. In the majority of cases, this will include older people.

RECOVERY is a remarkable, nimble and efficient trial that delivered results in a spectacularly speedy fashion, identifying four treatments that helped people with severe COVID and weeding out ones that were in-effective. And I love it, because the RECOVERY team does not exclude older people and people with frailty, as many trials do, and many of my own patients in hospital were enrolled. It's notable too that the RECOVERY trial is not funded by any pharmaceutical company but rather by independent organisations like the National Institute for Health and Care Research (NIHR), the Wellcome Trust, the Bill and Melinda Gates Foundation, and the UK Foreign, Commonwealth and Development Office. But older people were less well represented in trials of treatments in the community, and funding for trials of drugs to treat and prevent COVID-19 in care home residents arrived too late. We know that carrying out research studies in care homes is complicated – residents can't usually attend hospital easily for trial tests or treatments, and getting consent is trickier when someone has dementia, so teams doing such research need support. Older people must be represented in trials of all medications. It is not right that companies should be allowed to demonstrate the safety of their medications only in those who are least likely to develop side effects, when both we and they know that the drug once licensed will be used in a more vulnerable population, so from the start its safety and effectiveness should be demonstrated in those people too.

Lesson 7

Quick development and rollout of the vaccine was essential. During a pandemic, sufficient funding should always be made available to ensure that scientists are able to collaborate and develop vaccines quickly.

I hopped from one place marker to the next as I advanced through the entrance tent in the hospital car park. The queue for the vaccine was buzzy, full of chat despite the two-metre social-distancing restrictions. At the front of the queue I was greeted by Nick, a retired GP who grinned behind his mask, telling me, 'Lucy, I have had more training to deliver this vaccine into your arm than I got in the old days to perform a Caesarean section.' Barely a year after this virus had first been detected, I watched the drop of vaccine leave the syringe and move into my muscle. It felt like a miracle.

The development of the vaccine in record time showed what can be achieved when scientists and pharmaceutical companies across the world work in collaboration and when science is properly funded. Corners were not cut in the development and approval of the COVID vaccines, but scientists did not have to spend precious time applying for grants and funding. They simply got on with it.

And the speed of the roll-out of the vaccine was all the more impressive for being based on need! Those at the greatest risk from the virus were prioritised, and the roll-out was remarkable, notwithstanding the difficulties encountered by care home staff, for whom the urgency was pressing. No one was allowed to 'jump the queue' by paying privately to receive the vaccine; resources were allocated to those who needed them most, regardless of ability to pay – at least within the UK, though there are lessons to be learned about sharing vaccines more effectively with other countries, especially those with slim resources – for a pandemic is, by definition, global.

Lesson 8

A time of great crisis can also bring great innovation. Changes made during a crisis that are beneficial to patients should be retained.

How can anything good come out of this hateful virus? I take a deep breath. Here goes. The Rapid Response team supports people in crisis – a sudden inability to move after a twisted ankle, a husband with dementia whose wife, his carer, has been admitted to hospital – and the team talks through all its patients twice a day, every day, online; we can see some faces and hear everyone's voices, quickly, quickly, with no time for chat. Mariella the team leader is out on a visit in a valley but she's got reception; she checks that everyone knows what they're doing and please can they take on another patient this evening in Ebberly Cross, where is that? Someone knows; it's in the back of beyond, but the location is shared and Marco says he can get there. And now the new Hospital at Home team can use that technology too. I'm in my car by the gate to a field and I can see the whole team's smiling faces on my laptop. Later, I can look up Jerry's blood results while I'm standing in his bedroom. There are meetings online to hear about how places on the other side of the country are using innovations, better care in the community: what went wrong – well, we won't do that; wow, what do you carry in that kit bag? We could do with that; OK, says someone in Kent, I'll put a link to our list in the chat. Recognition that without social care the NHS doesn't work. A realisation that care homes are places of skill and life and love. They are homes.

Our medical director sits quietly at the late-evening handover, saying little and listening intently to young doctors who are both competent and stressed. The primary care networks – district nurses, GPs, complex care nurses, social workers, therapists and village agents, community psychiatric and palliative care nurses – are all on a weekly call to help the 'too difficult' brigade. Heather has sent round the list; they'll tell me if they need me there, or I can drop in online to tell them about David, whose sister has told me is 'a complete nightmare'– and the network team roll their eyes. 'We know David' – and I can tell them that David is going home tomorrow. 'Now that we didn't know. Thank you for the heads up.'

International medical graduates, the diversification of the medical workforce, the kindness, knowledge and patience they have brought with them. FaceTime for families who can't come in – no, not because of COVID; they're in Canada. Phone follow-ups for clinic – well, what with the traffic and the cost of the car park and Gerry doesn't like the hospital anyway, so a phone call is fine, thank you, doctor. Teaching surgical nurses medical things because our patients are all over their wards and they like learning. Meetings outside whenever we can, a walk with a colleague – past the boiler room and the Path lab in the sunshine.

Lesson 9

Measures taken to curb the impact of a pandemic may have unintended but serious consequences on the health of many older people. These consequences must be identified as quickly as possible and mitigating action taken.

There has been loneliness and loss of strength and a cancer that has grown under the radar because going to the doctor for tests is . . . and more loneliness and not being able to hear because getting the hearing aid sorted is . . . and more loneliness and not feeling up to much because I'm not so confident these days . . . and yet more loneliness and forgetting what day it is because one day is much like another. So here is the work to start talking and walking again, and getting out and having a check-up, and the yoga class is back on, and choirs and the Silver Swans dancing class, and craft club and Greek lessons, and the book group and the men's shed and the repair shop, where more is repaired than old clocks and a model boat.

Lesson 10

NHS workforce planning must cover three crucial elements: ensuring there are enough staff, ensuring all NHS staff have the skills they need to care for the ageing population and ensuring that staff are cared for mentally and emotionally and are supported to remain working in the NHS. The impact of not doing so may be catastrophic for individuals and society.

There are not enough of us. There are not enough doctors or nurses in the UK. Yes, more are being trained, but slowly and not enough. And of those doctors and nurses we do have, many have not had training that allows them to care well for older people. It's not all about complexity, some of this is simple stuff. I think of Michael, who came into hospital because his bladder would not empty. It had become as tight as a drum and painful, and he is now sitting on an Emergency Department trolley with his trousers undone, holding his jumper over his lap to preserve some dignity. Michael was given codeine tablets after a knee replacement last week, and no one told him that codeine would most likely cause him to become constipated, and no one gave him some simple laxatives to go with that codeine. So his bowels haven't worked for days and now his bladder has stopped working in sympathy, and that didn't need to happen. Our Emergency Departments and wards are populated by many older people whose admission could have been averted by better training for all those caring for them.

But then I think about our delirium team and how they detect those quietly muddled patients and teach other staff about what works when people are frightened and confused. I think about the Parkinson's specialist nurses, and of another nurse, a young one I hadn't met before last week, in the extra bay at the end of the Emergency Department, where Edgar lay because there was nowhere else for him, and he had been fretting, ill and tired. That nurse had tucked her phone between his pillow and its slip, to play the Massed Bands of the Royal Marines – she told me that Edgar had been a colour sergeant – and now he slept. I think of the University of Bristol Medical School, who used to send three students at a time for six weeks to the hospitals of the Severn region in order that they learn some geriatric medicine. Now we are sent twelve students at a time, who stay for eighteen weeks, and our Academy team keep them busy. Those students learn about dementia and delirium, about falls and frailty and that there is such a thing as 'too much medicine', and about poverty and continence and fractures and the annihilating exhaustion of being a carer this day and every day. They learn about what matters most, which is different for everyone, and about strokes and heart failure and hypothermia, and they learn to take blood from tiny veins that slip sideways, and they meet Hubert and Wilf, Jill and Margaret, and social workers and therapists and ward assistants. Many of the patients they meet will go home, but at least one of their patients will die, and those students offer to wash up the coffee cups after a meeting and they say, 'I wasn't looking forward to this placement,' or 'I didn't want to do eighteen weeks of gerries,' and they say, 'I really enjoyed it. I learned a lot.'

I believe that that Bristol course is the longest, most comprehensive and most popular undergraduate training in geriatric medicine in the world, and whatever variety of doctor those students go on to become they will carry that experience forward. I think of my geriatrician colleagues across the UK and other countries, who are increasingly working alongside surgeons, cancer specialists and cardiologists, setting up joint services to share expertise. They look at the single organ and then stand back and look at the whole person and talk with that person, and together they modify or adjust a plan that was designed to fit a person who has just one illness in order to fit a person who has six. There is so much we can do that will make the future better.

Finally, on holiday in Ireland I stretch out on damp moss by a summer lake, watching the wind gusting clouds across a bright sky, and add my own lesson. A long time ago in a physics class we did an experiment where you take a small spring and put it on a hook and measure its length. You hang a little weight on it and watch it stretch.

Then you take the weight off and the spring returns to where it was before, ready for the next weight, which is heavier. And you repeat this process, the weight a little heavier each time, and the spring stretches further, returning each time to its original length until suddenly it doesn't. And that is its elastic limit, and you can take the spring off the hook and squash it and try to push it back into shape, but it will never be quite the same again.

I used to do annual appraisals for doctors from many different specialties, reviewing their year, their plans, plaudits and worries, and I would sometimes hear a hesitation. 'It's just that –' or 'No, don't worry –', and we would talk about the stretched spring. We all have an elastic limit and many of us find it by reaching it. I found mine in a care home during a pandemic. But we can watch for signs in ourselves that we are approaching that limit – bad behaviour or tears, impulsivity or poor sleep, or being overwhelmed by small things (there are many signs) and when we recognise those signs we need to take some weight off that spring.

How? Telling someone is a good start. Telling ourselves and being honest is the best start.

13. Positive Intent

I look round from the computer on wheels – where is Aliyah? I'd like to show her Mr Hudson's blood results and she was with me a moment ago. I spot her further along the ward corridor just outside A Bay, where we had been earlier this morning, and she is standing with her back to me, her hands open at her side. I watch as she tips her head up, and stands, small and still, and I know something is wrong.

She turns as I say her name, and her beautiful calm face is pale, and she blinks and answers my question. 'No, I am fine.' Her gaze darts away and she is not fine, a tear is sliding down her face. And she says, 'I am OK,' but she is not OK, and we step to the side of the corridor where I put my hand on the sleeve of her blouse and ask what has happened.

Aliyah says, 'It does not matter.'

I say, 'Aliyah, something has happened. It does matter.'

She starts to speak. 'The patient we saw, Mrs Redman with the pneumonia, she had a question about her antibiotics –' Aliyah looks up at the ceiling and I can see her eyes fill again – 'and she said she could not understand my accent.'

Aliyah sweeps the back of her arm across her face and tucks a strand of hair back under her headscarf – silk, cream with green lilies, held in place with precise clips. Her fingernails are perfect ovals, clear lacquer. She says, 'It doesn't matter. It's not important.'

I cannot remember now exactly what I did. I know I did not get it right. I know I told Aliyah that I was sorry, that that should not have happened. I know I offered to speak with the patient, but Aliyah asked me not to.

'She is going home today. I'll do her discharge summary now; it does not matter.'

I know we got on with the ward round. We saw more patients together. We assessed, planned, explained. Aliyah pulled up scans and X-rays, showed me inconsistencies on drug charts, told me what a family had told her the preceding day about the son of a confused patient. She wrote notes, requested blood tests, filled in forms – a referral to another specialty, an order for oxygen to be delivered to a patient's home. She smiled at Bernie when he told us he needed to get back to his beehives. She prescribed intravenous fluid and listened to an occupational therapist describing her concerns about Gerald's squalid flat. She fetched a reel of tape, the better to protect Rita's cannula from her restless fingers, and I saw her later, kneeling beside an old, old lady, talking quietly as she searched for a tiny vein that no one else had been able to find, and the old lady looking at Aliyah, at her head bowed in her neat headscarf, while she did her job, and there was a look of such trust, and I wished I could bottle that trust, and use it to scrub away the stain, to heal the ugly corrosion created by that woman in A Bay, because I had seen earlier the way she had looked at this young doctor, and I knew that that woman did not have any difficulty understanding Aliyah's accent, which is as clear as my own.

What would I do next time? There will be a next time. Next time I will find a more private place in which to ask what has happened, because alongside the sting of that woman's words (words which meant not 'I do not understand you' but rather 'I do not want to understand you', and a whole lot more besides), I caused Aliyah to have to hold herself together while people walked past us, casting us curious glances. Would I confront the patient? My training has taught me that the response to such an incident should be led by the recipient – it's Aliyah's call, not mine – but I am in a position of strength, and I think it is fair to step in when Aliyah is off the ward or when the patient is leaving hospital. In my imagination I hold the door open for that patient, the woman from A Bay, as she leaves, and I walk alongside her to the lifts, and explain that she must not speak to a member of our staff in that way. I want to tell her that Aliyah was born in a country torn apart by a war generated by other powers; that her cousin in the same class at school was mutilated by a bomb; that she did her medical training – a good training – in another country that was not her own, learning quickly in a new language, even a new alphabet, far from her family; and that continuing con-flict – rubble, standpipes, the streets patrolled by vicious men – has prevented Aliyah from returning to the city where her parents live, and her grandma too, who she loves and misses with all her heart. I want to say that she has come here, with her kindness and her skills, and is studying for her postgraduate exams and she likes cupcakes and *Call the Midwife*, and hopes to become a paediatrician, and, Mrs A Bay, you will not speak to her like that. And then I think, I should not have to say any of that, that woman does not need to know anything of Aliyah except that she is a fellow human being and must be treated with respect.

Of course it happens that someone working in our health service may have an accent that is difficult to understand, as may our patients, and I have watched painfully awkward interactions between patients and those caring for them, hampered by issues with hearing and by masks because many of us do more lip-reading than we realise (I find my own hearing is strangely affected by wearing a mask – covering my mouth seems to stop my ears from working properly, and I might take off my own mask to listen better). There will be a complicated issue to explain, which is being described in complicated terms, and the use of jargon. I think of a young carer bellowing at an older man, reading from her checklist, 'What is your fluid preference? Your *fluid* preference!' Eventually giving up and asking, 'D'you want tea or coffee?' It can feel awkward to say, 'Please can you repeat that? I didn't understand.' But we need to be able to say this because everything we do, all our care, hinges on understanding. And we can do so without being rude – we can say, 'I'm sorry, when you are being so kind, but I am having difficulty understanding these words.'

I watched with admiration a young doctor from Senegal as he prepared for an exam, a demanding one that involves the assessment of communication skills, with actors playing the part of patients in situations that are stressful – the sharing of bad news or a medical error demanding a sensitive apology – and that young Senegalese doctor prefaced his interaction in our practice sessions by introducing himself, and saying to the actor (me or a fellow candidate), 'I am aware that my accent is quite strong – if I say anything, anything at all that you do not understand, please stop me and ask.' It seemed kind to me that he pre-empted embarrassment, acknowledged the barrier, and I realise now that his words are good words that any of us can choose to say, and his acknowledgement of an issue with language was dignified and honest and fostered trust.

I am aware, I hope constantly, of my own privilege. I know that my white skin elevates my position of power. I have not been subjected to glances, wariness or overt hostility, the sly phrases or filthy words. I have not been subjected to racism. I have not had to explain my name, my clothes, my presence. I am aware too that I may be more readily forgiven than others for my errors.

I rang Barbara to apologise for a mistake I had made. I had seen her in clinic. She was a woman in her eighties having funny turns. She had had a fall a couple of months previously – a tangle involving the cat coming in, Barbara going out and the runnel of a sliding door – that had shaken her up, and since then she had not been herself and had had episodes of feeling unwell. There was no loss of consciousness and her family didn't think she looked grey or clammy, but she would just stop talking and hold on to a door frame or kitchen sideboard. One of her sons would help her to sit and stay with her until she felt better. She was a martyr to her nerves at the best of times, said her son. It sounded to me as if Barbara was having spells of anxiety, feeling understandably overwhelmed, frightened that she might fall again. Her ECG was normal and I'd checked her blood pressure both lying down and standing up and listened to her heart. I'd written a firm letter to Barbara and copied the letter to her GP, reassuring them both that these were not sinister events. When I came to sign that letter a couple of weeks later I noticed on the electronic system that two days after I had sent her home from my clinic, all full of cheer, Barbara had been admitted again, having collapsed, her heart rate only thirty beats per minute, and she now had had a pacemaker inserted.

I spoke to her on the phone. She was feeling better – no more funny turns.

'I'm really sorry, Barbara,' I said.

'Not a worry,' she replied. 'You were so lovely and kind.'

Lovely and kind, Barbara, but also wrong, and I know that others, lovely and kind, might be accepted as a doctor, and trusted, until something goes awry, an oversight or a mistake, and the breezy forgiveness afforded to me might be less forthcoming for someone whose skin is a different colour.

What have I learned from watching my patients and their families, my colleagues and friends? What have I learned from the diverse populations during my training in London in the 1980s and 1990s, and as I watch the inhabitants of my rural community now, in which until recently almost all cultural diversity has been concentrated in the staff of its local NHS?

I have watched competence and care overcome prejudice. I have watched language become modified, seen attitudes shift, small perceptible changes led by ward sisters and specialist nurses, by care home managers, by kitchen staff who arrange celebratory feasts and embrace new recipes, and by cleaners and Health Care Assistants who get on with the job and laugh and learn and teach the rest of us. I've heard lengthy surnames converted into fond nicknames, have wondered if that is OK and been reassured by the owners of those names that it is OK, I like that name. For years I have frowned at the equality and diversity module that is part of my annual mandatory training and have timed myself as I pay lip service to a tick-box exercise, identifying legally defined 'protected characteristics' (religion, race, yes; vegetarianism, no) in a process that now takes me – I check – forty-three seconds. I have wondered how that exercise can possibly make any difference, but perhaps it does, because everyone in our organisation, the largest local employer, must read those words and understand that this matters. And everyone knows that everyone else has read the words too.

I've learned that I don't know enough and will never know what it feels like to be on the receiving end of racism. I've learned to look out for it, I hope, and I have learned, from courses and conversation with friends, family, colleagues, about being actively anti-racist, although even typing those words makes me aware that I am making a claim that requires more of me than I have hitherto given. I have participated in 'bystander training' and been taught that intervention is necessary and learned techniques for such intervention – to stop the situation, to allow my student or colleague to leave the room, to divert or distract, saying, 'Javier, I think you were going to make a call to radiology', to allow Javier to walk away. I have learned words with which to challenge prejudice without escalating bad behaviour. I have been taught that asking 'Did I miss something?' is one way to draw attention to an underhand comment. Even better, it can be a powerful move simply to ask the perpetrator, 'Are you OK?'

I have learned too that my older patients may be no more or less likely to be racist than many of the younger people for whom we care, but that many have been left behind by the evolution of language and they may use words and phrases that jar, and may or may not have malign intent, because sometimes those words are simply words that did not carry connotations of offence seventy or more years ago when that person was developing their vocabulary, yet they are very offensive now; or maybe they are words that were indeed always offensive but that offence was not given due consideration. It can be difficult but necessary to convey understanding, to explain how those words cause hurt and cannot be used. I've learned that such explanations may not work, especially when someone has dementia, but I have also learned that if someone with dementia is cared for in a place that is tolerant, and they do not hear that language, then sometimes their own terrible language will abate. I have also learned that there are people who are filled with hate and bigoted, and they will express that hatred more freely when they are unwell, either because they cannot control their words, due to an illness like dementia or delirium, or because they perceive that their role as a vulnerable patient grants them an opportunity to be vile, and those situations are very painful, and I have watched good people handle such situations with great kindness and at considerable cost to themselves.

I have learned, and am taken aback by learning, that as well as the micro-aggressions faced by many of those with whom I work, those from minority ethnic groups lose out on 'micro-affirmations'. I am more likely to pay a compliment, to praise work well done, when I am working with a trainee who looks like me. Having understood that, I think more about my behaviour and try to ensure that I am even-handed, without becoming tacky or inauthentic.

I have learned about 'unconscious bias'. When I first encountered this term it seemed to me that it was a euphemism, because many of us carry biases that we would like to claim are unconscious, but which are, in fact, perfectly conscious but unspoken, being shameful or illicit, and we might sit down with ourselves and give our beliefs and biases a good dose of scrutiny. But even when we have confronted ourselves and our conscious biases and feel we have faced them down, there is more to be done, for our past influences our present.

I am struck by the words used in a training programme run by the Royal College of Physicians of London. It's an online programme designed for senior medics responsible for the fair assessment of doctors who are training to become specialists, and its message is clear and helpful. The programme begins: *Everyone has unconscious bias.* This feels like a good place to start. I feel safe here with everyone. As I read through the slides, one scenario after another is presented – an exam candidate who is visibly pregnant and cannot reach across the patient to examine his left side properly; another with a stammer interrupted by the examiner, who feels awkward as she witnesses him struggle to speak; there's a candidate to whom the patient has taken a dislike because the candidate is not white. There is a candidate who is older than the others. 'How many times must he have tried to pass this exam?' comments an examiner behind his hand in this scenario, and we are asked to consider whether the examiner's assumptions will affect his assessment and what to do about this, for the exams are carefully moderated and there are mechanisms for examiners to challenge one another's behaviour, or to recognise and report that the attitude of a patient might have affected a candidate's chances. However, there is no feeling of witch-hunt to this process. There is an air of exploration, of understanding.

The programme notes continue, *It does not make you racist, sexist, homophobic, or a bad person to have been influenced by your past experiences or cultural and societal stereotypes. We are all biased, and awareness of this will help us to mitigate its effects.* I am impressed, although not surprised, by the thought that has gone into this course. It includes descriptions of tiny interactions, influenced by feelings of kinship, that may cause us to notice the nervousness of a candidate who reminds us of our younger selves, so we calm them with a few words, yet we might mistake the formal demeanour of a candidate of a different heritage, for confidence, when that formality actually conceals a quaking heart (these exams are career-defining and expensive), and that candidate, outwardly unlike us, is, in fact, exactly like us, and would have benefitted equally from the same comforting words. We are challenged to spot such inequities, which are subtle but in a tightly marked assessment may be the difference between a pass and a fail.

The course reminds us that *reasonable adjustments* can be made provided a candidate has declared in advance their need for assistance (a candidate with hearing loss is permitted to use a stethoscope with enhanced features; the examination couch can be moved to allow the pregnant candidate to examine her patient more effectively), yet the academic standards of the exam must be preserved. The candidates must come up to scratch, and so must the examiners.

The course notes continue:

Think about the assumptions and biases you have.

Consider ways in which this could impact your academic judgements.

How can you make sure that your bias does not get in the way of judging a candidate on the basis of their ability?

As I complete the course and save its certificate for

my appraisal portfolio, I think of the challenges it has posed. I think about the implications of bias beyond my role as an assessor, beyond my role as a doctor. We all have unconscious biases. We can think about them, detect them, bring them to consciousness. And then we can change them.

We can also think carefully about the words that we use and what they might reveal or suggest of our feelings, and how those words may be interpreted by the listener. And sometimes this may mean making changes to our language and our actions for which we feel ill-prepared.

'Hello, beautiful lady,' said Mum, and the beautiful lady looked down at Mum in her wheelchair, his Gandalf beard flowing exuberantly from his chin. He leaned down, the better to hear her question, which I knew would relate to the price of the chipped and weathered terracotta pots that were arranged around his feet alongside a lidless pressure cooker and a pair of melamine trays featuring robins in brambles, and other essentials. We'd been for a jaunt along the river in her little town, and Mum had spotted these treasures as I wheeled her homewards across the car park of the small shopping precinct near her house, and I knew she'd want those pots.

To be fair, Mum had to assess all comers by their shoes, socks and legwear; her spine had telescoped dramatically in the last years of her life and her view now did not include the sun or the moon, the tops of trees moving in the wind or human faces, unless they chose to sit by her, and even then to meet her gaze they might have to tuck themselves a little lower, bending sideways like wedding guests trying to plant a kiss under a cart-wheel hat. The pot seller was wearing sandals and a flowing skirt with yellow daisies. Even so, 'beautiful lady' seemed a bold greeting. He couldn't hear Mum's enquiry as to the price of the pots, so he leaned closer and now Mum could see a large grey metal cross dangling round his neck and was distracted from the purchase of old terracotta.

'Where did you get that lovely cross?' she asked.

The pot seller looked disconcerted and replied, 'Umm . . . in a charity shop.'

Mum was delighted. 'Ah, Croatia, I've been there . . . and are you a regular churchgoer?'

He replied apologetically in the negative and she sniffed. I handed over a fiver for the pots as quickly as I could before she could get on to subjects beyond gender and religion – abortion perhaps or Brexit.

Mum's capacity for embarrassing her children had always been limitless. When I was nine, she made a skirt for me out of an old green brocade curtain for a tap-dancing performance and seemed impervious to the fact that every other mother had followed the instructions and sourced the red polka dot fabric demanded by the dance teacher.

'It moves nicely,' said Mum. 'I've cut it on the bias.'

She jumped over small children when one of my fellow pupils fainted on stage during Parents' Day and lifted the child out through an adjacent window so the performance could continue. Mum compelled international ferries to delay their departure, drove up the bus lane at Trafalgar Square, broke (broke!) into our school to retrieve a raincoat after the end of term. She struck up conversations with strangers, always, on buses or trains, at concerts, in libraries and waiting rooms, on ski lifts or kayaks or the flight deck of an aircraft carrier, and habitually began such interactions with, 'So where are you from?'

Ah, such a question! And at first I think that surely anyone can see that her question does not mean 'Where are you from? Where are you really from?' with its terrible background sound, like an old LP on a turntable, a hissing 'I do not care where you are from – I do not want you here.' I think of Mum's Christmas cards hanging in lines along her hallway, through the kitchen, up the stairs, from people all over the world, strangers who have become friends, for whom that question was the start of getting to know one another. I think of the disappointment expressed by many, especially by older people, when they are told of the difficulties posed by that question, and they say, 'But I'm just being friendly,' and then they say, 'Isn't it just being curious and interested in someone?'

My daughter wisely cautions me. 'I don't think you can write about this, Mum. It's too difficult. You just can't say, "Where do you come from?" People need to stop asking that.'

I know I must treat this subject with respect, but I want to learn. I realise that there will be those who will say, 'This is nonsense. Of course it is OK to ask where someone is from,' and many will be hurt by the imputation that their words carry an unpleasant meaning. These are good people, who are indeed curious and interested and friendly. And there will be others who will say, 'Can't you see that this question comes with poison arrows? We do not need to discuss it,' because they have been put down, bullied and suffered cruel discrimination. I have thought about it and read and listened to those for whom this question can pose problems, and I hope that I understand now a little better why it is difficult sometimes to be asked, 'So where are you from?'

I listen to Jamil, as he explains. 'Well, OK, Dr Pollock, it feels as if you're checking up on whether my training has been good enough.' Jamil is right. I am partly doing that, because as well as being interested in the life that has taken him across continents, there can sometimes be an issue with those who have had their training in a different country. Some medical schools place more focus on the science of medicine than on physical examination or communication skills, for example, and I would like to ensure that my expectations of that young doctor are realistic, so that I can provide support if it is needed. But then I realise that every time I work with a new doctor, wherever they trained, I am listening and watching, because even within UK medical schools there is variation – for example, in some there is almost no teaching in geriatric medicine – and in any case each of these doctors is different, and despite the delightful claim of a Health Secretary some years ago, that he would ensure that all doctors will be above average, this cannot be, and there will be one who is charming but scatty, who needs reminding of details, and another who is methodical but whose lumpen questioning will not elicit a subtle emotional truth from their patient, and yet others who have simply had a disastrous morning, their child ill with chickenpox or a near miss on the motorway. I'm aware too that I may make a mistake, for any number of reasons, so the younger doctor with whom I am working is looking out for me, as well as forming their own opinions about my competence. Jamil and I may talk one day about where he comes from and where I come from, as part of a conversation of discovery, but I can see that it may be judgemental if I ask that question early in our working relationship, before we have learned other things about one another.

Jamil also explains (and he is courageous to do so) that there is an implication. 'I can see that you're not from round here – you do not fit in. To be honest, Dr Pollock, if you think I'm really good and you say where do you come from, it sounds as if you are sort of surprised that I might be any good.' I feel uncomfortable when he says this, because I recognise that I may indeed have been thinking that very thought and I am ashamed.

I am learning, slowly, to think about what I am asking and why. I must check with myself whether I would ask this question of a senior colleague. Or of someone who is white. For my patients, for the many who are good, kind, curious people, and for myself, I learn that there are better questions. Have you had a good day? Or a long day? Or both? What are your plans for the next step in your career? Do you enjoy working here? Do you have a holiday coming up? Do you have any time for hobbies? What makes you happy?

I'm so proud of our country when we get it right, when we build communities that are diverse and accepting, societies in which we work together and learn more about one another, celebrating both our individuality and our similarities. I love that what Jo Cox said in her maiden speech to Parliament in 2015 is true, that we are 'far more united, and have far more in common with one another, than that which divides us'. Yet it is simultaneously true that we are all different, and that one black, Asian or white person is as different from the next black, Asian or white person, as I am from my neighbour or from the tired woman who runs the petrol station early in the morning – it is not race that differentiates but simply our unique characteristics, which have nothing to do with race and everything to do with temperament, experience, opportunity.

We have such a long way to go. I listen to a GP, as she describes a consultation with a patient whom she has known for years. The patient has had problems with drugs and alcohol, and it had taken that GP a long time to build a trusting relationship with him, but they get on well together now; he tells her everything. She explains that for this new symptom he needs to be seen by a specialist at the hospital, and the patient tells her, 'Well, that's OK, but I don't want to see one of those foreign doctors.'

The GP smiles as she recalls this interaction, and says, 'I was wearing my sari. Like I do every day.'

I have such a long way to go. I watch a short video made for a social enterprise organisation, Patient Voices, dedicated to unearthing insight into all aspects of health and care through first-person stories. Among the compelling stories collected by this team over two decades – stories of healing, loss, fear and courage, trouble and resolution – is one made in 2021 by Sun Sander-Jackson, a nurse who now leads the inclusion team at the hospital in which I work. At first I struggle to understand some of Sun's words. There's a bit I can't quite catch, then I realise that she is talking of her younger self: 'little nurse me'.

'The day I left home,' says Sun in the video, 'my mum

whispered into my ear, "You will be a star. Rise up over the sky and shine through."'

Sun continues, 'Little nurse me, confident and full of life, arrived in Somerset.'

She looked at the beautiful scenery, smelled the fresh air. 'It was a bit cold, but I don't care. I have a warm heart.'

She describes the hope and pride with which she started asking, 'Can you feel my heart?' And the reply was: 'I can hear your accent.'

'Can you see my smile?'

'I can see you are Asian.'

'Can you see my potential?'

'I can see you're not from here.'

'Can you pronounce my name?'

'I will call you "nurse".'

Sun describes how she would 'hold a beautiful white hand, brush their blond hair gently so they would look beautiful for their family,' and how she 'put a plaster on every wound to the heart', and how 'walking home under a dark sky, little nurse me was not sure if the heavy rain fell from the sky or from her eyes'.

'Do I belong here?' she asks herself over and over again.

Sun describes a knock on her door. She is not so little any more, and here is a new nurse, a nervous smile. 'Can you help me? I am not from here . . .'

Sun's story of dignity, of community and understanding, of strength, stops me in my tracks. In her gentle, quiet voice she describes the growing sense of belonging, the healing of her heart, the plasters falling away.

'I can't feel the scars unless I touch them.'

Sun whispers her message to the new nurse. 'You will be a star. You will rise up over the sky and shine through.'

I am rendered breathless by her generosity.

You can listen to Sun's story, and find others here: Patient Voices: Little nurse me grows: https://www. patientvoices.org.uk/flv/1349pv384.htm

14. Uncertainty

I'm at a fund-raising event in a garden in London, and I can see an older woman sitting on a bench who's in trouble, so I sit beside her and ask if there's anything I can do.

When she speaks her voice is very quiet. 'I need my tablets,' she says, 'from my handbag.'

So I lift up her handbag, which is just under the bench, right by her feet, although she can't reach it, cannot move at all, and I get out her tablets. I already know what they will be from the way she rolls her eyes to convey apology, awkwardness, thanks, even though her face is expressionless and rigid. I pop two of the Madopar out of a packet, and there's a bottle of water in her bag just for this moment. She manages to get the bottle to her lips, the tablets are swallowed, and we sit together for a few minutes until her movement is restored, and now she raises her eyebrows at me and pushes a strand of hair off her face.

We talk. She's come from Cornwall, a long way – and we share words of admiration for the specialist who helps with her Parkinson's disease.

'How did you get here?' I ask.

'Oh,' she says, 'I drove.'

I blink.

Parkinson's disease in its later stages can torment with its unpredictability. It seizes you then lets you go from hour to hour or, later, even from minute to minute, and people who have that illness must play grandmother's footsteps, using the moments when its back is turned to dart forward, do what they want to do, and then the Parks snaps back round and freezes the patient with its stare, daring them to try to move, to wobble and fall. The medicines are partially effective – tablets enhance the supply of dopamine, the key neurotransmitter that is inexplicably depleted in this illness – but they have side effects, and the benefit they provide is short-lived, as the chemicals involved are metabolised quickly, so only a few hours after each dose the brain encounters another shortage of dopamine. People with Parkinson's disease find they're on a bumpy sea – at the peak of the wave, with too much dopamine, they develop unwanted movements, limbs twitching or writhing, eyes blinking. As the dopamine wears off, movement is slowed – in a bad trough someone with Parkinson's may freeze completely. Maddeningly, painful cramps can be caused by both too much and too little dopamine. But in the sweet spot movement is restored, enough perhaps for a walk in a wood or a trip to the cinema or a drive from Cornwall to London.

People who have Parkinson's disease, and the specialist doctors and nurses who look after them, spend a great deal of time working out how to smooth these waves, adjusting doses, timings and formulations to keep that supply of dopamine steady – but people with this illness get caught out. Something they have eaten may disrupt the absorption of the tablets, or changes in the levels of beneficial bacteria in the gut may affect the availability of the drug, or the dopamine supply is used up more quickly than usual by unexpected exertion or conversation or by smiles or hugs or holding the new baby. And the unpredictability of this disease and its treatment applies not only to movement but to other features such as hallucinations, distressing salivation and sudden drops in blood pressure.

I watch with such admiration the adaptability and patience that many older people muster in the face of uncertainty. I hear Marnie's plans to get to her granddaughter's wedding, her subtle enquiries as to the distance from the church to the village hall, where there are loos, and any obstacles that might lie in her path, because those three broad granite steps at the church porch that will provide a perfect setting for a family photograph will be a time-consuming barrier for Marnie. I meet Pat, planning for Roy – every invitation to a community centre or a pub lunch, every hospital appointment or trip to the audiologist evaluated for its potential for upset, for Roy to get lost or cross, and I see how Pat anticipates Roy's mood and will change their plans if it is one of his bad days.

I watch as Richard makes arrangements for Jan for trips and holidays that are surely unrealistic, because she is too frail, yet he makes them happen and returns triumphant with a photograph of Niagara Falls, Jan smiling beneath a misted rainbow. But I intervene with Mum, who has booked a trip to Spain, a week-long camino path pilgrimage to the cathedral in Santiago de Compostela, after I read the requirements – stout walking boots, a day pack – and I mention that she has been unable to walk for more than thirty yards for some time, and then only with a stick and a steady arm to hold, and I remind her too that each of my stepfather's stoical steps now takes him little further than half the length of his shoe. Mum says, 'We can sit on a rock and wait until they come back to collect us,' and while there is being adaptable and optimistic, there is also being wilful and having not enough regard for others. Mum concedes and chooses a hotel in Devon instead, beside the sea, and I feel mean but relieved.

There is a graph on a slide provided by a cardiologist during her talk, which shows trajectories of illness, our independence plotted against our age, and a hundred years ago our lives might have ended quite suddenly even when we were young, so the line on the graph starts horizontal – all is well – then it falls abruptly, a vertical drop cause by a lethal infection (polio, say, or tetanus or typhoid) or by an accident. We have largely eradicated such existential uncertainty from youthful lives, and so we plan our futures – Friday night, the summer holidays – confident that we will wake up tomorrow, as fit and able in six months' time as we are today. The same is not true for older people. Some illnesses have a gradual but still predictable course. For those with an incurable cancer, for example, or progressive kidney failure without dialysis, the illness is likely to cause a gradual decline in mental and physical energy, so the line on their graph slopes smoothly downwards, and sometimes it can become relatively straightforward to predict when that line will reach the bottom of the graph. But the graph for heart failure is quite different. Heart failure is a condition often characterised by periods of relative stability punctuated by sudden episodes of decompensation, followed by treatment that brings relative recovery, so the line of life on the heart failure graph looks like a row of irregular battlements, with each dip followed by a step back up. I have watched my patients as they cope with the uncertainty that brings, because they and I both know that alongside the episodes that might only thwart a Christmas plan, one of those episodes will be the last and there'll be deterioration without recovery, and that dear heart will say 'enough', and that event, that terminal decline, may happen over a period of days or weeks, with some time to plan, or it may happen quite suddenly.

Even for older people who do not have any of these conditions that focus the mind so sharply on mortality, as the years pass and we move into our later eighties and nineties, the prospect of suddenly not being is a real one. We have to come to terms with that idea that we might have watched television or ordered our shopping online or played bridge with three friends and go to sleep one night and not wake. Conversely my most frail patient, who looks as if a breath of wind would carry her away, this old, old woman transparent with age may turn out to have a core of steel and defy expectations to live another year or longer.

I read of Ulrich Beck, a German social scientist who died in 2015, having spent his career studying our attitude to risk. So much is now controlled – shipwrecks and cholera and runaway horses – and things that are not controlled are at least predictable; sophisticated forecasts can tell us that tomorrow the sun will shine and we can make hay, confident that the following days will not bring a downpour and mouldy spores to lace the cut grass. Beck asked of his own country in 1992, *Isn't Germany . . . an Eldorado of bureaucratically organised care and caution?* But Beck was not speaking words of admiration for his orderly, risk-averse country. Rather, he was sounding a warning; our perception of safety, that all risk can be eliminated, is misplaced. We may mitigate one risk only to find that in doing so we have increased the risk of something else, and many of the risks we now face – from climate change or financial turbulence or mass migration in response to violence or hunger – are too big to be managed by single states and require global coordination. Beck wrote, *Searching for predictability in the face of an open future is a daunting task.*

Beck's words ring true on a personal scale too, in our kitchens or on the familiar pavements during a short walk with a small dog. As we become older, predictability becomes evasive, and the task of finding it may seem daunting. How do we best come to terms with that uncertainty?

Kim says crossly of her mother (there's a long history there) that she's always fretting – she worries about the boiler and the gas bill and the possibility of mice because it's easier to worry about those than about dying, but I'm not sure that's true; I think Kim's mum's capacity for worrying is limitless, and dying may well be on the list of things she worries about, though the others are easier to voice.

Kim's mother is not alone. My patients do not all face the future with equanimity. I think of Thomas Hardy's Tess Durbeyfield, whose life held such cruel complications. Tess looks in a mirror as she acknowledges anniversaries, the date upon which she was assaulted, the dates of the birth and the death of her baby son, and her own birthday, and she suddenly thinks *that there was yet another date, of greater importance to her than those; that of her own death . . . a day which lay sly and unseen among all the other days of the year, giving no sign or sound when she annually passed over it; but not the less surely there. When was it? Why did she not feel the chill of each yearly encounter with such a cold relation?*

What have I learned about uncertainty from older people and those who love them? How do we deal with the fact that on one day that feels like any other day there may be an ending? How do you make things as good as they can be when you don't know how long you've got?

I have learned that most older people with whom I talk do not fear death itself – if there is a feeling of chill, it is the manner of dying, rather than its fact, that is the culprit. I have thus learned that talking about the manner of dying is often helpful. It can be helpful to know that death – expected death – is usually peaceful, and that it involves increasing fatigue and often long periods of sleep, which evolve into periods of uncon- sciousness from which we may wake, and we may talk or listen a little before sleeping or losing consciousness again, and that at some point in one of those periods of unconsciousness (periods of which we are unaware and of which we have no recollection during those increasingly brief spells of waking) we will breathe out and we will not take another breath. It helps to know that in older age even sudden death is often quiet, an extinction of light that seems almost simple and does not appear to involve distress or maybe even awareness, and a book may lie still open in a hand. It helps too to know that most often, when someone is dying, physical suffering can be alleviated – that the symptoms such as pain or breathlessness that may accompany death are the symptoms of illness rather than dying and can be addressed.

I have learned also that for some of my patients transition to a next world does, in fact, hold dark horrors, and for some confession – to a priest, a friend, a relative, even a stranger, a nurse in the night – is a powerful balm, but a few cannot summon hope of redemption, and once, only once, have I witnessed in an older person an ending full of fear, even to the end. She was consumed by fear, and I wish she had not been for it served no purpose for her.

I have noticed over several decades that many of us have stopped believing in hell but retain confidence in heaven, and I have seen that for many an end to existence, whatever happens next, does not seem to pose as much concern as one might think. I am struck by the serene philosophy of many of those who have lived very long lives, which seems sometimes to match that of the very young. I am told a story by a mother of her twelve-year-old son's interview for a scholarship at a highly academic school, her nervous wait in the car, and she asked him afterwards how it had gone and what the questions had been. The boy replied, 'Well, I think it was OK, and at the end they asked me what was the thing I most feared and I said "Oblivion" and they looked impressed and wrote that down, but I meant the ride at Alton Towers.'

Many of my patients retain or develop – because they didn't always feel like this – a calm and accepting view of the future, whether of non-existence or an afterlife. I am asked by a retired clergyman whether, in my experience, people of faith approach death with more confidence, and I think that for many the conviction that comes with rock-solid faith is secure and beautiful. Yet others seem to manage perfectly well without it, but what may be shared regardless of faith or its absence is a sadness at saying goodbye, at leaving this world that holds familiar faces, this planet with wavelets upon which sunlight dances.

I have learned too that older people and those who love them may fear being 'kept alive', overburdened with treatment that might postpone death, and it can come as a profound relief to realise that this does not have to be the case. When considering what treatment is appropriate towards the end of a life, medical teams must take heed of their patient's wishes and views, which can include a rejection of life-prolonging treatment. We have work to do, both to speak and to respect those wishes.

I have learned that many of my patients find relief in planning and resolution. I have learned that for many comfort is found in sharing plans for a quiet resting place or a spectacular send-off. I think of Maisie, who arranged for her body to be cremated and, mindful of the behaviour of ash in a breeze, had her remains made into golf balls, to be lofted into the sea by her grandchildren from a clifftop near her home. I think of Terry, who was dying of lung cancer but would not allow this fact – 'I am fighting it, doc. I am going to win this' – and we spoke of his family and how they had not visited, 'because they care more for the dog than for me,' but after a few more sentences Terry and I considered that perhaps they had not visited because they did not realise that he was ill, was dying, that his insistence on fighting his battle alone was keeping them away. His certainty in his victory over cancer was misplaced, and so Terry picked up the phone and later that afternoon they were there round his bed, with roars of laughter and tears wiped on an oily handkerchief, and Terry's brother bundling him into a wheelchair, all bony wrists and ankles and a chest drain collecting beery-looking fluid into a cylinder, his brother taking him out 'for a breath of fresh air' as Terry patted his pyjama pocket for his Rizlas and rolling tobacco.

I sit in clinic with John, who has had a heart attack, and he would like to know why exactly that happened and what are his chances of having another, and, more importantly, when will it be. I can answer the first two questions, but I am stuck on the third and I make the mistake of saying that I do not have a crystal ball. John gives me a disappointed look and shuffles the paper on which he has been taking notes back into a blue Manila folder. He had expected better and I should not have used such flippant language in the face of his wish to know his future. I could have acknowledged his anxiety and spoken about the medication he is on, which will reduce but not abolish the risk of another heart attack. I could have shared with him the difficulty of living with uncertainty and helped him to plan and to make the most of whatever time he has, because if he and I do not do that, John's time will be spent worrying and waiting – the efforts to defer or avert another heart attack will be worth nothing if he must spend that time in a state of fear.

Jennifer Ouellet is an assistant professor of medicine at Yale. She was named Outstanding Junior Clinician Educator of the Year at the American Geriatrics Society in 2023. The junior clinicians she teaches are anyone and everyone who might care for older people, and what she teaches them is what matters most to their patients.

One of Jennifer's senior colleagues, Professor Mary Tinetti, came up with the five Ms to describe the work of geriatricians. We focus on the Mind, Mobility, Medications and Multicomplexity, because our patients often have several conditions, but may also have a party to attend or a concert in which to perform or a son whose release is imminent from prison, and we may not be able to address one issue without at least acknowledging the others. Tinetti's fifth M was 'What Matters', and this is where Jennifer Ouellet has concentrated her energy.

'"What Matters" is one of the pivotal Ms,' said Jen

in her acceptance speech. 'You really can't make decisions without knowing what matters to our patients and what they're hoping that their healthcare can help them achieve. That provides us an anchor in the face of uncertainty in the work that we do.'

I have realised over the years that for many of my patients Beck's daunting search for *predictability in the face of an open future* is a search that needs to be firmly abandoned. We can gather knowledge and understanding of our bodies. We can be aware of averages, that people with this or that condition might usually live another three years, or five, but we must also accept that not one of us is precisely average. Doctors need to be honest and to share uncertainty. This is not to say that we should duck a frank conversation when someone's prognosis is clearly very limited – we can explain that our patient is likely to die within days or weeks at the same time as ensuring there's understanding that we may yet be proved wrong. We can put figures on the likelihood of an event, and each of us will look at such figures with relief or with alarm, as a 10% risk of a heart attack to one person may seem dangerously high, yet the same figure may be cheerily dismissed by another. But with regard to many of the events that can destabilise life in older age – falls and fractures and infections that can precipitate a sudden decline in function – and in terms of recovery from such events, which may be smooth or stuttering, we can only do our best and do the work to reduce risk and to ameliorate what we can. Our colleagues in palliative care put it well when they talk with their patients of 'parallel planning' – we can each 'hope for the best and prepare for the rest'. And, of course, 'the rest' is the difficult bit, the unknown. But as Jennifer Ouellet puts it, a shared understanding of what matters most – individual, idiosyncratic, human – provides a steadying anchor.

For many years I have watched my patients as they weigh up their futures, and thoughts of Hardy's 'sly and unseen' day are put aside. The decision is made, unvoiced, to live lightly and well.

I listen to Edie, who has been in and out of hospital with her sagging heart and an infection that crept from a sore on her leg to take up residence in one of the discs between her vertebrae, an infection that took weeks to sort out, during which time she had COVID too, and recovered, and went home to her fat white cat, and we touch upon the future when I meet her in clinic to check that her infection has cleared completely and to adjust her heart medicines once more. She's wearing a dress of stretchy fabric, autumn flowers with a zip down the front, and her white cardigan, and cream sandals on the last hole of each buckle over her feet. 'Edie,' I ask, 'do you ever feel a bit afraid – afraid of dying or what happens next?'

Edie looks at me sideways, a look that says, whyever would I think about that, even though she almost *has* died, twice. Then she leans in. 'I says my prayers every night.' She pauses and adds, 'I'm not religious, mind.'

Edie looks around to check that no one will hear her confession of undue spirituality. 'But I says, thank you, God, for my lovely life.'

I am smiling at this, its suggestion of accomplishment and preparedness, when Edie adds firmly, 'And I'll talk to you again in the morning.'

15. Sadness and Hope

In 1957 my father's middle sister, my Aunt Cecily, had a baby called Harriet, and Harriet was wrapped in a soft blanket when she was born, by a midwife who arranged that blanket carefully and tucked its ends in firmly in order that it would not come undone when the baby was put into the hands of my aunt, who could then look down on the perfect face of her baby and would not have to see that behind that still and perfect face, Harriet's head was incomplete. She had no brain and no chance of life.

Despite the care of that midwife, Cecily descended into despair and became unable to look after her older daughter or herself. She could not eat or sleep, and she fell silent and sat with her eyes open, her limbs remaining in whatever posture they had adopted hours previously. Pills proved ineffective and eventually Cecily was admitted to a psychiatric hospital, where she was diagnosed with catatonic depression.

Dermot is an anaesthetist.

'I'll tell you my favourite list,' he says. We have been talking about job satisfaction and Dermot has revealed some great saucy theatre gossip, but now he is serious and he leans forward to confide.

'My favourite list is ECT.'

I look disbelievingly at him because ECT, electrocon- vulsive therapy, involves Dermot anaesthetising people who have severe intractable depression and giving them a muscle relaxant so that an electric shock strong enough to induce a convulsion can be delivered to their brain twice a week for a period of six to twelve weeks.

'You actually like doing that list?' I ask.

Dermot replies, 'I like watching those patients get- ting better.'

My aunt's psychiatrist in 1957 arranged for the admin- istration of ECT, which since its inception in 1938 has been regarded by many as barbaric. Even now there are debates as to its effectiveness, although there have been randomised controlled trials that show it to be of benefit for select groups of patients, but there remain concerns about its side effects and it is recommended as a treatment only when all other treatments have failed. For Cecily the ECT worked, and our house is dotted with her pen-and-ink sketches, paintings and silk-screen prints. An angular lion that she carved from stone sits, small and solid, on our doorstep.

It was not the first time Cecily had ECT, nor the last – she developed a psychotic depression in her late seventies when her second husband became unwell with a rapidly progressive dementia, but she emerged from hospital one spring after a final course of ECT to watch trout swim in the chalk stream near her home once more.

Depression is the commonest mental health problem suffered by older people and one of the more treatable, although treatment is not always successful. The diagnosis and treatment of depression in older people usually falls to GPs and geriatricians, but for those whose depression does not respond to initial treatment, or whose illness is atypical or catastrophic, we turn with relief to psychiatrists who specialise in the care of older people and their teams, who understand the complexities that ageing brings to the management of mental illness. The treatment of depression is complicated enough without throwing in physical illness, frailty or pain, and too often the double blow of dementia. Depression may be mistaken for dementia (by the sufferer as well as by their family or professionals – how frightening that must be). Sometimes the opposite happens, as dementia can mimic depression, and very often depression may accompany dementia. In addition, these sad conditions in combination do not respond to treatment in the ways that might be expected of one alone. The work of restoration may be laborious and incomplete. We stumble at the first fence, as even the identification of depression is not straightforward.

I see Avril out of the corner of my eye while I sit at the nurses' station. I've been listening to Rashid, one of the medical students, presenting a new patient. Rashid has hit it off with Brian. 'He played good cricket, Dr Pollock,' Rashid tells me, and he's gone through Brian's medication list and asked me a perspicacious question about why Brian is still taking a tablet, tamsulosin, to help him pee when he has had a long-term catheter for over a year. Rashid and I have talked about how easy it is for medicines to remain on a patient's list long after the need for them has gone, and I've shown Rashid a Royal College of Physicians article that described these as 'historical prescribing remnants', which evokes the painstaking archaeological search through records that may be required to expose such errors. I score the tamsulosin off Brian's chart and Rashid works out how to amend his discharge summary to let Brian's GP know of that change.

My attention has moved now to Avril. She is sitting by her bed, her left leg stretched out on a stool, an off-white plaster extending from foot to thigh. The television is on but she isn't watching it and her book is unopened. I know that this morning Avril declined her session with the physiotherapist, explaining that she hadn't slept and was too tired, and she said the same yesterday and the day before. I watch as Avril looks out of the window. Her eyes are empty; she is not watching, just looking.

Scott Murray is the Liaison Psychiatry Nurse Specialist

and Dr Niall Campbell is a consultant in liaison psychiatry at the Borders General Hospital, and together they wrote a sensible article about depression:

> *Before we go diagnosing everyone with depression, we should remember to allow what's normal.*
>
> *It is normal to feel afraid in hospital, being surrounded by the sick, frail and dying. It's normal to feel awful after surgery and normal to feel a bit despondent if we're not progressing as fast as we would like. It's normal to be fed up being in a 6-bedded bay, surrounded by equally bored and sick people, when it's noisy and you can't hear or see the telly because you don't have your glasses and hearing aid. It's normal to feel miserable because it's been a week since you've had a visitor.*
>
> *Being low in mood will often be a normal adjustment reaction to being unwell, to suffering some loss, or just to being in hospital. Before we call everyone depressed, let's help people to 'Normalise not Pathologise' their reactions.*

Rashid and I talk about whether Avril is looking depressed because she is in hospital and she'll feel better when she gets home, or whether she is now so depressed that she cannot get well enough to go home and whether she might need active treatment (an antidepressant tablet, as we have no access to psychotherapy for inpatients, and precious little for outpatients either) in the hope of improving her mood enough that she may be able to gather the strength to tackle her physical recovery.

'I could do a GDS,' Rashid offers. 'I need one for my portfolio.' He is bright and engaging with his spiky hair and a gold earring.

'OK then, Rashid,' I say, 'but please can you approach that gently and talk with her? Don't just do the question-naire.'

Although the Geriatric Depression Scale is a tool rec-ommended for the detection of depression, it makes me shiver.

Rashid is gone for ages. I see some other patients and he returns, his concern visible.

'Well, that was sad. I hadn't really looked at the ques-tions properly before we started so I was just reading them out and it's asking does she feel hopeless and does she feel helpless and does she feel *worthless*.' His merry face is troubled. 'It felt a bit heartless really.'

I ask what Avril scored.

Rashid looks at his notes. 'Eleven,' he says. 'That's loads. More than five is depressed. But I don't know. Some of the questions didn't help, because it says, "base your answers on how you've felt in the last week," and she's been in hospital for about a month and she can't stand up because of the leg, so of course she'll say yes to being bored and helpless.'

'What else did you talk about?' I ask Rashid.

'Oh, she was a librarian, and she used to live with her friend, but her friend died, and she really likes Italy, so we talked about that a bit and at the end she said she thought she wasn't ever going to get to Italy again.'

Sometimes – maybe often – we are so bound up in the medicine and the nursing, the blood test results and the recording of oxygen saturations, the administration of a little cup of pills and checking that the pressure mattress is working, that we don't notice our patients' descent into despair. And, too often, my patient does not feel able to tell me of the hopelessness that lies heavy on her bed in the night and that robs her of volition in the day.

Rashid and I go to see Avril together, and as I walk towards her I note that Gwennie, who was in the bed opposite, has been moved to a side room because she is dying and that Marilyn in the bed next to Avril has been distressed and calling at night, and Marilyn's shouting has gone on for several nights, I know, as we've been trying to work out what to do about it, and I also know that Noreen, on Avril's other side, is bound up in her own problems, and is heavy and bad-tempered and mutters ill-willed comments about the nurses, and her family visit but are sullen and hostile. Sometimes a bay of patients carries a therapeutic energy all of its own, a camaraderie, and at other times the dynamic shifts in a bad direction. I perch on Avril's footstool and we talk of the plan for the plaster and how last week's chest infection is resolving, though the cough may persist for some weeks yet. Avril tips her head down and sideways, looking at the hem of her pink dressing gown.

'Avril, I think you must wonder whether you're ever going to get out of here,' I say, and her eyes meet mine, wide, and she gives a tiny nod and leans forward, and glances at Marilyn.

'It's like the Seven Circles . . .' she whispers, before tailing off.

'Of Hell, Avril. I know, and I'm really sorry.'

She shakes her head, a very small movement, and she says, 'I can't . . .'

I take her hand and I say, 'Avril, I need to tell you something. I have done this job for a long time. And I can usually tell who is going to get better and get home. And you, Avril –' I turn her hand so that our hands are clasped, to make a grip that she cannot help but mirror, to make a pact – 'you are going to get better. I don't always get this right, and it's going to take time, but from what I know you are going to get walking again and you are going to get home.'

We make assumptions about what our patients know or are guessing, and it's too easy to get those assumptions wrong. We do it when we suspect someone may be dying, and too often that person shares our suspicion, or his family guesses, but we do not talk about it. We behave as if all is well, tomorrow will be another day, and we put out forms for blood tests when we should instead drop everything and talk about death. But we miss the opposite situation too. We have our 'board round' each morning, when nurses, doctors and therapists discuss the plans for each patient, the targets of home or a move to a rehabilitation setting because things will take time but will eventually come right. We may not realise that our patient is unaware of our optimism or does not share it. I worked for years with Salvador, who had come from Spain and settled in Britain. He cared with passion for the patients in one of our community hospitals, who might be there for several weeks, arriving like half-drowned kittens after debilitating illnesses and traumas. Salvador would take me to see the new patients on my ward round each week and would throw open the door to a room and announce – loudly, everyone would know it – 'This is Mrs Brandon. Mrs Brandon is a *fighter*,' and often I suspected that Mrs Brandon hadn't reckoned herself to be much of a fighter, but now here was this jolly Spanish doctor announcing a new future and there would be the trace of a smile, the bracing of shoulders. Well, if you insist. Sometimes we just need the right conversation and encouragement. It sounds almost trivial but it isn't.

For others around whom depression has wrapped its tethers, medicines can work. Frank, thin and nervy, beset with palpitations that didn't show up on heart recordings, needed mirtazapine for several weeks before his sleep and appetite were restored (antidepressants aren't a quick fix as a rule) and he went off to the races in his winkle-pickers and told me of ice cream in the sun and backing the winner in the last race of the day. Over the years I have watched patients like Frank get better and would like to believe that their improvement has been down to my prescription. I have seen people unravel when the medication they have been taking for years has been discontinued, inadvertently or in a well-meaning attempt to tackle side effects, and they may need rescuing because a proportion of people absolutely need and depend upon that antidepressant – for many antidepressants incontrovertibly work. For others there are better alternatives.

I like my colleagues in old age psychiatry; they seem to share a ready kindness. There's a sympathy to them; they've seen horrors, heard many sad stories. Depression and other mental illnesses can spring from nowhere into a life previously sunny, but these conditions are too often fuelled by poverty, neglect, grief, cruelty or pain. Psychiatrists and the nurses and therapists who work with them somehow maintain a gentle optimism that things can be made better. Dr Aziz tells me, 'You say no one wants to be referred to a geriatrician. You try being a *psycho*geriatrician.'

They make me smile.

I must write carefully about depression. I have not had depression myself and although I have cared for and treated a great many people who have depression alongside other conditions, I am not a specialist in this illness. So I present this chapter with respect to those who know much more than I do, and with respect to people who have contended so courageously with this illness. I hope it will help to share some of the things I have learned from my patients and their families, and from my own friends and family, and from good colleagues – things that I have found helpful.

I talk with Dr Lucy Knight, who is an old age psychiatrist. Like many she has a waning enthusiasm for a medicine-based approach.

'Pills can work,' she says, 'for somewhere between one in three and one in nine people, and we do use them, but to be honest we need to have more humility. We don't really understand depression.'

I raise my eyebrows and Lucy explains.

'Well, it's a diagnosis that reflects a series of constructs developed out of observation and debate and consensus. We don't have sound science; we don't have scans and biometric markers. We don't even properly understand the effects of medications on the brain. Sometimes I think the main effect of antidepressants is just to drop your sodium.'

She gives me a wry smile for which I have sympathy. A low sodium level is a common and frustrating problem in older people and is often seen in those who have neurodegenerative conditions like strokes or dementia, but it has several other causes too, such as heart failure. Thus many conditions that increase our likelihood of becoming depressed are also associated with a low sodium level, and antidepressants, alongside several other medicines, can make that sodium worse rather than better. Prescribing for people with depression can become a patch of thorns.

Lucy continues, 'There's also this huge overlap of depression with frailty, because fatigue is such a big part of both conditions, and there's another big overlap of depression with cognitive problems, and we know that antidepressants don't generally work for people with dementia.'

I ask Lucy for her approach.

'First I'd say try to understand why it's happened.'

Dr Mark Upton, one of Lucy's colleagues, agrees.

'I ask myself why is this patient presenting with these symptoms now? Because on the face of it, if a diagnosis – say depression, mood changes, cognitive changes – does not make sense from the history, then the diagnosis as a whole needs questioning.'

Lucy says, 'Stop making things worse. Try to reduce the other medicines as far as possible – plenty of them can lower mood. Look at the environment – hospital is pretty toxic obviously, but there may be difficult things going on at home too. And loneliness kills.'

Her face brightens.

'We all need to feel useful. I'd say ninety per cent of the time we need to do less of something medical and more of something social.'

At home that evening I am in the kitchen, evaluating the options presented by a fridge that seems to contain only condiments. Our younger daughter is due to return to university imminently, and I hear her say, 'I am going to miss you sooo much.' I turn to reciprocate and find that she is talking to the dog. Later, I tell her about Lucy's views about depression, about the social aspects, and my daughter pauses while she makes us cups of tea.

'We learned something like that at college,' she says. 'Three things for when you're feeling down. Do something for yourself. Do something for someone else. Go outside.'

'It's given me the heart to live again.'

Christine uses the back of her arm to sweep back her hair; it's blowing around her face, the wind funnelled between the buildings of an East End housing estate. Clouds scud in a blue sky. She's on TV being interviewed by psychologist Professor Tanya Byron. The programme is exploring different ways of tackling mental health problems like depression.

At the start of the interview Christine looks shy and uneasy. 'I was very depressed after my husband died – you know.' She is swaying from foot to foot, and while she talks she's trying to stop the little seeds from blowing away, which she has been pressing into the soil in a pot on the bench. She cups her hands over them. 'I said to my doctor I haven't got no life, because we used to do everything together.'

Tanya looks sympathetic and asks, 'Did you feel you needed someone just to listen?'

'Yeah,' Christine says uncertainly, and she looks around, her eyes saying, 'no,' because it wasn't listening she needed, she's just being polite. She continues more firmly. 'And to give me some aim, because I used to just get up and be depressed, just lying on the settee.' She gives an apologetic giggle. 'I didn't even put the telly on.'

'How did you feel then?' asks Tanya.

Christine's eyes dart from side to side. 'I felt like I was off me head really.'

Tanya asks, 'Did you like it, coming here?'

'Yeah . . . at first I was all right when I was here, and then the feelings would come back when I was at home . . . you know –' Christine suddenly looks terrified. The memory is there at the edge of her mind, bug-eyed cruel depression scraping at her door.

Tanya rescues her by asking, 'And were you a gardener before?'

'Oh no,' says Christine.

'So this is a whole new skill?' says Tanya. 'And do you love it?'

Christine looks sideways again but now she is smiling. 'Yeah. Because when we come here you don't need to go on about problems; you just do the gardening and have a laugh, and we laugh at silly little things. It's given me the heart to live again.'

Her eyes crinkle. Her hair swirls round her head and she grins as she looks at the people standing nearby, conferring over seed packets, and they too are laughing as the wind catches at a headscarf, a beret.

Christine didn't need listening to – or, rather, not in a room, one to one, her bad thoughts circling the building, whining to be let in. She needed companionship, purpose and laughter. And her loss was still there, of course; it will never leave her. That loss may even be in the room at home, but it lies quietly by the door and does not need to trouble her now.

On other occasions the grip of depression is fiercer and will not be unlocked by words or activities or pills, and depression becomes a fatal disease. I did not have a solution as Mairéad slid downhill. She had always been anxious – 'Mum lived on her nerves,' her daughter Fionnuala reported – and in recent years Mairéad's memory had slipped away. Over the last year or so she had lost interest in grandchildren, novels, music; her earrings lay in their porcelain box, unchosen. Nothing had helped – her GP tried antidepressants, and a community psychiatric nurse had visited, but Mairéad frowned at his questions, turned her head away and later wept, inconsolable. And now she was in hospital following a fall and did not even glance at the foil-wrapped fancy biscuits brought in by Owen, who sat in his Ireland rugby shirt beside his wife to coax her to eat. We looked for causes of delirium – infections or medicines that might have caused her mind to step further away from the love of her family – and we checked that she could hear and her blood tests were normal and her brain scan was unchanged. Fionnuala showed her mother pictures of the cat stretched out in a patch of sunlight at home, but Mairéad turned away again, a tear slipping on to her cheek. Her nurse Innocent asked me after the ward round, 'Do you think there's such a thing as terminal sadness?'

Someone asked about tube feeding to buy time while Mairéad's medications were adjusted once more, but her family were firm. Mairéad would be aghast, and in any case we know that such feeding in those with dementia is of no benefit; it does not prolong life or improve the quality of that life. Tom, the liaison psychiatrist, visited her on the ward and explained that Mairéad would not respond to a further change of medication. He reiterated the evidence that depression in those who also have dementia is likely to prove intractable in terms of treatment with antidepressants.

Her rosary, the priest, a YouTube ceilidh – all were met with indifference. Tom talked with Owen and Fionnuala, reassuring them that they had done their utmost and must not feel guilty that they had been unable to find a key to unlock Mairéad's mood. We arranged for her to return home in the hope that perhaps she would be happier there. I heard some weeks later from the community team that Mairéad had died in her own home with her daughter and husband beside her and the cat on the windowsill. It was dementia rather than 'terminal sadness' that was written on Mairéad's death certificate, but I think that sometimes they become so intertwined as to be indistinguishable.

For long periods between her episodes of life-threatening depression, Aunt Cecily was funny, kind and interested. She maintained her mental balance despite other sad events that included loss and betrayal. She had another daughter whom she adored. She arranged trips to the theatre, the ice rink, went camping in France, read voraciously. I have a dressing gown in a Liberty print that she sewed as my wedding present. She tied her bootlaces in a special knot and played the organ in her village church. She held art lessons in her kitchen, encouraging children to mix eccentric colours using powder paints in muffin trays. And I am aware now that she treated her mental health with care and was respectful of its fragility. Cecily took at least one antidepressant tablet every day of her adult life and was clear that she would not have survived without this. Alongside a pharmacological approach to her depression, she administered her own therapy, and when I was in my early twenties and was despondent – a bad relationship, exams and an overdraft – Cecily wrote out for me the letter of Sydney Smith, written to his friend Georgiana Morpeth in 1820. Smith empathises with Morpeth's 'low spirits' and delivers twenty instructions. They're beside me now, written in my aunt's neat script with her rOtring pen:

1st. Live as well as you dare.

2nd. Go into the showerbath with a small quantity of water at a temperature low enough to give you a slight sensation of cold.

3rd. Read amusing books.

4th. Take short views of human life – not further than dinner or tea.

5th. Be as busy as you can.

6th. See as much as you can of those friends who like and respect you.

7th. And of those acquaintances who amuse you.

8th. Make no secret of low spirits to your friends, but talk of them freely – they are always worse for dignified concealment.

9th. Attend to the effects tea and coffee produce upon you.

10th. Don't expect too much from human life – a sorry business at the best.

11th. Compare your lot with that of other people.

12th. Avoid poetry, dramatic representations (except comedy), music, serious novels, melancholy, sentimental people, everything likely to excite feeling or emotion, not ending in active benevolence.

13th. Do good and endeavour to please everybody of every degree.

14th. Be as much as you can in the open air without fatigue.

15th. Make the room where you commonly sit gay and pleasant.

16th. Struggle little by little against idleness.

17th. Don't be too severe upon yourself, or under-rate yourself, but do yourself justice.

18th. Keep good blazing fires.

19th. Be firm and constant in the exercise of rational religion.

20th. Believe me, dear Lady Georgiana.

For my aunt, Smith's instructions were to be taken seriously, and she selected several as an adjunct to the heavyweight medical treatments of her depression. Not all hold their place now 200 years later (and I suspect that too often, we compare our lot with that of other people in the wrong direction, looking enviously at glossy social media posts rather than recognising our own relative fortune). Their tone is light, but I do not think they mock or undermine the suffering of those for whom depression holds not just 'low spirits' but desolation and horror.

From time to time I think of these instructions. Some years ago, after another failed bid for funding for a new colleague, I wobbled on a swivel chair to take down our dismal office curtains, calf-scour yellow with a pattern of ill-defined smears. I remind myself remorsefully that I may need to attend to the effects of alcohol as well as those of tea and coffee. I watch the bubbling exhilaration of those who have discovered cold-water swimming, vibrant women who wade out of choppy seas or lakes frilled with ice, and I see Instagram posts from men who assert that their well-being has been enhanced by lowering themselves into barrels of frigid grue, with February clouds spitting down upon them. I find their claims so compelling that I run my shower hot, and then push the handle right the other way and try not to gasp. I turn myself under a stream of cold water until my skin becomes pink with indignation, and whatever was occupying my thoughts when I got into that shower seems less important when I get out.

I'm aware, however, that my patients may find themselves far beyond the reach of measures that may simply lift a low mood. Sadness is an emotion; depression is an illness.

We're discussing Gordon in one of the team meetings online. There's a GP present, Jane, but she hasn't yet met him. There's Gabriela, the complex care nurse, and a social worker, and the deputy manager Della has joined us from her office in the large care home where Gordon has lived for the last year.

'He was all right when he moved in,' says Della, 'but he's stopped eating now. He's in his room – won't come out.'

Gordon has had some blood tests, all normal.

'He's got dementia,' says Della. 'But he's going down-hill more quickly, you know, faster than I'd expect.'

'Does he have visitors?' asks Gabriela.

'His wife used to visit,' Della says, 'but she died a while back, quite soon after he came in.'

'Does he know she's died?' I ask.

'No,' Della replies, 'his daughter won't let us tell him.'

I see Gabriela blink and lean back in her chair. Jane the GP rubs her hand across her forehead because this is sad, and there may not be a right answer. Who knows what Gordon is thinking – maybe he has forgotten that he ever had a wife, so her absence is not distressing him. But maybe he's thinking that his wife does not love him, has forgotten him, has run off with someone else. Maybe he thinks she is ill or suffering, I should be with her, or maybe Gordon guesses she has died but no one is talking about it and he is facing that knowledge alone day after day.

A team at Alzheimer Scotland put it well: *The purpose of the grieving process is to adapt over time to the loss of someone . . . The aim is to accept the reality of the loss, work through the pain and adjust to life without the deceased.* For some people with dementia the grieving process may begin but cannot move forward, as that person may not be able to remember or build upon the previous day's tiny step of healing. Gordon's daughter may not be unrealistic in her fear that her father will suffer pain, may have to be told of his wife's death over again. Yet, as the team explain, *loss of cognition should not be confused with the absence of emotion. We know that, however severe the dementia is, the person is still able to feel emotions.* The change in Gordon's behaviour suggests that he knows something is amiss, is feeling a painful loss, and just as someone who has dementia may need support with other facets of life, they may also need support in grief and may take longer to find their way through the process of mourning. It may be better that those around Gordon acknowledge his loss and attune themselves to his emotional state, saying perhaps, 'I wonder if you have been missing your wife? Tell me about Gina – what was she like?' But they need to do that after discussion with his daughter, and with her help if she can give it, and they need to be consistent yet responsive. The team suggest that we *accept that the person may want to talk about the deceased person frequently or infrequently and that they may have far more understanding of the situation than you think.*

And the authors of that piece are wise when they advise, *Be prepared to revisit the experience or to never again address it, depending on the response of the person with dementia.*

What have I learned about depression in older people? I have learned that it is slippery and can evade both detection and treatment. I've learned that it may develop in the context of illness or bereavement or a cruel shock, or may less commonly swoop, unheralded and devastating, into a life in which depression was not anticipated, and become all-consuming. I've learned that it takes many forms, may announce itself through withdrawal or as agitation or restlessness. It may be accompanied by terrifying delusions of destitution, persecution, even of being dead already. I've learned that it can be difficult to tell with precision, especially in older people, when low mood, worry or malaise have become something more pervasive. I have also learned that sadness and depression are two entirely different things. Sadness is a necessary part of a complete life. Depression emphatically is not.

I have learned that depression marches hand in hand with loneliness, and that sometimes we can see it coming. Often we can intervene and make changes for ourselves or on behalf of someone else, and the sooner those changes happen, the more chance they have of working. I have learned that medication is effective – indispensable – for some, but that for others a different approach will unlock this illness.

I've learned that continuity matters, that it is better to be offered the help we need by someone who knows us, who has taken the time to understand our situation, hopes and fears. I've learned that the fact that continuity matters and is effective does not mean that it happens. There is work to be done.

I've learned not to trivialise a condition that for many people is bleaker than those who have not suffered it can ever comprehend; it's a condition that can leave someone with apparently only two options: a choice between an unbearably desolate life or a despairing death by suicide. I have learned that talking about suicide does not make it more likely to happen – that, in fact, a simple question from a friend, a professional, a stranger (have you thought of taking your life?) can be protective.

I have learned that depression tells lies fluently and relentlessly to those over whom it asserts power, for depression does not wish to offer other choices. I've learned that those choices are revealed most often by a voice, a word, a smile – a tiny ember of human contact can grow to provide a healing warmth. I have learned that depression may be – though not always – driven back and if not banished, then at least contained. I've learned that for many, beyond even the grimmest present, there can be hope.

I am shown a project, The Recovery Letters, written by those who have had depression to those still in its grip. James Withey's depression was severe enough to cause him to be admitted to a psychiatric hospital, and he wanted to hear stories from people who had found their way through, including from those who had been suicidal, who had recovered or who had learned how to manage this illness. James wished to know – and later to show – that it was possible to live a life with meaning after despair. James asked those with experience of severe depression to write letters and to share their knowledge with others – *to give hope that you can recover.*

How beautiful the letters are. They are direct, full of empathy and understanding. Their authors repeatedly state, I do not know you, I do not pretend to know exactly what you are going through – but at the same time their words convey a deep connection, a familiarity with the bleak plains that stretch around those who have depression.

Peter Hobden's letter explains, *When I was asked by someone 'How do you feel?', it was a silly question without an answer from where I was – you would* need *feeling to give an answer. To ask such a question of us means they don't even know where we are. This place, so real and ghastly to us, is cruelly invisible to others.* Peter describes the profound relief he felt as his depression abated: *like bursting the surface of a bottomless ocean and gasping for air, feeling alive again.*

William Dean Ford writes, *Life and love and friendship and fun don't have to be things that happen to other people while you watch from the sidelines . . . Everything comes from believing change is possible.*

I read one letter after another. Simple, complex, halting or fluent, gentle and firm. The letters speak of loneliness, of guilt and hopelessness, of how difficult it is to tell another person our feelings. And they speak of recovery, joy, laughter, truth and beauty.

Barbara writes, *If your experience of depression is anything like mine, then right now you are scared, at the bottom of a dark pit, with no way out. Now just look up. Right up there, at the top of your deep, black, pit, there's a glimpse of sunlight. That's your hope. And there are hands reaching down. Those are my hands.*

*

You can read the Recovery Letters and find links to James Withey's books and other writing supporting people with depression here: https://www.therecovery letters.com/

16. Understanding

I'm cross, again. The Foundation Years doctor who admitted this patient has finished her shift and left for the evening, so I'm seeing Josie on my own, and the young doctor has made a mess of the medication list, which is extensive but clearly inaccurate. I perch on Josie's bed to explain that her kidneys are not working very well, which is probably just dehydration because there's been a heatwave and she's been off colour with a urine infection, but Josie's in her seventies and has heart failure as well, so we need to get this right.

'I want to check something, Josie. I think there's been a muddle about your medicines because you're on some tablets that are only for men.'

As I say that I feel a sudden lurch, a realisation that I have got this badly wrong. Josie raises her chin and turns her head away from me, closing her eyes. I see the strong line of her jaw and a necklace of smooth pale green marble discs above which her Adam's apple is prominent, and I notice now, so stupidly, her broad wrists, and I burn that I have caused her distress. We're in a bay. The curtains are pleated, disposable and pose no barrier to the transmission of sound. And my voice is loud; I know it has carried.

My hands fly to my face. I whisper, 'I'm so sorry.'

Josie gathers herself. She is kind. She has grey-blue eyes. She has had to explain herself before – to explain not her meaning but her being.

'It's sort of good that you made the mistake,' she says, and adds, 'It's a long story.'

She had some surgery a decade ago to make her body more feminine, but then suffered a heart attack, which caused such damage that her surgical team felt that further procedures would be unsafe. As she speaks, I realise that I know nothing. I don't know which procedures Josie had. My mind is scrambling to make sense. There's a part of me saying that it doesn't matter, that I don't need to ask intrusive questions – Josie is Josie. Leave her alone; just treat the illness – but then I realise that Josie has a prostate, which explains two of her medicines, which are given to men who have the benign enlargement of the prostate that commonly happens with age, and that matters because if Josie has some male anatomy it makes it more likely that her kidneys have failed because the flow of urine is obstructed, which is less common in women – or, rather, in people with female anatomy. I'm tripping myself up. Josie *is* a woman. So I need to re-evaluate the plan made by the young doctor who saw her earlier and arrange a quick scan of Josie's bladder to make sure it's emptying, and even as I'm making that plan I am thinking about the other medicines on Josie's list, one of which is oestrogen hormone replacement therapy, which I hadn't particularly noticed since lots of older women use HRT, and another is an antiandrogen. I hadn't recognised the name, but now it makes sense – it's an antiandrogen to block testosterone, Josie's male hormone. Are both those treatments safe in someone who has had a heart attack? Or relatively safe, because I can guess that without those hormones Josie's life might become unsafe in different ways, in how she sees herself or in how others see her.

I uncoil my stethoscope and listen to Josie's breathing and her heart. I lay my hand flat to feel her abdomen under her blouse, which is cotton, a sixties block print in green and white, and I wonder what if she *has* got urinary retention and needs a catheter. Will that be complicated because of the surgery she has had? I feel wary thinking about that. I can usually contemplate anatomy with equanimity (everyone's the same but also a little bit different), but Josie's anatomy is somehow a more private matter, and my wondering feels uncomfortable, even salacious.

Josie is in a female bay. Naturally – her name is a woman's name and her gender is stated on her documents as female. Do the nurses know? Do they need to know? Did the young doctor who saw her earlier realise? She has not mentioned anything in the notes, but she's only in the first year of training after qualifying so I am not surprised that the inconsistencies between Josie's gender and her pharmacology may have gone over her head. Or maybe that doctor knew exactly Josie's situation but being more than thirty years younger than me she does not deem it worthy of comment. Josie is Josie.

I ask her nurse Shailesh to do a bladder scan. He is Indian, thin and elegant. I'm worried that Shailesh may make the same mistake as I did when it's time for the drug round, so I say, 'Josie is on some special medicines, unusual treatments because . . .'

Shailesh puts up his hand and bends his head to me, saying quietly, 'I know. A lovely lady.'

After meeting Josie, I do some reading and realise that I am not alone in knowing nothing. We do not know the longer-term effects of various hormone treatments – we can extrapolate from the effects of antiandrogens that are given to men with prostate cancer and the effects of oestrogen HRT on postmenopausal women, but we don't know about the effects on heart disease, stroke risk, bone strength or the risks of certain cancers when these hormones are used to help someone to live in a different gender. We don't know the long-term effects of various surgical procedures – for example, we don't know the risks of breast cancer in those who have had a mastectomy, having been unhappy or even miserable in a body with breasts.

There's a lot more we don't know.

I read the words of Joanne Lockwood, herself a

transwoman, who writes powerfully and movingly of the benefits of inclusivity, diversity and understanding. Joanne and her team work with businesses, the armed forces and government organisations to explain and educate, and to provide practical ways in which we can work and live better together. Her website SEE Change Happen is full of positivity and optimism – and trust.

Joanne asks good questions about the future for older trans people. She observes that we don't know what might happen when someone develops dementia – will that trans person forget that they have transitioned from one gender to another? Might they wish to retransition? What happens if someone loses capacity to decide what gender they are? What if family members disagree about someone's gender? If they never did accept Dad as a woman? Who decides? How should care staff respond? Joanne makes good suggestions about advance care planning – perhaps such planning is something trans people can use if they are concerned that they may need support in later life to continue to live in a chosen gender. As I read this I remember that there are many people who belong to one religion or another and follow its practices and choose to make good plans for the future, and they write to make it clear that they should be supported to continue in those religious practices, and yet I wonder whether that future self, who has forgotten their past but has current opinions and wishes, is the one whose desires should be respected, regardless of the strictures that their past self wanted to put around their behaviour? Because acceding to their request for a forbidden food or a pair of trousers will make them happy today and their past self won't know anything about it. But I can see the distress too that someone would feel contemplating a future self who may behave in a way painfully at odds with their precious and carefully defended current practices and beliefs.

My head's in a spin, and so I read more of Joanne's words, which are wise. She advises care staff to *Just be aware of the complications and intricacies of the person and the people around them.*

Joanne lists barriers to good care for people who are trans, and as I read them I realise that they are, of course, the barriers to good care for anyone who does not fit the mould, who does not look like us, speak like us or think like us. She mentions inexperience, biases and misunderstandings. She highlights difficulties with IT systems that do not allow for nuance, and concerns about confidentiality. But top of Joanne's list, her biggest barrier to good care for anyone we perceive as 'different', is one I recognise: fear of getting it wrong.

'It's all part of a process,' my nephew Laurie tells me when I have once again screwed up his pronouns.

'Don't worry, Aunt Luce. You'll probably get it right in the end.' He twists his fingers in his curly hair and I am grateful for his patience and understanding.

My friend Robbie explains how his daughter had been

dating a 'nonbinary . . . person? Is that the right thing to say?' Robbie looks worried, and says, 'I am so desperate not to turn into my dad, not to say, "ooh, they/them."'

He imitates his father, raising his eyes skywards and his mouth going down, and his whole head doing a little vertical circuit. It's not subtle but it is funny, and Robbie is feeling his way uncertainly to a better understanding of his daughter and her friend, and it's fine to acknowledge this uncertainty and to laugh at ourselves and to be kind.

Change is difficult. To many it feels as if the sands are shifting too quickly and it's hard to keep up, to identify and scrutinise our prejudices. For others the adaptation of attitudes seems lumbering, painfully slow, and each day they may be angered or hurt by unnecessary and thoughtless cruelties or by cultivated intolerance.

David Watson is on the ward. He's wearing crisp blue and white pyjamas which contrast with the sagging pale green numbers, poppered and gaping, in which his neighbours are clad. A paisley dressing gown hangs on the back of his chair. His feet, puffy and purple, are nonetheless sporting smooth leather slippers. David has been managing his heart failure dutifully. He shows me his weights, recorded at home every morning. He has typed out his medication list – there are annotations regarding dose adjustments, the sudden appearance of a rash. He was a bank manager before he retired.

'Do you live alone, David,' I ask, 'or with . . . ?'

There's a beat. 'A friend,' David says.

Despite his careful curation, David's heart is deteriorating. His kidneys have joined in now and there's trouble brewing. I suggest we discuss his Treatment Escalation Plan. It's not something he's thought about before. Would he like someone else to be here for this conversation? He waves away the offer.

David listens attentively as I outline options and explain some limitations.

David nods. 'Not the resuscitation attempt and not machines,' he says, 'but yes to the rest.'

I show David the form. There are boxes. *If I am unable to speak for myself* reads one line, *please contact . . .* and there's a space for 'name'.

David says, 'Luke Greening.'

Then I show him the next box which says *who is my*, ready for wife, son, daughter-in-law, usually an easy question. David pauses. This time it's not an easy question and the pause lengthens and David's eyes look down and flick left, right, trapped. 'A friend . . .' he says, 'my friend.'

I say, 'OK, friend,' and am writing that down when David puts his hand up to stop me. Our eyes meet.

'Partner,' he tells me. 'Luke is my partner.'

I read the words of Sir Ian McKellen addressing the Pride in Ageing project in 2019. Sir Ian explained, 'I can remember a time when the number-one rule if you were LGBT was never to talk about it – because you were breaking the law.' Sir Ian's words are quoted by Lawrie Roberts, who works for the LGBT Foundation, in a presentation he made to a group of doctors, trainees in geriatric medicine in 2022. Lawrie explains some of the barriers faced by those from the LGBT community. He outlines the evolution of the law: in England homosexual activity between two men was decriminalised in 1967, and in Scotland it remained a crime until 1981, and homosexual activity is still a crime in many countries. At that Pride event Sir Ian continued, 'Although the laws have changed, attitudes haven't altogether.'

My patient David was thirty when the Sexual Offences Act was passed in 1967. Even then this was less a decriminalisation of homosexuality and more to do with enshrining people's rights in their own private spaces. Arrests actually increased after this date; you could still be prosecuted for 'unnatural offences', 'public indecency' and 'procuring sex', which covered any sexual contact between men including touching or kissing and any intent to invite gay sex, such as chatting up or winking at men in public.

Lawrie's presentation contained more stark facts. Aversion therapy was offered as a cure for homosexuality on the NHS until 1980, and homosexuality was listed as a mental illness by the World Health Organization until 1992. Sir Ian McKellen described his own experience to the Pride in Ageing audience: 'I was criminalised, and that can leave a brand on you – you never really get rid of that.'

I am caught by his phrase. A brand – the tattoo needle or a hiss of flesh burning. There is such pain, and I can see that my patient David, in his eighties and coming to the end of his life, has felt that pain too. McKellen continued, 'You want to feel that you are surrounded by friendship, love and respect.'

I'm with three medical students in my office. We are talking about dementia and the restlessness or agitation that can happen late in the afternoon and evening, when someone has seemed serene all day, even chatty, but now is pacing, vigilant and defensive.

I ask the students to imagine themselves in a summer garden. The sun is setting. What sounds can they hear?

'Traffic!' says Ashraf.

'Anything else?' I ask. 'Might you be able to hear birds?'

They nod and so I ask, 'What is happening to the birdsong?'

Ashraf smiles in recognition. 'It's getting louder!'

I explain that the phenomenon of restlessness as the day comes to its end is called 'sundowning' and is familiar to those who live with or care for someone who has dementia. I think it is an atavistic behaviour; birds do it – think of the alarm call of the blackbird, and you can hear it from a field of sheep too, the crescendo bleating of lambs and ewes in the gathering dusk, as predators are stirring. We must search for our offspring – or for our mother or for refuge – as night falls. Even when someone with dementia cannot define what is unsettling her, she may rise from her chair, uneasy, implacable.

Ashraf clicks his fingers. A penny has dropped and he's delighted. He says, 'My boyfriend in Bristol had a patient just like that!'

That evening I suddenly feel very old. Ashraf's sunny and uncomplicated announcement of his sexuality in our teaching session has inexplicably shaken me. When I was Ashraf's age, the East End GP with whom I was learning introduced me to Frank, who had fought at Gallipoli, aged fourteen in 1915. He had lied about his age to join up, Frank explained; he and his brother were hungry ('starving really') and the army had food. Their father had been wounded in the Boer War, shipped back to England in 1899 and died a few years later of his injuries. At Gallipoli, up against the Ottoman Empire, Frank had been a driver. Two mules.

The date of my own birth is closer now to the outbreak of the First World War than to today's date. Soon my birth year will be closer to the death of Queen Victoria than to the present. I have a sudden swooping sensation of lifespan, feeling abruptly as if I'm at a hinge between two eras and that time is rushing past and I am not keeping up. I know that my surprise at Ashraf's candour reflects my age and experience, but even so I should not expect a gay person to be coy about his relationships. I want to deny that my reaction betrays prejudice.

My children look dubiously at me when I try to explain this.

I get flustered. 'I'm not saying he was wrong,' I tell them. 'I'm really happy that he felt able to say that. It's just . . . it's just *new*.'

My children roll their eyes. It's not new to them.

I watch another of Lawrie Roberts' presentations, this time addressing a group working on part of a National Lottery funded project, Ageing Better, which produced a welcome focus on many aspects of ageing in Britain, tackling everything from digital exclusion to loneliness, from intergenerational working through to carers in communities at risk of isolation. Lawrie's default expression is a gentle smile; he is here to promote understanding. He outlines the assumptions commonly made about those who are lesbian, gay, bisexual and trans, and even when he is describing the hurtful phrases encountered by LGBT people his tone is one of forgiveness.

One of Lawrie's slides lists 'bad' questions to ask:

Are you a man or a woman? What were you originally? How do you know you are gay/bisexual/trans/ queer? How did your parents take it?

Some of the bad questions make me smile too.

Are you . . . you know . . . um . . . ? and *Do you know [insert the name of the other LGBT person you know]?*

We can ask better questions.

How would you like to be addressed?

Avoiding assumptions such as 'So Sue is your sister?' is a good start.

The presentation continues with advice about what to do when we make a mistake. *Apologise! Just say sorry. Wow, I really messed that up, I'm sorry.*

Not *Sorry, but I need to know if you're a man or a woman* or *I'm sorry if that upset you – but are you actually gay?* Just: *I'm sorry I made a mistake.*

Lawrie suggests that it's kind to express gratitude if someone has corrected us. We may need to hold ourselves in check – it's awkward to have got something wrong and we may need to 'calm our defences' to prevent a rush of humiliation from turning into anger at the person we now feel should be blamed for putting us into that awkward situation. We can take a breath and say, 'Thank you for telling me,' or 'Thank you for explaining that.'

And then, says Lawrie, move on. It's hard to get it right and we may need to commit time and mental effort. Unfamiliar personal pronouns, for example, do not come easily. Lawrie suggests writing down good phrases or practising out loud. I think of my own Laurie, my nephew, and how I have blundered around his pronouns for years now and I resolve to do better.

'Some of these little children have four mothers.'

I was attending a day-long conference covering the

ethics of early life at Great Ormond Street Hospital, and
I listened to a psychiatrist – he was German, I thought,
or Dutch perhaps. I'd only recently started chairing the
Clinical Ethics Committee at my hospital, a committee set up to advise clinicians when the right course of
action seems uncertain, and I was aware that my knowledge should be relatively secure as regards the medical
ethics and law surrounding the end of a life, but I did not
know enough about the questions that arise at the start.

It had been a riveting day. There had been presentations about the selection of IVF embryos – permitted
for genetic misalignments incompatible with healthy life
but used, illegally in the UK, to guarantee gender or hair
colour. I'd learned the guidance around termination of
one or more fetuses to allow the survival of others in a
multiple birth. I'd heard about the care of desperately
premature babies. When might it be right to stop without even trying to fan a tiny glow into a flame? And now
this psychiatrist was talking about 'new families', about
children born through IVF or through the donation of
eggs or sperm, to straight people and gay people and
single people.

He smiled as he explained the four mothers. 'They
may have the egg donor mother and the surrogate
mother, and then the two lovely lesbian lady mothers.'

He grinned. 'I have only one mother,' he said, 'and
that is quite complicated enough.'

The psychiatrist went on to explain the serious

research which shows that, in fact, such children are no more or less likely to develop complexities in their life than those born to conventional parents, a heterosexual mum and dad. They're no more or less likely to grow up gay, or to be depressed or anxious. Some will have mental health problems, others will not.

This summer, years later, I have a day in London. I'm giving a talk this afternoon, but I have time to walk from Paddington station through Hyde Park and I do not recognise it. It's June and the grass is unmown. Paths criss-cross the northern half of the park through meadows, the grass thigh high. I reach a junction of two sandy tracks and stand for a moment. There is only green – long grass, distant trees – and the falling notes of a chaffinch. There is a patch of nettles, a butterfly. It's glorious. Nearer the Serpentine and around the Albert Memorial order is restored. The grass is shorn, there are deckchairs, and teams are gearing up to play softball. A pair of Egyptian geese shepherd their goslings round the feet of people walking alongside the lake.

There's a noticeboard, a QR code inviting me to learn more about the park. I scan it and read the title page on my phone screen, *The Queer Ecology of the Royal Parks*. There are guided tours that explain how trees can change gender, how slugs are hermaphrodite, that birds often pair up into same-sex couples. There's a picture of *Queer ecologist Connor Butler* kneeling to show a dung beetle to the photographer, and there's a statement of Connor's aim *to encourage everyone to take time to appreciate the smallest details in nature and to show love for the often-unloved species on our planet.*

I think of David and Josie and the burdens they have carried through lives defined by prejudice. I think of Ashraf, and Connor, and Hyde Park with its billowy meadows. This is better.

17. It's Complicated

'The problem for my sister and me,' says Alysha, 'is that our mum got things in the wrong order. She had us and then decided she didn't want children.'

I listen as Alysha outlines the arrangements she and her sister have made, taking it in turns to support their mother, who has made clear in one way or another, throughout their lives, her resentment of their existence. I hear Alysha – this gentle funny woman with her long lash extensions, her juggle of a demanding and poorly paid job, her teenage kids, her partner, her uncomplaining good humour – and I hear her determination to do the right thing by her mum.

At the other end of the county Ros is in a similar situation. Her mother lives in Ros's house, ninety-six and coolly unpredictable, with a stash of phrases and behaviours that have been honed over years.

'I realised when I was still young that my mother wasn't a safe person for me,' Ros tells me.

'How young?' I ask.

'Around seven,' Ros replies.

Yet Ros has made herself safe, has created a shield that shimmers around her to deflect the worst of her mother's emotional assaults. I wonder what Ros's shield is made of – understanding perhaps, awareness of her mother's psychiatric illnesses and of the bitterness and regret that fuel her anger.

But my patient's daughter Carole tells me, sniffing, 'We have our own lives to lead.' And when I've put the phone down I look at the map, at the few hundred yards between Carole's house and that of her father. Carole is retired, she's told me that already, and I'm aware that there are reasons, reasons I will never know, why Carole feels that her fortnightly visit is as much as her father should be granted, even though he has become frail and needs help, so he will have to join the long list of people waiting for attention from social services.

It's complicated.

I talk with Juliet, who looks out for her mother, visits her each day, collects her shopping, folds the laundry, is there to meet the electrician because a fuse keeps tripping. Juliet puts out the bins, goes to the pharmacist for her mother's prescriptions.

She smiles. 'Nick's coming down this weekend. Golden boy. Mum can't wait.'

Juliet likes her brother – he's carefree and funny.

'Oh, Luce,' says Juliet, 'it's OK really but, you know . . . I take Mum to the podiatrist. He takes her to the races.'

The therapists hear it most when they are trying to work out how someone can remain at home, how to cobble together enough help from a family and from care agencies or charities; they hear the nuances, the hesitations, the flat refusals. They meet the niece who has given up her job to care – she will do everything for her aunt and uncle, will not have it any other way. The therapists meet Stuart, who is looking after his mother, and I recognise that Stuart fits into a pattern with which I am at last familiar, a son who now looks after his mother when, in fact, it has been his mother who has looked after him all these years, because he has never moved away from home, has not got married. Stuart's first job didn't work out, the boss didn't take to him, and there's a reason for that and I feel for Stuart, shifting anxiously from foot to foot in his green raincoat as he tries to make sense of what's going on, what he's being asked to do for his mum, because he was a bright enough lad, his teachers said, but always a target for the bullies, and he never was able to get his head around the moods other people might be in. Nowadays a child like the one Stuart was might be given a diagnosis, but back then – well, his mum has looked out for him, and now, half a century on, she can't remember what's what, can't boil a potato and there's a problem with continence, and that's a difficult situation for Stuart to be in, becoming a carer when he's always been the one who needed the care.

Aidan, the occupational therapist, puts down the phone in our shared ward office after a call. I've been writing up notes while Aidan has been listening to a daughter-in-law. He rubs his hand across his forehead. He says, 'You never do know, do you, when you pick up the phone, what the story will be?'

Neil is a big fellow in his camouflage army jacket, and he runs his hand round the collar of the T-shirt underneath, because the ward is warm and the conversation is running down awkward crevices. The skin of his neck looks hot and creased and red, his gold rings tight on thick fingers. Neil explains how his mum calls him to fix the TV, to get her some milk, to see to a rat that ran across the patio. But the TV is on when he gets there. There is milk in the fridge and the neighbours don't know anything about a rat.

Neil does not fit on the plastic chair we have provided, and he adjusts himself, his hefty boots planted on the lino floor. He looks up at me and at Sarah the social worker, and tells us, 'Like, last weekend, I was going fishing, had just got it all set up down the beach, and my phone goes and I know it's her. And she says the boiler's broken, and I think, well, it was fine yesterday. But then it's cold, I can't leave her, so I pack up and go to her place and she's right it's cold. Because she's switched the boiler off.'

Neil sighs, a troubled, aching sigh, and says quietly, 'She's all I've got and I'm all she's got. I moved out when I was sixteen. Couldn't stand her.'

There's a balance and we don't always get it right. Our patient is our patient and we want to do our best by them, to support them in their decisions and actions, and to act in their best interests when they do not have the capacity to make decisions for themselves. But our patients come with families or friends or neighbours, and what is right for our patient may not be at all right for someone who is close to them. The burdens that are carried can be welcome – may not, in fact, be a burden – and then sometimes a family member takes on a role and the halo they wear is heavy but it's a halo all the same; and on other occasions the burden is intolerable but cannot be removed and becomes somehow tolerated. We feel our way every day to a compromise, an exploration of who can do what and how long that can last and whether it is the best way and whether it is fair.

Raymond is determined to go home again – he's had the four days in hospital that usually suit him, and now he's decided to leave, but everyone's worried. The receptionists at his GP surgery know Raymond well; he's had their number on speed dial for years. He wants Dr Tony to call him, and, no, he cannot give them some more details – it's a private thing and he knows his rights. Tony has managed this situation adeptly by setting up a weekly call. Tony rings Raymond every Tuesday afternoon and for ages he's listened to Raymond's grumbles and gripes and adjusted his medicines, for Raymond does have medical problems – he's enormously overweight, has diabetes and poor blood flow to his puffy feet, which he can't reach, and he's had a heart attack in the past and is a sitting duck for another one. But over the past year or two Tony's holding mechanism has proven no longer up to the task, and we've had a message from the ambulance service. Raymond rings 999, complains of chest pain, the paramedics are round at his flat almost every week and sometimes they bring him in and sometimes they don't, but nothing changes, and Raymond's chest pain is evaluated each time; it isn't a heart attack or angina or even indigestion and it resolves when he wants to go home. In the last few months Raymond's been issued with an alarm system, a wrist-worn button that he can use if he's in trouble, but this has proved to be an unwise move, for Raymond has pressed the button again even as the paramedics are leaving his house. The team who handle those lifeline calls would call Raymond, and at first they would send someone round and later they realised that a conversation would usually resolve the issue and that they could answer his demands by listening. But Raymond has become unsatisfied by that response; he does not want to be fobbed off with chit-chat and he knows now that if he presses his alarm button they will ring him and if he then doesn't speak but just breathes into the telephone, ignoring their questions, they will have to send someone, a pair of proper paramedics in high-vis tabards with their big box of tricks, the neighbours watching, for who knows whether Raymond might be lying on the floor with a hip fracture or a stroke?

Raymond's had a spell in a local residential home but discharged himself, being displeased with the regime, the food, the staff ('All foreign'). Back at home he has carers coming in three times a day to help with a wash, a meal, his tablets. We have talked about loneliness, which he denies. He claims he is happy with his own company; he likes watching telly and the traffic going past the window.

I creep up on him with the subject of death.

'Are you worried, Raymond, that something bad is going to happen?'

He gives me a look like, *Are you daft or something?* Which could mean, *Of course I am worried. I live in mortal fear of death every day.* But when I suggest that perhaps he might be afraid of dying, Raymond grunts.

'If it happens it happens. I'm not bothered.'

And in the end we conclude that Raymond likes the attention and it feels improper to state this; everyone feels uncomfortable calling out Raymond's bad behaviour, but it is bad behaviour, and when the paramedics are with Raymond they cannot be with someone else who is sicker, so we try to pull together an agreement that the paramedics won't bring him in if they can help it, and if they do, Raymond will have the minimum tests necessary in the Emergency Department to exclude a heart attack and he'll be sent home. We put an alert on his notes, but it's a forlorn plan, and most of the time Raymond will have his way.

I meet a woman on the bus to London, who tells me of her mother-in-law, who is playing her sons off against each other.

'She asks my husband to do something, to take her to the shops or to pin up the rose on her house, and if he hesitates for a second, it's, "Don't worry, Donald. I'll ask your brother to do it."' The woman looks out of the bus window. 'There's a farm at stake here; everyone knows it and no one can say it.'

Sometimes – maybe often – we witness a scene, when we are working with older people and their families, that seems difficult to explain. We see only one episode, one scene in one act, an extract from a family drama upon which the curtain lifted decades ago, a drama that will continue long after our role as audience has finished.

Eunice has three daughters and she's taking a long time to die. Her daughters, all in their sixties or seventies even, visit separately at carefully syncopated times and do not speak with one another, but they bombard the staff between their visits with phone calls. Is she on oxygen? What has she eaten? Has she walked to the bathroom? This is all despite the evidence of their own eyes of Eunice, ninety-three, pale and silent, in bed, unresponsive since her last stroke two weeks ago, peaceful but irretrievable, and their questions persist despite many conversations in which we have explained to each daughter in turn that Eunice is dying. Eventually, early one morning, Eunice has died and I think it's probably better if I phone one of those daughters myself rather than leaving this task to Eunice's nurse, who is from an agency, or to the Foundation Years doctor, who joined us only last week, because there's something going on here and I'm not sure what it is. I ring Pamela, the eldest, who is matter-of-fact. 'So that's it then.' I ask whether she might tell her sisters, but she declines this task, so I call Velma, who is shopping but guesses why I have rung and says she'll talk to Pamela but she won't speak to Sheila. So then I ring Sheila, the youngest, who is at home on her own, and I ask first if she is sitting because (I go slowly) I am very sorry that I have some sad news for her.

At which point there is a gasp.

'You've rung to tell me!' she howls. 'This is the news I've been dreading for forty-four years!'

'I'm so sorry, Sheila,' I say, though I am baffled by the specific duration of her dread. I wait as Sheila's wails gather pace and volume, running into one another, with choking and snot and the full soundtrack of distress, which suddenly comes to an abrupt stop.

'Have you told my sisters?' she demands, and I confirm that I have.

Sheila sniffs and there's a pause. 'I bet I'm more upset than Pamela.'

We need to understand enough both of what matters most to our patients and of what is important to their families or others close to them, but we do not need to know everything. We accept people as they present themselves. I almost always ask my patients what they did for a living. Beyond the relevance of occupational risks – the lung diseases of coal miners or chicken farmers, say – their answers inform our conversation, help me to pitch my explanations, and often cause both of us to smile. But I am aware that my patients do not tell me, 'Ah, I have spent more of my life in prison than out of it.' They do not say, 'I supported my children, paid the bills through prostitution.' I will remain unaware – and should remain unaware – of Shaun's inclusion on the sex offenders' register; I am ignorant that this is the cause of his long wait in hospital after an amputation, as the social worker scrabbles to find new accommodation for Shaun within certain restrictions: not near a school or a playground.

My friend Laura explains her search for peace, with her mother Connie.

'I realise now that Mum probably had dementia ages before it was diagnosed. Eventually they thought she had a frontal variant of Alzheimer's, which explained a lot. She just lost her empathy, her interest in other people, long before it affected her memory. And that made her so tough to be with. She never asked about her grandchildren, never said how are you. She just went straight to what she wanted. I wish I'd realised sooner that it was as much dementia as her own personality, being like that.'

Laura looks away, across the garden of the pub to which we have walked. 'I know it sounds silly, a bit pathetic really, but I was always looking for her to be my mum, even though I'm a grown woman with kids of my own. I even had a row with her about it and she was all, "I do ask, I do ask how you are, how's the family," but she just didn't. She couldn't. In the end I realised I was – I don't know – it was like I was looking for affection, and I was doing all the worrying about her and I kind of wanted her to worry about me for a change. I was hoping a little plant would grow, but it was like hoping a plant would grow on a rubbish tip, in a toxic environment full of old oil cans and broken electrical stuff. It just wouldn't. And once I'd understood that, it felt better, and later, after Mum had died and I was able to put those last years into a better context, I got a new image and it was like reshaping that rubbish dump, covering all the bad stuff with a layer of better memories, the best bits of her life, and in my mind I was able to create a new landscape, putting in a lake, planting trees.'

*

There is often neglect in the scenes that I witness, and usually that neglect is not intended. It comes about because all parties in a relationship are at a loss, do not know that they need to ask for help or do not know where to turn for that help, or help has been requested but is not forthcoming. Sometimes there is carelessness or selfishness, and occasionally there is real abuse, evil at work, someone who is conspiring to cause harm. But that is rare, and most often I see something quite different.

I listen to the story in an outpatient clinic. Malcolm's nights are spent with an ear always listening. He has persuasive techniques to get Hazel to take her medicines. He explains his attention to her tight support stockings; it's a right job getting those on, and how he settles her in front of *Countdown* before taking the dog for a spin round the block, and he's worried, Malcolm, about whether Hazel's doing OK, and he wonders would it be all right if Hazel did not have the scan for which they have been given an appointment. He hasn't told her about it yet because she will fret – she does not like the scanner, calls it the clam shell – and my part in the story is to explain that the scan is not so necessary after all, not if it will cause Hazel distress, because whatever we find on that scan is unlikely to change things materially for Hazel.

'Well, that's a relief, because I was feeling . . .' says Malcolm, as he adjusts the sleeves of his jacket, old tweed over soft cuffs. He gives an uncertain smile to make light of what he is saying. 'You know, I was thinking, am I up to this job?'

I look at this steady man, who has found himself conscripted late in life, called up into a new role for which there has been no training – or, rather, none beyond that provided by a fifty-eight-year marriage. And it's not just one role. Malcolm is domestic bursar, chef, party planner, pharmacist, cleaner, driver, nurse, project manager. Carer.

I tell him, 'Malcolm, you are doing a great job. You are doing all the right things.'

He pulls a face, awkward at the praise, then changes his mind and puts his hand on my arm, gives it a squeeze, and maybe he is about to say something but no words come out and he looks down to find the satchel with Hazel's appointments and her medicine list, and he takes her hand.

I find myself saying it over and over again – to daughters, wives, partners, husbands – you are doing all the right things. You are in a very difficult situation, and you are doing all the right things.

'What will happen to the anger after she has gone?' Chris asks me. He has confided that his mother punishes him with her disappointment; she lists all the careers he could have had. In turn Chris punishes his mother through his absence. He talks of the unlikeliness of resolution. Chris is rueful. 'Too much water under the carpet,' he says, and winks as I laugh; it's a suitably messy image. But he looks sad and I feel I have little to offer. I know it would be good if Chris could dismantle, defuse, some of that anger before his mother has gone, because afterwards there will be regret.

I have been told a Hawaiian mantra and have found it useful myself in a sad situation when words were hard to find, so I tell Chris the sentences of the hoʻoponopono: I'm sorry; thank you; I love you.

They are very good words. They don't always work but they're a good place to start.

I'm sorry. Thank you. I love you.

18. Here's to the Future

There's a smell of sweet spices, and stairs that lead to a basement space at the back of a GP surgery in a small park in north London surrounded by high-rise social housing. Tony greets me. He is the manager of the Third Age Project and his office is jammed with folders and files. Plastic boxes of coloured pens, first-aid kits and bags of dressing-up clothes are higgledy-piggledy under the desk, and Tony tells me of the Bollywood dance class and the sessions run with black actors as they set out on their careers. He describes the choir and ukulele groups and the annual panto performed by members of the project for local primary schools. A posse of Somalian singers visited recently – four young women whose leader laughed with Rose when she told them her age. 'That's more than all of us added together,' said the lead singer, and Rose was pleased about that and proud. In the meeting room the ceiling flutters with butterflies and birds made of wire and coloured tissue. Tony explains how the Third Age Project works – he's been involved for years, ever since he retired at the end of his first long career. 'Anyone can come,' he says. 'Well, if they're over sixty. It's like a social club really, but we ask people, "What can you offer?"'

I'm surprised and say that I can see that might be an uncomfortable question for some people.

Tony smiles. 'Exactly, and they might say, "Oh, I have nothing. I'm old. I have arthritis." And I tell them, "You can offer friendship."'

The same year I'm invited to speak with an Age UK Camden book club. This invitation is irresistible both for the warmth with which it is issued, but also for the location of the club's meetings, which is a building that I know but have never visited. I am made welcome by Maria and given cake. We sit at a long table in the corner of a large public space, and I listen as the book club members discuss Damon Galgut's novel *The Promise*, and the conversation flows across lifetimes and continents – several present have connections to South Africa – and there's a consensus that this Booker Prize winner is both brilliant and bleak, and everyone nods when someone says they are glad to have read it, but wouldn't recommend it to anyone else, and someone else says quite a lot of things in life are a bit like that. Later, it's my turn to talk and I am asked not to be shy but to speak up, even though there are other people sitting nearby and that is how I came to be talking loudly about laxatives in the British Library.

'I've given up the unequal struggle,' says Patsy, and I leave her room to find a piece of paper, my hands wobbling as I pick up a marker pen from the desk.

I am snappy with the receptionist, a capable woman with purple-framed glasses and purple-tinted hair who greeted me warmly this morning. I don't want to talk to the nurses – one is standing by the computer on wheels, showing her student the medicines administration system, which is different here in the community hospital to the one we use in the big hospital from which Patsy was transferred seven weeks ago. The physiotherapist is coming towards me, his face open and enquiring; he is about to ask me about one of his patients, but I put my hand up to stop him.

I write in big letters. I snatch the Sellotape dispenser from the desk and walk back up the ward. I hold the piece of paper in my teeth while I tear off some Sellotape and I stick the piece of paper to the door on top of the label that reads Anne Wright. It's crooked and the tape has ridged up, but I stick another bit of tape on and the piece of paper says *MY NAME IS PATSY.*

My eye is caught by a newspaper article. It's by Tony Blair and William Hague, officially on opposite sides of the political debate in the UK, and it seems optimistic that they're writing together so I read on for their blueprint for *innovation to power the future of Britain.* The article describes plans for investment in science and research, in international collaboration and proposals for improvements to government infrastructure, harnessing artificial intelligence systems to create more effective public services.

Their suggestions cover education and procurement, pensions and planning, and I smile, because the report 'A New National Purpose' promises to apply the power of data and advances in biotech to healthcare to *create a more predictive, preventative, personalised and participatory model.* I am relieved to see that reference to personalised care, for we are all people, and we deserve care that recognises us as individuals, care that acknowledges that we may be known by a name that is not the name on our records. I'm glad too that participation is highlighted. We deserve treatment that respects our wishes, that is not imposed upon us by someone in a position of power who chooses to ignore our story, our values.

'I haven't told you about my nan,' said my colleague Jess. 'She was a super lady, honestly a cracker, brought up her kids after her husband died young. Didn't suffer fools, mind you. Lived in Warrington all her life, still independent at ninety-two – bowling club, making fish pies for her neighbours, you know the sort.' Jess looked out of the window to the red-brick wall opposite and the weeds growing in the high gutter. 'Then last year she had a massive brain bleed. Unconscious. I looked at the scans; she was never going to get better from that. Mum and I had gone up together and told her doctors what she'd want, which was to be left alone. So keep her comfortable and let her go peacefully.'

Jess paused and looked at her hands. 'But the next

thing I know, she's got an NG tube up her nose and the nurse told us the doctor had said he thought she should have a trial of tube feeding. And we had told them. We had said that wasn't what she'd want.'

I click again on Blair and Hague's report and my pulse quickens as I read the article behind that reference to *predictive, preventative, personalised and participatory* care. It's a piece in the *Journal of Biotechnology* by three scientists, and I realise that its authors do not share my understanding of the word 'personalised'. Their vision is of a different sort of 'personalised care', one which uses information about our individual genomes, combined with the results of tests, to predict which diseases may befall us and to design treatments that are better targeted to our individual genetic make-up. And their interpretation of the word 'participatory' is different too, referring not to our need to participate in decisions about our treatment, but rather that we participate by contributing our digitised data to the healthcare database of the future.

The authors of the paper conclude, *our vision . . . is that each patient will be associated with a virtual data cloud of billions of data points and that we will have the information technology for healthcare to reduce this enormous data dimensionality to simple hypotheses about health and/or disease for each individual.*

Simple hypotheses. I want to scream.

*

327

The dog and I walk by the river. The swans have raised cygnets, six this year, now graceful beige adolescents. Beyond them swallows swoop to drink and fly towards and round the dog and me, taking advantage of our footsteps that have caused insects to rise from the track. I become calmer and think about personalised care, as those scientists envisage it, and the advantages it will bring. I think of the advances on the horizon for people who have cancer – treatments that will allow a biopsy to be taken of a cancer that threatens our life, and how the DNA might be extracted from those cancer cells and be used to create a compound unique to just that cancer, our own cancer, no one else's, that can be injected back into us to trigger our immune system to recognise those cancer cells and destroy them. I think about how some commonly used treatments simply don't work in large groups of people because they carry a genetic variation that disables the drug, and when we know our individual genetic information we will be able to stop taking something that isn't helping and be treated with something more effective instead. I think about how we can participate, as those authors proposed, contributing our anonymised data safely and willingly so that researchers can better understand which treatments have value and can challenge orthodoxy. I think of a team in Exeter, Jane Masoli and her colleagues, who explored the huge databases of anonymised information already available from primary care systems in the UK, to demonstrate that in adults above seventy-five years with moderate to severe frailty, and in all those over eighty-five years, there was no increased risk of death with high blood pressure; their polite and understated conclusion was that *the priority given to aggressive BP reduction in frail older people requires further evaluation.*

I watch a heron standing still and patient in the reeds, and I think of artificial intelligence and its ability to suggest rare diagnoses that might elude doctors, and of early studies indicating that for selected conditions consultations performed by AI systems compare favourably to those offered by humans. I have already experimented with ChatGPT, an AI system, challenging it to advise me how to create an advance care plan for a relative with dementia. Its answer was empathic and mostly correct.

At the pumping station, far out on the liminal land through which the river flows, the dog and I turn for home. The fields now are lush with flowering grasses, but for weeks in the winter they will be submerged and this track will become a narrow causeway across the floodplain.

My rage abates. Of course we need science and biotechnology and billions of data points, as we seek to improve the lives of older people, our future selves. But side by side with the science we need a deep and abiding understanding of what it means to be human.

Bill is sitting on a grey sofa in his dressing gown and slippers. The house is tiny, one of hundreds built in cul-de-sacs that sprout in all directions on the patch of land between town and motorway, short streets that bear the names of the natural features they have obliterated. I have passed Bramley Way, Pippin Close, Orchard Drive.

Enid opened the door. There's a cat litter tray at my feet as I introduce myself and take off my coat. Bill has lung cancer and has been in hospital three times in as many months to have fluid drained from his pleural space, space where there should be only silky transparent tissue to cover his lungs and line his chest wall so that Bill's lungs can expand and contract, smooth and frictionless. The cancer has caused a build-up of fluid in that space, and now the disease has marched on, angry cells dividing and thickening, and his right lung is encased in cancer and filled with it too and has no room for air, and Bill is breathless and in pain.

But he is smiling.

'I'm all right really,' he says, and I admire the cat while I check his pulse. There is a smell of something delicious from the kitchen, and Bill tells me, 'Indian family next door. Nice people, gave us their recipe.' As I examine his feet, I ask, 'Bill, what did you do for work, when you were a younger man?'

He holds his hands out, saying, 'I made . . .'

I wonder what he made, bread or bricks or shoes, for his hands are held out as if he's holding a box, while he finds the words, which takes a moment because either the disease or the drugs or the pain are slowing him down.

'I made . . . particle accelerators.'

I laugh out loud because I love being so wrong and being confronted with my prejudices and preconceptions.

Bill wriggles his eyebrows up and down at me and winks.

Yet there's a lesson for me here – I know as little about Bill's hopes and wishes as I do about his job. His living room is filled with the paraphernalia of illness – pills and syrups, dressings and letters, and appointments for tests demanded by protocols that are blind to Bill's situation. There's a sheet of dietary advice, triggered by a routine test suggesting that he may be at risk of diabetes; blood bottles that have arrived with a letter requiring him to complete the annual questionnaire relating to his decade-old hip replacement.

We will talk now, Bill and Enid and me, about what matters to him. We will scrub round hospital visits and rationalise his tablets. We will talk about a campsite in the Peak District and a thunderstorm, and about making the most of Bill's life right to the end.

It's easy to lose our way as we become older, navigating the complicated paths of healthcare. Both medical teams and patients can become taken up with processes, many of which have negligible or even negative effects on well-being, and we forget to ask the central questions. Why am I doing this? What is the purpose of this scan or that tablet? Do we, doctor and patient, understand and agree our goal? Will this proposed activity get us where we want to be? As doctors I wonder what it is that allows us, even when we have heard our patient's voice, to ignore it? What pride or fear, what arrogance or ignorance, might cause us to insist that our patient must have this test or undergo that treatment? And as patients, as families, friends, spouses, children, how do we ensure that our twenty-first-century medicine offers all that we need but does not impose more than we want? How do we find the voice to express how we feel? How do we know what to ask and when to ask it?

There's a terrible joke, which goes, how many Irish mothers does it take to change a light bulb? And the answer is: don't mind me. I'll be grand in the dark.

We can talk about what matters most. We can be bold, engaged, empowered. We can request information and be guided rather than led. We can demand illumination. We will not be grand in the dark.

I look back through photos on my phone. There's one of a small dog sitting on the blanket that covers the legs of a woman in her hospital bed – he has bright eyes, one ear up, one down. There's another dog in clinic beside a wheelchair – he has a winning smile, this stubby little dog next to thick tan tights and black-laced shoes. There's a photo of a ward receptionist, her arm round the shoulder of an old man who is standing with a walking frame – it's taken from behind, so you can't see their faces, but her head is tilted to hear his words. There's a Health Care Assistant from the Philippines putting an ID sticker on a hearing-aid box. There's a photo of a hospital bedside table, and a mince pie and a glass of mulled wine. Maggie had made it in a big enamel jug so everyone could have some, and the same jug features in another image but filled with Michaelmas daisies on the nurses' desk. There's a man's urinal bottle made of compressed cardboard and someone has written on it in biro, *Ray's bottle*, and drawn a smiley face figure with sticking-up hair. There's a junior sister; she's plaiting the hair of a fidgety woman on a red plastic chair, and I know that as she plaits, she's working, explaining to the new nurse the staffing rotas and how the iPads work for recording observations. There's a physio assistant walking beside a tiny figure; you can see her maroon dressing gown, her back bent over, and she's wearing a pretty bonnet because she had an operation to mend a bleed between her skull and her brain after a fall. And she's usually busy at home and hops on the bus to do her shopping, but she wouldn't walk after that operation and refused to be transferred to the community hospital in her own town, and the physio assistant had watched as Orla put her hand to her head, where the neuro-surgical team had shaved away her hair in preparation for surgery and understood suddenly that Orla was shy and ashamed of her appearance with half her hair cut to stubble, so Maggie had fetched a bonnet from the Beacon Centre, where the chemo teams work, and Orla is up now and walking.

Algorithmic medicine alone does not work for older people – it doesn't work for any of us whose medical problems are more than a matter of biology. Reducing our thinking to the binary – yes, so we take this pathway; no, so we will take that one – does not work. The answer so often is not yes or no but maybe. The answer is, I'm not sure. The answer is, I can't decide, or it depends, or I would like to talk with my family. The answer is, you are asking me the wrong questions.

It is at the interface of the algorithm and the human that our futures lie. This is an interface between perfection and imperfection, for human lives are not perfect and it is the things that are right alongside all that are wrong that make life worth living.

I'm watching *The Graham Norton Show* late one evening. Arnold Schwarzenegger is a guest, as is Jay Blades from *The Repair Shop*, and Jack Whitehall, who is funny and charming, and Dame Judi Dench, who is there to talk about her book about Shakespeare. There is banter – it transpires that Dame Judi played a part in the courtship of Whitehall's parents. Graham Norton asks her how much Shakespeare she knows. Dame Judi tucks her white hair behind her ears – she has a socking great diamond stud in each side – and is modest. We all speak Shakespeare all the time, she says, often without knowing it. And when we are in a corner, Shakespeare has a way of summing up our emotions. She talks of his

HERE'S TO THE FUTURE

relevance when we are in love, or jealous, or angry, and as she speaks it is clear that at eighty-seven years old these emotions are not faded memories for her but real emotions she could feel today or tomorrow. Of course she could.

Norton demands a performance. A sonnet, please. Dame Judi rubs her face with the back of her hand. She looks down, then away and straightens herself on the red sofa and puts her hands on her knees and begins.

> When, in disgrace with fortune and men's eyes,
> I all alone beweep my outcast state,
> And trouble deaf heaven with my bootless cries,
> And look upon myself and curse my fate . . .

Her eyes are looking far away, not at a camera, as she continues. The words of self-disgust and envy ring fierce and sad down the centuries.

> Wishing me like to one more rich in hope,
> Featured like him, like him with friends possessed,
> Desiring this man's art, and that man's scope,
> With what I most enjoy contented least;
> Yet in these thoughts myself almost despising,
> Haply I think on thee —

There is the smallest change in her expression, a memory permitted to rise.

– and then my state,
(Like to the lark at break of day arising
From sullen earth) sings hymns at heaven's gate;
For thy sweet love remembered such wealth brings
That then I scorn to change my state with kings.

There is silence before the applause.

I look again at my phone – more photos, taken over many years, representing the tiniest fraction of what I have witnessed. There's a bag of crisps between two people sitting on the edge of a hospital bed, a thin hand reaching out to hold up the name badge of one of the activities coordinators, the better to read her name again as he gets to know her. And they talk of cars and Iron Maiden, this young woman and this very old man, and he eats the crisps while they talk, even though he has eaten nothing for days.

There's a photo of an A4 piece of paper on a bedside table – it's been crumpled up, then smoothed out again, read and reread. Its message is written in capitals, the letters clear but decorated with extra flicks and embellishments that reflect an education outside the UK.

It reads: *YOU ARE IN HOSPITAL. YOU DO NOT NEED TO WORRY ABOUT ANYTHING.*

Mum died while I have been writing this book – at home, in a bed installed downstairs, where she could see, if not her garden, then at least its penstemons and asters in a blue glass vase at her side. Over the following months my sister, brother and I emptied her house by the river, in a process that anyone who has done such a task might recognise, combining as it does a requirement for stern practicality against a background of elegiac loss punctuated by howls of helpless laughter. Mum's house is distinctive for its scraps of paper stacked in old chocolate boxes and wedged into photo frames. Italian vocabulary, snippets of songs, names of friends and strangers for whom to pray, all in mixed media – pencil, pen, Tippex. There's a clutch of them on her bedside table upstairs and dozens more in the bathroom and kitchen. I set some aside. The jokes that don't make sense go in the bin. Later, at home, I read one I've saved. Mum's writing has always been dire, but I can make it out and I smile, for it is a quote from a Victorian tale, *The Water-Babies*, and it is also known as the Golden Rule. It has appeared in different cultures across the world for centuries. *Do as you would be done by.*

I think back to that day at Great Ormond Street when I learned so much about ethical dilemmas relating to children and young people. A group from Cambridge University had been studying the psychological well-being of children from 'new families' – children born through assisted fertility techniques or using surrogacy, children raised by gay couples – and it turned out that

while these children may develop psychological challenges as they grow towards adulthood, they do so no
more or less often than children in traditional families.
The researcher looked out at the audience from the lec-
tern, the light catching on her brown wavy hair. Her
message has stayed with me. It is not only a message
about children. It resonates across generations.

'It seems it does not make much difference who provides the love,' she said. 'What matters is the quality of
the loving.'

This then is a job for all of us. We can all play our part
in finding the oil that will smooth that surface between
science and human. We can start conversations with our
families, our friends and colleagues, and with our future
selves, about what matters to us most.

We can choose to treat older people as we would wish
to be treated ourselves. In turn we may realise that the
decisions we make now about older people – their place
in our society, their treatment and care – will shape our
own futures.

The words of the far-sighted economist Ernst
Schumacher, written in 1973, have popped up on
Twitter, and I am grateful for the irony. *Wisdom*, wrote
Schumacher, *demands a new orientation of science and technol-
ogy towards the organic, the gentle, the elegant and the beautiful.*

Towards Bill then, and Enid. Towards Patsy, and Jess's
nan, and the members of an Age UK book club. Towards
the people in the photos on my phone. Towards all of us.

We talk of the ageing population as if that population is something apart from us, detached. It isn't. We are the ageing population – I am, you are. We are in this together.

Acknowledgements

The time spent researching and writing this book has been, for me, a time of gifts. The friends, colleagues and strangers whose stories are told have been generous with their time and knowledge, and I thank them all. There are many others who have helped – people who grow skills, gather evidence, change things for the better. People who shine light and respond to challenges with optimism and creativity, who laugh and hug, and work patiently, and listen. I am grateful to have met you.

Thank you to Laurie, Rachel, Gráinne and Lauren for their careful reading and wise advice on subjects about which I still have much to learn.

Thank you to Phil Dolan and Kate Barrington at AgeUK Somerset, and to all the AgeUK groups and their quiet unsung heroes.

Thank you to Sarah Stacey and Michael Dixon, for showing care that is all about the human.

Thank you to Jugdeep Dhesi, for instant warmth and friendship, and to Sarah Mistry and others at the British Geriatrics Society, for fellowship, sound science and a lot of laughter.

ACKNOWLEDGEMENTS

To Andrew Tresidder, for magic medicine, and to Clare Howard, Tony Avery and Jamie, Gimmo, and Steve the Chemist, three Aural Apothecaries, for understanding.

To Tosin Lambe, whose generosity stopped me in my tracks, and to James and Alex whose response to a personal tragedy has been to pour joy and comfort into the lives of others.

To Tracey, Shirley, Josie and Craig, who made a difficult time better with quiet love and good humour.

To @Jennifer10651535, for honesty, and to Sash and Lucy once again, for a haven.

To my patients and colleagues, for teaching me, and giving me time.

Thank you dear Louise Moore, for your confidence that this book would be written, and to Ariel and Paula for the steady hands on the tiller, and to all the MJ team.

Thank you to Cathryn Summerhayes, for the straight-talking and happy sparkle.

Thank you to my dear Aunt Mary, for a lifetime of stalwart kindness and wisdom. Thank you also to Mary Fryer, for a great deal of listening, food and friendship.

A long time ago, our youngest daughter came home from primary school and told me, 'Mum, Granny's mad,' and I replied, 'Well, yes, but –' and my little girl said, 'No, she's not 'mad' mad. She's M, A, D, Making A Difference.' Thank you, my dear and maddening mum, for the certainty that there's never not enough time to pop into an exhibition, and for making a difference.

Thank you to Vic and Josh, my loved and precious siblings.

Thank you to Giles, who sees through things, and sees things through.